50
facts you need to know:

USA

facts you need to know:

50

USA

Stephen Fender

ICON BOOKS

Published in the UK in 2008 by
Icon Books Ltd, The Old Dairy,
Brook Road, Thriplow,
Cambridge SG8 7RG
email: info@iconbooks.co.uk
www.iconbooks.co.uk

Sold in the UK, Europe, South Africa and Asia
by Faber & Faber Ltd, 3 Queen Square,
London WC1N 3AU or their agents

Distributed in the UK, Europe, South Africa and Asia
by TBS Ltd, TBS Distribution Centre, Colchester Road
Frating Green, Colchester CO7 7DW

This edition published in Australia in 2008
by Allen & Unwin Pty Ltd,
PO Box 8500, 83 Alexander Street,
Crows Nest, NSW 2065

Distributed in Canada by
Penguin Books Canada,
90 Eglinton Avenue East, Suite 700,
Toronto, Ontario M4P 2YE

ISBN: 978-1840468-84-7

Typesetting in Neue Helvetica by Hands Fotoset

Printed and bound in the UK by Clays of Bungay

Contents

Acknowledgements

It's a pleasure to recall colleagues, friends and members of the family who have helped me with this book. Trevor Burnard, Owen Fender and John Sutherland offered fruitful suggestions for the facts themselves. Michael Les Benedict, Hugh Ditzler, Tom Fender, Richard Follett, Charles Nager, Andy Reinhardt, Stephen Schaefer and Clive Webb were generous with their time and considerable professional expertise. Fiona Sandiford showed me how a good young journalist can help to make an old academic's prose readable. Tim Ranson's continued interest and support, not to mention his practical and theoretical help with the computer and internet, kept the project moving. To all I am very grateful.

About the author

Stephen Fender was born in San Francisco and educated at Stanford and in the UK in Wales and Manchester. He has taught in the States, in Scotland at the University of Edinburgh, and in England at London and Sussex, where he was head of American Studies from 1985 to 2003. He now lives in Dulwich, south London.

Introduction

National identity has become a hot topic in the United Kingdom recently. Do the British have a national identity? If so, what is it? If not, should the government and media and other opinion-formers set about constructing one? Americans have the opposite problem – a powerful national narrative from which it's hard to escape.

'Who can desire more content, that hath small meanes, or but only his merit to advance his fortunes,' wrote Captain John Smith in 1616, trying to persuade his countrymen to settle in New England, 'than to tread, and plant that ground he hath purchased by the hazard of his life?' The American dream was open to those poor in wealth but rich in merit, with the guts to risk their lives – or at least their savings and comfort – to own a piece of the new dispensation. When people did begin to migrate to New England they came as pilgrims to found a reformed Christian society, one they hoped would serve as a model for colonies to follow.

So piety, independence, self-reliance, hard work, the mentality of the self-made citizen, unsupported by inherited social or financial advantage, unencumbered by the high taxes needed to fund a welfare state – all of these qualities went into making up the American self-image.

Some of the facts in this book are here to test the assumptions underlying American national identity. Take American self-help, for instance. It's really community-help. Not only that, but the country really does have a welfare state, only it's where you would least expect to find it, in the military services. And only about half the number of Americans that the media claim go to church actually attend regularly. As for freedom from inherited privilege, American social inequality has been growing over the last twenty years, even if a recent opinion poll found that an increasing proportion of the population believed the opposite to be true.

Of course a mere 50 facts could never cover the vast spread and variety of physical, social, and political landscapes that we call America, let alone the enormous energy – creative as well as destructive – of the United States. The subject cries out for a thousand facts, maybe a hundred thousand.

So I had to go in for a representative selection. Some facts announce themselves as serious from the start, like there being one car for every adult in the US, or 65 million Americans owning handguns, or the high number of bankruptcies caused by medical fees. Others are not quite what they seem, like the one about Americans saying more than they need to.

Others again are put there to tease. The citizens of Rabbit Hash, Kentucky, elected a dog for mayor for a bit of fun, and to raise funds for the local historical society, yet this fact leads on to the more serious question of why corruption in local politics seems to involve mayors more than state governors. And maybe it's just a historical curiosity that the man who invented recorded sound, thus becoming one of the first people able to hear music played backwards, thought that jazz sounded better that way. Yet the fact opens the wider issue of why jazz, an even greater American invention than recorded sound, caused the establishment to fear it as 'the devil's music'.

Some of these facts suggest national shortcomings, others triumphs. At a time when America's popularity has fallen to an all-time low overseas, how stands the Union? Older Americans like me remember a time when our country was more progressive at home, less reckless abroad, happier and more content than now.

But old age tends to distort the present. It also tends to mis-remember the past as a golden age. The proper use of advancing years is historical perspective. What that perspective teaches us is that although America has made many mistakes in the past, few have gone uncorrected by the enormous counterbalance of the generous, clever and above all sovereign American people working through the country's democratic institutions. For after all, those national characteristics still motivate the people, and still represent Americans' sense of themselves. It is indeed what gives Americans the inspiration and energy to ensure that present-day America lives up to the high standards of its history.

Americans aren't born; they are made.

An English friend spending a visiting year in California recalled his son's first day in the local primary school. Celebrating their multi-ethnic entry, which included children from Hispanic and South Korean families, the teachers asked all the new pupils about their countries of origin. One question was: 'In what year was your country founded?' My friend's son was stumped. When *had* England been 'founded'?

Later we adults tried out all sorts of answers to that question. True, you could say that Great Britain was established by the act of union between England and Scotland (1707), and that another such act in 1800 forged the United Kingdom out of England, Scotland and Ireland. But England? Or Ireland, Scotland, Wales? Were they ever 'founded'? And if so, who were their founding fathers? That was another question put to the incoming school pupils.

But America was founded. It's not alone in this fact. Many other ex-colonies, or nations reborn after cataclysmic revolutions – France, for example or, just to mention two of the countries from which the families of those California pupils were drawn, Mexico and South Korea – can trace their modern origins to specific dates and historical figures.

Fittingly, considering how good we were to become at the practice, we Americans announced our founding in the form of an advertisement, written mainly by the Virginia country gentleman Thomas Jefferson and signed by 56 lawyers, doctors, clergymen and businessmen, including John Adams, Benjamin Franklin and Jefferson himself. It was called the Declaration of Independence.

The Declaration announced to the world that the United States were open for business. No longer would customers for the country's raw materials have to go through Great Britain or ship their goods out in British sailing vessels. More to the point, given the conflict that the declaration would soon provoke, friendly countries could now form alliances directly with the new nation, sending troops and weapons to aid in the fight for liberty.

In due course the advert was followed by a legal instrument, the

Constitution of the United States, designed to codify the relationship between the federal administration and the various state governments. As the poet Walt Whitman put it: 'The Americans of all nations at any time upon the earth have probably the fullest poetical nature. The United States themselves are essentially the greatest poem.'[1] He meant that literally. Americans – even ordinary Americans – were poetic because together they had come up with the greatest artefact of the collective imagination, the complex constitution and polity of the country itself.

What this means is that America is as much a contract as a country. Immigrants sign up to the idea of America, and must take a test in its laws and traditions before they can qualify as citizens. Anybody who buys into the idea becomes an American, wherever she or he was born.

By the same token, birth in the United States confers no special privileges. You can break the contract just as well as assent to it. During the protests against the Vietnam War, self-styled patriots sported a bumper sticker saying: 'America: Love it or Leave It!' This didn't mean go back to where you came from. It meant: whoever you are, whatever your background – native or immigrant, old money or new money, city-dweller or hayseed, black or white – put your money where your mouth is and get out if you don't like the mutual contract between government and governed. It was all there in the title of the House (of Representatives) Un-American Activities Committee. You could be, or become, un-American by breaking the agreement.

Would the Houses of Parliament ever establish an Un-British Activities Committee? In 1940 they tried to outlaw the British Communist Party, which had come out officially against the Second World War, then being fought by the British with their backs to the wall. But Winston Churchill argued against the ban, saying that the Communists were Englishmen, and he didn't fear Englishmen.[2] He couldn't imagine anyone born in Britain being un-British. That's because he was thinking of Britain as a natural evolution, an organic process, of which birth was a part. You couldn't go back and decide to be born somewhere else.

The British publisher Robert Maxwell, who was born in a peasant village in Czechoslovakia, volunteered for service in the British

Army in the thick of the Second World War and took part in a number of dangerous engagements, gaining promotion from Corporal to Captain. When he won the Military Cross for gallantry, Field Marshal Bernard Montgomery himself pinned the medal to his breast. Becoming a British citizen, Maxwell educated his children in England, and ran his business from there. In 1964 he was elected to the House of Commons as the Labour Member of Parliament for Buckingham.[3]

When he died in November 1991, some time before the full discovery of his financial irregularities, his obituaries were generally favourable apart from one fact, which ran through them as a common theme. Try as he might, they said, he could never quite pass himself off as British. 'Robert Maxwell loved England,' wrote Anthony Delano in the *Daily Mail*, 'but never learned to understand what it meant to be an Englishman.'

A psychoanalytically more up-market comment along the same lines came from Laurence Marks in the *Observer*, who wondered whether the 'ease with which he assumed social camouflage' had 'eroded his sense of identity'. Marks called Maxwell 'a fantasist' whose 'most fantastic invention was Robert Maxwell', reworked 'from peasant youth to British Army infantry officer, and thence to publisher of recondite journals, Buckinghamshire MP and inter-national financier.'

Maxwell himself was painfully aware of the difference. He 'used to stand up at public functions and announce: "All of us here are Englishmen together". "The difference", he would continue, "is that you are Englishmen by accident. I am an Englishman by choice".' Far from being a fantasist, he never felt completely assimilated in his adopted country. 'Because I'm a foreigner and successful,' he once remarked, 'people say there must be some mystery or there must be some fraud. Neither is so. I am just successful.'[4]

So what about Henry Kissinger? Born in Germany just fourteen days before Robert Maxwell, Kissinger never felt the need, as Maxwell did, to smooth out his gravelly European accent. Does he still feel like an outsider in America? Whatever they may hold against him for his foreign policy, will his memorialists say that he never learned to understand what it meant to be an American? You only have to ask the questions to understand the American difference. How absurd it would be to expect anything remotely similar being said and written by and about Henry Kissinger. He became fully-fledged as an American when he was naturalised as a United States citizen on 19 June 1943. Since then, he has been at the centre of the American establishment, even serving as the country's senior official representative to the rest of the world, as Secretary of State. As an American, he was made, not born.

Throughout history, around one-third of all migrants to America have returned home.

There's a photograph by Alfred Stieglitz (1864–1946) frequently reproduced in exhibitions and coffee-table books about American life. It's called 'The Steerage', and shows a scene on a transatlantic steamer. Jauntily dressed women and men look down on a cargo well crowded with women in shawls, balancing children on their hips, amid laundry hung out to dry over the rigging. Invariably this picture is seen as documenting poor peasants on their way to America, weary and bemused after a long voyage, but grimly determined to endure the landing at Ellis Island and to make good in the New World.

In fact, they were on their way back to where they came from – and so were the people looking down on them. Stieglitz took the picture on his first trip to Europe in 1907. Why has that picture been read so often the wrong way round? Because back migration has been the untold chapter in the great American story about itself. We like to think that people of other countries have been so desperate to come to the US that we now suffer a crisis of illegal immigration. In fact, averaged out over the country's history, around a third of migrants to America have gone back. Sometimes departures actually exceeded arrivals, as in the year 1931–32, the worst of the Great Depression, when only 2,155 British aliens entered the US, while 12,311 left it.[1]

Why this surprisingly large backwash? Some were turned back at Ellis Island after failing one or more health checks. Some were deported even after long years of residence in the country, as is now happening to illegal immigrants from Mexico, when they are caught. Others failed in their enterprise, having used up all their savings without finding a job or house for their families. Charles Dickens offers a harrowing portrait of some glimpsed in steerage on his own return voyage from America in *American Notes for General Circulation* (1842).

Some of them had been in America but three days, some but three months …

Others had sold their clothes to raise the passage-money, and had hardly rags to cover them; others had no food … but the bones and scraps of fat … from the plates used in the after-cabin dinner.

These unfortunates were forced back by the law or bad luck. It comes as more of a surprise, though, that quite a few migrants returned home because they wanted to. Some, like Frances Trollope (mother of the novelist Anthony Trollope), who wrote the highly critical *Domestic Manners of the Americans* (1832), came out as migrants but turned themselves into tourists before returning home to write up their experiences. Others, perhaps like the better-dressed figures in the Stieglitz photo, never intended to stay for good, but just to work hard for a few years to build up a nest egg to allow them to marry and settle back home. Nowadays, most of these would arrive holding one of the 28 kinds of non-immigrant visas; so their return wouldn't be classified as back migration at all.

The reason why back migration occupies such a small place in the American public consciousness can be traced back to the psychology of migration itself. America is a country of immigrants. So strong is the psychology of migration that it doesn't really matter if we are newly arrived or the offspring of families ten or more generations in the country. The way of thinking has been handed down from parent to child, has become part of the national narrative. To understand this mentality is to understand part of what makes America distinctive.

Emigration was and remains a shock to the emotions. Typically a young married couple would be leaving their extended families, their friends, all the social, political and geographical landmarks of their town, county and country. Before the last quarter of the 20th century they would have had little expectation of seeing their friends and family again. Their life in the new country would be uncertain, even hazardous. There would be housing and work to find, new friends to make, an unfamiliar social and economic environment in which to plan a future. For many, all this would have to be done in a foreign language.

Given this trauma, the new arrivals had to convince both those left back home and of course themselves that they had made the right decision. Letters home to the extended family described the move as an ordeal heroically and triumphantly overcome. Often they spoke of material promise: cheap prices, fruit literally falling off the trees and given away in season, improved health, low rents or even free land, good prospects for jobs. Good news had to be sent back at all costs, bad news suppressed.

Letters often came right out with this connection between writing and good fortune. In her first letter home, two years after she and her husband emigrated from Lancashire, Kate Bond wrote: 'Dear Mother, ... I would have wrote before this, but could not write you pleasant news, as Stephen has been *so unhappy* in a strange country.' John Rowlandson spoke for nearly all of them when he wrote to his wife from New York State in 1852: 'If I am successful you will soon hear from me again.'[2] And if not?

Another tactic for making the break bearable was to forget about the old home, even to disparage it. The past was past; there was no point in mooning over it. Sometimes this attitude took the extreme form of refusing to believe that the old country had a future at all. Migrants would be astonished, often even strangely disappointed, to hear that some progress – whether political, economic or material – had actually been made back home. 'I see that the Reform [of the franchise] Bill has had a second reading in the House of Lords', wrote John Fisher to his brothers in 1832. 'I am afraid it will not pass.'[3] But it did.

Migration arouses such powerful feelings because it's felt as a rite of passage. Like birth, adolescence or coming of age, it's loaded with both dangers and also vast opportunities for development – an experience of such emotional force that it changes you forever. The two strongest features of such crucial moments in human life are that they cut you off from the past and there's no reversing them. To become a child again after the strains of adolescence, or dependent on the family after once having become independent, would seem not just undesirable but somehow against nature.

Of the over a million British who back-migrated from America up till the end of the 19th century, only a handful of letters or other records remain. That means that either they wrote very few letters home, or their families didn't keep them. They had nothing good to report, and they were ashamed of their return. So were their families, probably. So in this sense, back migrants failed to write themselves into the record.

But just in case they tried to speak for their own experience, the more successful migrants were on hand to disparage their ill reports. 'There was two men that was passengers in the same ship as us,' Andrew and Jane Morris wrote home from Germantown, Pennsylvania, in 1831, who 'talked about what great things they would do when they got to America.' But after landing in Philadelphia, 'they got drunk instead of looking for work ... and then began to curse the country and all that was in it.' Lacking money to pay for their return passage, 'they sold themselves to the captain until their father came to Liverpool and pay their passage. So I leave you to guess what tales they would tell when they got home.'[4]

So having set out in search of economic and social freedom, these back migrants returned in bondage, 'sold' to the captain, thrown back on parental patronage. Through their own laziness and moral lassitude they had failed every test of the American adventure. No wonder, given this mindset, that self-reliance is such a powerful component of American culture – and also why (by our own admission, and running counter to our global role) we remain highly sensitive to criticism from abroad, while largely ignorant of what's going on in the rest of the world.

But that's the negative side of American immigration, the black hole in the national memory. The other side is the powerful effect of the standard ideology, even on recent arrivals of groups hostile to American policy on the global scale. Recent surveys agree that even Muslims have assimilated far better in the US than they have in Spain, Germany and especially Great Britain,[5] where four home-grown suicide bombers killed 52 Londoners on 7 July 2005, another four tried to repeat the performance a week later, and 24 were allegedly involved in a plot to blow up ten airliners over the Atlantic in August 2006.

Time will tell, but America has yet to suffer an attack from the much more thoroughly assimilated Muslim community in the US. 'American Muslims, by and large, are wealthier and better integrated into American society than their European counterparts', writes pollster John Zogby.[6] 'One major difference between the United States and Britain,' reports Neil MacFarquhar in the *New York Times*, 'is the United States' historical ideal of being a melting-pot meritocracy. "You can keep the flavor of your ethnicity, but you are expected to become an American," said Omer Mozaffar, 34, a Pakistani-American raised here who is working toward a doctorate in Islamic studies at the University of Chicago.'[7]

So those migrants who stay the course, who survive the rite of passage, feel they have bought into a new life. They have no intention of undermining what they have invested in so heavily.

America is a country with 50 capital cities. Few Americans can name them.

Every American state has its own capital. Just as the American government is famously split between the three estates of Executive, Legislature and Judiciary, so federal – that is, central – power is balanced against that of the states and cities. State powers are defined negatively as everything not the responsibility of the federal government. Or as the Tenth Amendment to the Constitution has it: 'The powers not delegated to the United States by the Constitution, nor prohibited by it to the States, are reserved to the States respectively, or to the people.'

The origins of this odd formulation lie far back in history. The states – originally the colonies – were political entities long before the federal government came into existence. The first stab at a federal constitution, the Articles of Federation, denied central government the power to tax and allowed each state one vote in the Congress of Confederation, regardless of population. So when the Constitution replaced the Articles in 1788, the framers had to tread warily around the states' prerogatives.

The solution they agreed was that the federal government would be allowed only the right to levy taxes, to declare war, to regulate interstate commerce and to pass any law 'necessary and proper' to facilitate these expressed powers. In time, of course, this was extended. The bitter struggle over 'states' rights' led to the Confederate states seceding from the Union over the issue of slavery. After the Civil War, then during the New Deal, and again in the 1960s and 1970s, the government moved to extend and enforce minimum standards in civil rights and social services.

This leaves a lot of power and responsibility to local government. Cities take care of their own town planning and local tax assessments, rubbish collection, the police and fire services, while each state government is in charge of higher and further education, public health, roads and highways within its borders. State governments charter banks and corporations, run elections, and even organise their own system of justice in the courts.

Powerful as they are, however, very few people can name the state capitals. For every one who recognises Sacramento, capital of California, there are thousands who know Los Angeles, not least because it's near Hollywood and has over eight times Sacramento's population. Fewer could name Wilmington, the largest city in Delaware, but how many would recognise the state's capital, Dover, with a population of 34,288? Or the capital of Illinois, Springfield, with 115,668 inhabitants, as against Chicago, with 2.8 million?[1] In fact so obscure are many state-capital names that school children are forced to memorise them, often with great difficulty. Websites meet their needs with quizzes and electronic flash cards matching states with their capitals.

So what happened? Did the state founders simply fail to predict future growth, picking a community that seemed to be thriving, only to see it overtaken by other cities with populations stimulated by factors little understood at the time, like industrialisation? This may go part way to explain the choice of Carson City (population 67,701), designated as capital of Nevada when the nearby Comstock silver lode drew tens of thousands of miners to the town in the late 1850s.

Carson, though, was soon outpaced by Reno, 26 miles to the north, when the latter got connected to the transcontinental railroad in the late 1860s. As for Las Vegas, the largest American city to be founded in the 20th century, its growth came from the railroad, an air force base, gambling and tourism, and now also high-tech businesses.

But if state authorities were after size and prominence, they could have shifted the capital to the largest, fastest-growing city in the state whenever they wished to. In fact they seem to have been looking for something almost exactly the opposite. Call it a quiet life. Sometimes they were trying to avoid actual military danger, as when the capital of Michigan was moved from Detroit to Lansing, still with only 119,128 inhabitants, to get it further from the British in Canada, who had briefly held Detroit during the War of 1812. More often they were determined to steer clear of the power of commerce and later industry, the very stimuli to continuing growth, for fear that these influences would upset the balanced process of government.

And something similar has been governing the evolution of even the largest American cities. The fact is, the United States has no metropolis, in the strict sense of that word. If this seems surprising, compare the US to three European countries. The British, French and Italians – despite their radically different political premises as, respectively, a constitutional monarchy, a republic and (in effect) a confederation of medieval and Renaissance city states – see nothing unusual about centring political, financial and cultural power in one place.

Think of how national institutions are concentrated in London. The biggest city in the United Kingdom is also its capital. The stock market is in London. It's where the head of the national church lives. Most of the large corporations have their national offices in London, as do the labour unions. It's where films and music are produced and distributed. Theatre and opera are largely centred there. Above all, London is the centre of broadcasting and newspapers, which are circulated throughout the country every morning. Paris is all of these, minus the church. So is Rome, with the church put back in – only this time the biggest world church of them all.

Look around for an equivalent metropolis in the United States, and where would you find it? The stock markets are in New York and Chicago. Publishing and theatre are centred on New York; so is dance and the graphic and plastic arts. Hollywood has the movies; Los Angeles, Atlanta and Nashville share the music. There are no national papers, just many powerful regional ones, like the *New York Times*, *Chicago Tribune*, *Washington Post*, *Los Angeles Times*, *Cincinnati Enquirer*, and many more.

Television has its national networks, shared by local stations, but they're hotly pursued by cable and satellite, now nudging 50 per cent of the audience figures (see fact 16). Finally, central government and the civil and military bureaucracy are in Washington, DC, which is not a state. The centre of 'the church' – the term is seldom used in that European sense – is everywhere and nowhere. It was a guiding principle of American settlement that there should never be a metropolitan centre for 'the church'.

In London a Member of Parliament might also be a stockbroker, a businessman, or a corporation lawyer, and even write a column in a daily or Sunday newspaper. American decentralisation means that we're likely to be much more specialised than this. To take just one example, Wall Street may be in New York, but the Securities and Exchange Commission, which governs the Stock Exchange and prosecutes its inside traders, is headquartered in Washington.

That distance is still important, even in this era of instant electronic communications and data sharing. Faith in the separation of powers, seen most clearly in the split between the Presidency, Congress, and the Supreme Court, pervades American life at every level.

To put it another way, despite recent accusations to the contrary, Americans are fundamentally anti-imperialistic. Which is why the US can boast of some of the most cosmopolitan cities in the world – New York, San Francisco, Los Angeles, Dallas, Atlanta, Miami, and many others, each with its art galleries, symphony orchestras, gourmet restaurants and chic cafes – but no true metropolis. And this is good news. If there's no one centre from which all kinds of power, whether political, financial, cultural, moral or military, radiate out to the provinces, that means there are no provinces either.

The US Supreme Court has ruled that burning the American flag is a legitimate expression of free speech.

In August 1984 the Republican Party met to nominate its candidate for President. For the first time in the history of either the Republicans or the Democrats, the convention was held in the socially and politically conservative city of Dallas, Texas. While the delegates were busy choosing President Ronald Reagan for his second four-year term of office, around 100 protestors marched through the streets, chanting slogans against the warlike posture of the Reagan administration, and the threat of nuclear war that they claimed it posed.

On their way through the city they stopped to make speeches, spray-paint the walls of big Dallas corporations supporting the Republicans and overturn a few of their ornamental potted plants. As the demonstration wound up in front of the City Hall, someone handed an American flag that had been looted from one of the downtown businesses to a member of the Communist Youth Brigade called Gregory Lee Johnson. After the others had doused the flag in kerosene, Johnson set it alight. While the flag burned, the protestors chanted: 'America, the red, white, and blue, we spit on you.'

For this offence Johnson alone was arrested, charged with 'desecration of a venerated object' in violation of the Texas Penal Code, and sentenced to a year in prison and fined $2,000. Appealing against his conviction, Johnson took his case all the way to the Supreme Court. They ruled, by a narrow majority of five justices to four, that Johnson's conviction was inconsistent with the First Amendment of the US Constitution, that 'Congress shall make no law ... abridging the freedom of speech'. 'The First Amendment literally forbids the abridgment only of "speech",' the Court ruled, 'but we have long recognised that its protection does not end at the spoken or written word.' Burning the American flag, in other words, is an expression of opinion protected by the Constitution.

The *Texas v. Johnson* ruling in 1989 overturned numerous flag-desecration statutes throughout the country, but conservatives have been unwilling to let the matter lie there. Scarcely a year goes by without Congress debating the subject. As recently as 3 March 2005, John Thune, the junior senator for South Dakota, announced that he would introduce an amendment to the Constitution 'soon', specifically banning flag-burning. In the event, he found more immediate causes to occupy his time that year, like fighting to overturn the Pentagon's decision to close down a large air force base in his home state.

Why should burning or otherwise 'desecrating' the national banner arouse such heated controversy? Because the American flag is literally an object of veneration. School pupils pledge allegiance to it. People face it, their hands over their hearts, with those in military uniform saluting, when the national anthem is played at the start of football games.

After the attack on the Pentagon and the Twin Towers, it began to appear widely as enamel buttonholes. President Bush never speaks in public without at least one prominently displayed behind him. In fact, according to the novelist Norman Mailer, Bush's politics can be summed up as 'flag conservatism' – not (needless to say) conservatism in the old sense of a cautious foreign policy and a balanced budget, but in waving the Stars and Stripes as a sacred talisman against the forces of evil in the world.[1]

A high proportion of households fly the flag on the Fourth of July – and often at other times too – whether on a substantial pole in the front yard or hung out of a window on a short staff. By law it flies from public buildings on all public holidays. Executive orders, codes and customs regulate how and when it may be flown, how raised and lowered, how folded when taken off its halyard. It must never be allowed to touch the ground. It's never to be used for decoration, as for example to cover a ceiling, or as bunting on a political speaker's rostrum, or for advertising purposes, or 'embroidered on such articles as cushions or handkerchiefs and the like'.[2]

American literature has long reflected the popularity of the flag as symbol of the nation. John Greenleaf Whittier, once so popular that several New England states named holidays after him, famously versified a legendary stand-off over the flag during the Civil War. As the story goes, when they entered Frederick, Maryland, in September 1862, Stonewall Jackson's Confederate troops caught sight of an American flag fluttering from the upstairs window of the house owned by a 90-year-old woman called Barbara Frietschie. Outraged at this emblem of the hated Union, they blasted away at it until it was in tatters, its staff severed. At which point:

> Quick, as it fell, from the broken staff
> Dame Barbara snatched the silken scarf;
> She leaned far out on the window-sill,
> And shook it forth with a royal will.
> 'Shoot, if you must, this old gray head,
> But spare your country's flag,' she said.

Abashed, Jackson ordered a ceasefire.

The reason why Americans revere the flag to the point of idolatry is that the flag represents the people, and the people are sovereign. Of course most countries claim to represent the will of their people, but in America this isn't just a play on words, much less a political fiction – it's literally the case. The American people occupy that space in their government where the sovereign would be found in a monarchy.

In Great Britain, when she opens Parliament, the Queen sits on a throne at the focal point at one end of the upper house, the House of Lords. It's from there that she delivers the Speech from the Throne outlining her government's legislative programme for the coming session. For the rest of the year the throne is empty, but the noble lords bow to it, as to an altar, whenever they pass in front of it.

The first words of the American Constitution, inscribed in two-inch-high letters, are 'We the people'. It then goes on, in normal-sized handwriting:

... of the United States, in Order to form a more perfect Union, establish Justice, insure domestic Tranquility, provide for the common defense, promote the general Welfare, and secure the Blessings of Liberty to ourselves and our Posterity, do ordain and establish this Constitution for the United States of America.

This is set out in the style of a contemporary royal proclamation, a formal announcement of some importance made under the seal of office by the Queen or King in council, binding upon all loyal subjects, and headed 'By the King (or Queen): A Proclamation'. In the Constitution the people speak as the supreme executive power in the land.

If you really want to understand the American attitude toward the Stars and Stripes, think of the acts and words – in law, in the press and in ordinary speech – that the British adopt towards the Queen. Of course there are cynics and satirists among them, republicans and anarchists as well – verbal flag-burners, if you like. But for the most part, and especially on anniversaries significant to the country and the Queen's person, the people of Great Britain strike an attitude ranging from dignified respect to enthusiastic reverence towards their monarch.

The Queen represents the country. That's obvious enough, and the national anthem underlines that fact, with its fervent prayer that God save her, and

> Send her victorious,
> Happy and Glorious,
> Long to reign over us;
> God save the Queen!

And the American national anthem? Well, that's about the flag, of course, the 'Star-Spangled Banner' that continued to wave over the ramparts of Fort McHenry after a day and long night's bombardment by British ships in Chesapeake Bay during the War of 1812.

> And the rockets' red glare, the bombs bursting in air,
> Gave proof through the night that our flag was still there:

> O say, does that star-spangled banner yet wave
> O'er the land of the free and the home of the brave?

The Supreme Court found in favour of Gregory Lee Johnson on the grounds that burning the flag was an expression of his opinion. 'That we have had little difficulty identifying an expressive element in conduct relating to flags should not be surprising', they wrote. 'The very purpose of a national flag is to serve as a symbol of our country; it is, one might say, "the one visible manifestation of two hundred years of nationhood."'

Nine per cent of US adults report having attended at least one Alcoholics Anonymous meeting in their lifetime.[1]

Peterborough, New Hampshire (population 5,883), has four groups of Alcoholics Anonymous, holding 26 meetings a week in all. One of them is called 'Our Town', after the play based on Peterborough by Thornton Wilder. Why is that? Is Peterborough a quarrelsome backwater where people drink themselves to death out of boredom?

Absolutely not. It's a thriving, sophisticated country community whose summer calendar for 22 June 2006 listed twenty other support groups for medical and psychiatric problems, alongside around 180 events running from museum and art gallery exhibitions, through to children's summer camps and music classes, reading groups, theatre workshops, 'food banks' and farmers' markets – not to mention instruction in everything from dog obedience to painting *en plein air*.[2]

AA is just taking its rightful place among all this rich variety of activities in Peterborough, and if it needs four separate meetings, that's all part of the AA tradition of allowing as many autonomous groups as wish to set up in the same area. There are no franchises granted, or territorial ownership allowed, to AA meetings.

The movement all started when two men from neighbouring Vermont met in Akron, Ohio, in 1935. William Griffith Wilson ('Bill W.' to AA members) had been a stockbroker, ruined by the Wall Street crash. Robert Holbrook Smith ('Dr Bob') was a doctor working in the Akron City Hospital. Both men had been fighting and losing the battle against alcoholism, until they discovered the Oxford Group. This movement attempted to work a worldwide moral revolution through small meetings in which participants confessed their sins and vowed to make restitution to those they had injured. Finally experiencing moments of conversion, Smith and Wilson began to achieve longer and longer periods of sobriety.

The men teamed up. Drawing on their own experience, they began to convert other drunks. By the end of the decade they had formed groups in Akron, Cleveland and New York that resulted in their first 100 sober alcoholics. From there the Akron group pioneers were so enthused over AA that they started highly successful meetings in Detroit, Chicago, Houston, and elsewhere. In time Alcoholics Anonymous went nationwide, then global.

How does it work? Effort is concentrated on the autonomous meeting, on the spoken word in dialogue. People are welcomed; they confess their condition, which is then analysed by the group as a whole. Members share experiences, offer practical advice based on what has worked for them. Anyone can speak in a meeting; there's no set order of proceedings. Meetings take their tone from the region. The biographer and literary critic John Sutherland attended AA on both sides of the continent. He remembered his spell in a New Hampshire meeting as 'oppressively private; infused to the point of moral implosion with a New England Puritan shame', while in southern California, the 'dominant motif [was] a kind of freewheeling zaniness'.[3]

The process is set out in the 'Twelve Steps', a summary of the founders' experience, reprinted in their 'Big Book', *Alcoholics Anonymous* (1939). The first three steps go like this:

1. We admitted we were powerless over alcohol – that our lives had become unmanageable.
2. Came to believe that a Power greater than ourselves could restore us to sanity.
3. Made a decision to turn our will and our lives over to the care of God *as we understood Him*.

Those references to a higher power threatened to pose difficulties, so had to be stated with sufficient generality to include Jews, Muslims, Hindus or members of any other belief – not to mention atheists. But the real difficulty lies in the one condition for entry. Meetings are completely open; you don't have to be invited or elected to them. There are no membership lists; you don't have to sign your name to anything; you can't be excommunicated from the group. But you *do* have to acknowledge that you are an alcoholic. This is far from easy.

After all, consider what alcoholism is, and how identified. According to the AA's Second Step, it's a kind of insanity. The National Council for Alcoholism and Drug Dependence defines the condition as 'a primary, chronic disease' influenced by 'genetic, psychosocial, and environmental factors', that is 'often progressive and fatal'.

How do you know if you've got this disease? Signs to look for include losing time from work through drinking, being unable to 'get through the day' without a drink, drinking alone and/or in the morning, getting the shakes, relieved only by a drink, and a sudden loss of memory. But chances are you won't diagnose yourself as alcoholic, because perhaps the chief symptom is denial.

When members join the AA meeting, and every time they return to it, they must introduce themselves – by first name only, to preserve anonymity – to the rest of the group: 'Hello, my name is Frank and I'm an alcoholic.' Again and again, participants have reported that admitting their alcoholism was the hardest, the necessary, first step. Others followed, like making 'a fearless moral inventory of ourselves' (Step 4), asking God to remove our 'defects of character' (Step 6), and (these two inherited from the Oxford Group), making a list of 'persons whom we had harmed' (Step 8) and making 'direct amends to such people where possible' (Step 9).

The Twelfth Step sounds like a call to mission.

12. Having had a spiritual awakening as the result of these [first eleven] steps, we tried to carry this message to others …

But it isn't. AA doesn't proselytise or engage in propaganda. The Twelfth Step is about mutual help among alcoholics, encourage-ment, support. Anyone tempted to fall off the wagon can call up a fellow member called a sponsor, who will drop everything to come over and talk them down from the crisis. The Twelfth Step builds on fellowship established through the meetings, a crucial element in the curative process.

Does it work? Who knows? AA's decentred organisation collects no statistics. But if the thousands of anecdotal accounts volunteered by family, friends and acquaintances are anything to go by, the answer is yes, often – and often permanently. One collateral clue to the movement's practical success rate is the increasing tendency of the courts to mandate a specified number of weekly AA meetings to those convicted, not just of drink driving, but also of aggravated assault, illegal possession of firearms and violence against children.

Alcoholics Anonymous is deeply embedded in American culture. At first sight this must look like a strange claim. After all, according to the standard version of American identity, the country got rich and powerful through millions upon millions of acts of individual enterprise. Absolutely true. It's equally true, however – see fact 45 – that this tradition of self-help has often been a communal affair. However much it may draw, as AA does, on individual effort, American self-help is often mutual help.

Besides, Alcoholics Anonymous has a strong flavour of the alternative about it, as though deliberately cutting across the grain of the national self-image. It's for Americans who cannot afford psychotherapy, which in any case has had only limited success with alcoholic addiction. Although it took early inspiration from the Oxford Group, it's not a religious movement in itself, having nothing to say about the origin and purposes of life, or of life after death.

Although a global enterprise, like a secret terrorist group, it has no overriding organisational structure, no hierarchies of management, no real estate. It has no budget to speak of. You can't leave a bequest to it. Funding comes from small collections at the meetings – a dollar in the hat, as they say – just enough to hire the church hall or schoolroom in which they take place. AA doesn't lobby for specific policies; it doesn't even promote itself. There are no qualifications demanded on entry, apart from a desire to stop drinking.[4]

Yet this austere aversion to property and other capital, this emphasis on mutual help, this egalitarianism, this insistence on the absolute autonomy of the meeting – all these have their roots deep in another American tradition. They can be found in the congregation of the Pilgrim Fathers, in the Quaker meetings, where anyone can speak in any order as the spirit moves them – even in fraternal organisations like the Masons, Oddfellows and temperance fraternities that flourished in the 19th century. All this is deeply traditional. As the sociologist Robin Room has put it: 'The United States has been a society of meeting-goers, of voluntary organisations arising spontaneously and autonomously for a myriad of purposes.'[5]

65 million Americans own handguns, and use them to kill 35,000 other Americans every year.

As the American pro-gun lobby is always quick to point out, the 'right to bear arms' is engraved in the Bill of Rights, specifically in the Second Amendment to the American Constitution. 'A well regulated Militia, being necessary to the security of a free State, the right of the people to keep and bear Arms, shall not be infringed.' The National Rifle Association (NRA), chief among pro-gun pressure groups, usually quotes only the second half of that amendment. There's a reason for that.

The idea has its origins in early 16th-century theories about how to govern Italian city states. In Chapter XII of *The Prince* (1515), Niccolò Machiavelli argued that instead of depending on mercenaries, whose professional interests lay in prolonging wars, the prince of the city state should arm his own people, form and drill them into a citizens' militia, and lead them into battle himself.

Not only would such an army have a stronger incentive to win, but 'a republic which has its own citizen army is far less likely to be subjugated by one of its own citizens than a republic whose forces are not its own'. Experience bears out the truth of this idea, he said. 'Rome and Sparta endured for many centuries, armed and free. The Swiss are strongly armed and completely free.'[1]

He was certainly right about the Swiss, whose citizens have retained their arms to this day – 200,723 fully automatic Sturmgewehr assault rifles to be exact – locked away in household cupboards. But these aren't handguns; they are intended to be used by Switzerland's citizen army. Every shell issued is counted and signed for, and heaven help the part-time soldier who undertakes a bit of hunting on the side, let alone goes in search of human game.

Local journalists 'could remember only two crimes involving guns in recent decades', writes Emma Hartley, 'one involving a man in a latex suit who was shot by his girlfriend, and a [shooting] spree at the national parliament – each was especially memorable in its own way.'[2]

Handguns are kept in a quarter of all American households. When you add shotguns for shooting birds and high-calibre rifles for hunting deer, elk and bear, the figure jumps to 39 per cent, the highest number and proportion of armed population in the world. Next comes, rather surprisingly, Norway (32 per cent), followed, more predictably, since this figure includes rifles kept at home by army reservists, Switzerland at 27.2 per cent.[3]

The American link between handguns and the local militia isn't quite so secure as in the Swiss example, Italian republican theory – or the Bill of Rights, come to that. For one thing, who ever heard of a modern local militia in the US? (The state national guards are quite different.) Secondly, the same Constitution that provided for local militias also mandated a federal army and a navy (Article I, Section 10). Furthermore, the Executive could commandeer local militias for the common defence (Article II, Section 2), and the federal government was granted powers 'to provide for organizing, arming, and disciplining' the state militias (Article I, Section 8).

In other words, that popular image of the Minutemen, ready to take their muskets down from a rack over the fireplace and defend their townships at a moment's notice, was a fond folk memory even by the time the Constitution was written and signed. For what Article I, Section 8 means is that central – not local – government would decide how many officers and men the militias would contain, by what regulations they would serve and the type of arms to be issued to them. So even before the Second Amendment the Founding Fathers were envisaging a different source for armaments than those kept at home on an ad hoc basis.

So though they constantly present themselves as defenders of the Second Amendment, pro-gun lobbying groups like the National Rifle Association don't have much to say about local militias. Instead they champion all sorts of gun sports, from target practice and skeet shooting to deer and duck hunting. So far, so uncontroversial. Where they plunge into the thick of contemporary politics, though, is in their insistence on private citizens' right to keep guns in their houses to ward off violent assailants.

This goal the NRA advances as a sacred trust, as though it were the very preservation of American civil liberties. Well-publicised speeches attack politicians in favour of gun control. At an NRA meeting in 2000, the association's president, actor Charlton Heston, famously held aloft an antique musket given to him by the association, vowing that presidential candidate Al Gore would have to prize it 'from my cold, dead hands' if he tried to deny him his 'second-amendment rights'. The scene figured in Michael Moore's film against lax gun control legislation, *Bowling for Columbine* (2002), where it was edited to suggest the comment had been given a year earlier, as a direct response to those grieving after the mass shooting at Columbine High School, near Denver. The gun control debate is full of dirty tricks like that.

The NRA also push their message in their wide range of publications. *The Armed Citizen* carries stories of vulnerable householders – a high school freshman, an 81-year-old woman – who shot and scared off intruders trying to kick their doors in or break their windows with (in one case) a bicycle. What these stories have in common is that the bad guys are never attacking with revolvers or pistols of their own, and when shot by the house-holders, don't get their heads blown off by a .357 Magnum soft point. Instead they run away. The police later pick them up and take them to hospital, where their 'condition' is reported to be 'stable'.

For all that, the NRA is an extremely effective lobbying force. In 2004 their influence blocked congressional renewal of a ten-year-old ban on the sale of assault weapons. When cities around the country began to initiate class action suits against gun companies, the NRA argued for a federal law to insulate manufacturers and distributors of armaments against such cases. The bill to protect 'Lawful Commerce in Arms' passed the House on 20 October 2005.[4]

Do handguns really scare off threats to the home, or do they just make death by gunfire more likely? The jury's still out. Each side argues from statistics selected from a wide range of figures based on different premises. Advocates for gun control claim that: 'Homicide of a family member is 2.7 times more likely … in a home with a firearm than in homes without guns.' In 1993 a Swiss professor, Martin Killias, published a study of eighteen countries that showed a weak correlation between gun ownership, homicide and suicide.[5] But as an FBI Uniform Crime Report of 1997 pointed out, other researchers found in those same eighteen countries a much stronger correlation between firearm homicides and car ownership![6]

More seriously, Gary Kleck has found that if you exclude the US from the international comparison, there emerges 'no significant association between gun ownership and the total homicide rate' in the remaining countries compared.[7] Still others – and not just the partisan NRA – argue a negative correlation between guns and violent crime, citing Switzerland and Norway (high ownership, low homicide), and even claiming that increased gun control goes along with rises in cases of armed robbery – up 44 per cent since a recent round-up of guns in Australia, for example.[8] All these international comparisons are weakened by the wide variety of crime included in the various studies: gun-related and non-gun-related homicide, armed and unarmed robbery, assault with and without a firearm, and so on.

The real wild card is suicide. Here – although naturally not included in NRA scenarios like those in *The Armed Citizen* – there really does seem to be a positive correlation with gun-toting. In 1999 over half of all gun deaths in America were suicides, and of all suicides committed in the US, over half were by firearms.[9] Norway, Finland, Canada and above all Switzerland – all countries where firearms are allowed, though often subject to strict licensing – also had high rates of gun-related suicide.

There may be something opportunistic about this. If you want to do yourself in, the gun in the house may be the first recourse. Granted, the same can be true of other sources of stress, like family quarrels, feuds with neighbours and of course self-defence. But the decisive factor is likely to be the stress in the first place, and its underlying causes, like unemployment and high medical bills. With its relatively weak social services, America is a bad place to be down on your luck.

At least once a week, 42 per cent of Americans eat out while they are en route to somewhere else.

America has no monopoly on fast food. You can get it at East Asian sushi and noodle bars, or as a shish or doner kebab or falafel wrapped in pitta bread almost anywhere in the Middle East. Snacks like these are common in open markets and busy streets all over the world.

But apart from such outlets as hot-dog carts in New York and Washington, DC, American fast food is more often associated with the open road than the crowded city. It originated in roadside diners catering to busy travellers on their way to somewhere else. Typically, these provided a long counter to accommodate single men or (less often) women, maybe truck drivers or travelling salesmen. Additional seating, often arranged in booths, provided for families and courting couples.

The kitchen, just behind the counter or close to it, would have a griddle for cooking pancakes, bacon and eggs in the morning, then hamburgers or small steaks later in the day. There would be an oil fryer for the french fries, an electric mixer for sodas and milkshakes, a coffee pot of course, and racks of pies and cakes behind glass or under fly-proof screen covers on the counter.

That's how we remember them, anyway, and how they can still be seen as retro recreations on 'Main Street' in Disneyland, in restored 'colonial villages' and up-market shopping malls.

Today's fast food is very different in the huge global operations like McDonald's, Burger King, Wendy's, Hardee's, Taco Bell and Colonel Sanders' Kentucky Fried Chicken. And the cooking no longer takes place behind the counter. Or at least not cooking as we would recognise it. 'Assembling' would be closer to the truth.

According to Eric Schlosser, author of *Fast Food Nation* (2001) and *Chew on This* (2006), Taco Bell's ingredients arrive as frozen, pre-cooked meat and dehydrated refried beans that look like bran flakes. Just add hot water and you're ready to roll. Burger King's hamburgers go in as frozen patties at one end of a conveyor belt, emerging from the broiler 90 seconds later, fully cooked. 'The ovens at McDonald's', he writes, 'look like commercial laundry presses, with big steel hoods that swing down and grill hamburgers on both sides at once.'[1]

Driving all this engineering are the needs for consistency and low price. The industrialisation of food preparation yields economies of scale and an identical product from coast to coast – and even in foreign countries, except where local dietary proclivities force a substitution, like lamb for beef in India. Consistency entails keeping the product chemically stable over the time taken to deliver and store it.

It also means making sure it tastes the same from place to place. Whole industries exist to provide the right balance between sweet and sour, salt and bitter, not to mention the subtler overtones in the science of artificial flavours. To meet these demands McDonald's strawberry milkshakes contain no fewer than 59 ingredients running from 'A' to 'V' – from amyl acetate, through ethyl heptylate and methyl naphthyl ketone, to vanillin.[2] And sugar, of course. Lots of that. Even the non-dessert and non-drink items on the fast-food menu – the burgers, tacos, ribs and fried chicken – contain sugar in their complex make-up.

The drive for low prices involves the local labour market too. Fast-food outlets hire teenagers at the minimum wage, which has stuck at $5.15 per hour since 1997, despite several attempts, strenuously resisted by the fast-food moguls, to increase it. As recently as 4 August 2006, the Senate voted down a proposal to raise the minimum wage to $7.15 per hour by mid-2009.[3]

The word 'McJob' has actually entered the latest edition of the Merriam-Webster Collegiate Dictionary, where it's defined as 'low-paying and dead-end work'. Jim Cantalupo, then boss of McDonald's, dismissed the term as 'an inaccurate description of restaurant employment', and pointed out that 'more than 1,000 of the men and women who own and operate McDonald's restaurants today got their start by serving customers behind the counter'.[4]

Then there's the health risk. The high fat, salt and sugar content in most fast foods is making an already-overweight nation fatter and sicker (see fact 40). Playwright and film director Morgan Spurlock dramatised this threat in *Super Size Me* (2004), a film log of himself making a hog of himself eating only McDonald's food for a month. Though starting with above-average health and fitness, he gained 25 pounds and developed severe liver trouble.

Still, for all the financial and gustatory engineering going into these worldwide franchises, the 'fast' in American fast food has always had as much to do with movement as quick preparation. To reinforce their association with travel, many of the old roadside diners themselves were manufactured to look like the dining cars on streamliners – long and slender, with fluted stainless-steel exterior walls. Like their customers, they too were mobile – up to a point. 'Having acquired one,' as Bill Bryson has written, 'all you had to do was to set it on a level piece of ground, hook up water and electricity, and you were in business. If trade didn't materialize, you simply loaded it onto a flatbed truck and tried your luck elsewhere.'[5]

Even McDonald's began as a roadside burger stand in San Bernardino, California, alongside fabled Route 66. Fast food's later move into the suburbs still kept the car motif uppermost. So-called 'drive-in restaurants' – like the one in George Lucas's movie *American Graffiti*, where in 1973 they were already the subject of nostalgic reflection – were really just hamburger stands and soda fountains in the round. Even modern McDonald's and Taco Bell have their 'drive-thru' facility, where you can order at one window, then drive round to collect your meal at another, without ever leaving your car.

The fact is, we don't eat in fast-food joints every day, which is why Spurlock's trial run wasn't really a proper experiment at all. We eat out for a break, when shopping – above all, when travelling. And travel imposes its own strains, even anxieties, especially for a nation forced so often to travel against its will (see facts 8 and 44). On the road, people want solid, meaty comfort food, and they want it as they're used to having it – the exact same choice, flavours, price – especially on a long trip. Add to that cleanliness, fast service and a child-friendly environment providing everything from high chairs to toys and play areas, and you have a pretty powerful appeal to the travelling public.

After all, imagine the scenario. You've driven 350 miles, you have another 200 or so to go. It's lunchtime. In the back, running low on blood sugar, the kids are growing increasingly restless and out of control. You've got an hour to spare at most. In conditions like these, even the most avid gourmand might prefer an American fast-food joint to a cosy little restaurant with one Michelin rosette and a set-price menu for €65 a head, *boissons non compris*.

Only 18 per cent of American adults own a passport.

That's according to the European Travel Commission, which promotes American travel to their countries. Amazingly, this figure may be an overestimate, since it includes partners of American service personnel posted overseas, who may not have gone along for the ride any more willingly than their husbands and wives. Or it may understate the number of Americans going abroad, since (for the moment) passports aren't required for travel to Canada, Mexico or the West Indies. Never mind. It seems that fewer than a fifth of Americans old enough to make up their own minds can or want to travel to another country. This compares with half the Australian population who own passports, 70 per cent of Belgians and Dutch, and 80 per cent of the British.

This reluctance to travel is pretty odd for the biggest global superpower in history, given that it needs to manage military, commercial and even cultural enterprises all over the world. It's even odder when you consider how often Americans move house (see fact 44), and how fond they are of stories and movies like *Huckleberry Finn*, *On the Road* and *Easy Rider*, in which young men grow up through travel. Clearly Americans are mobile. Like Daniel Boone and Huck Finn, we may still prefer lighting out to staying at home in 'sivilizashun'. But conventional travel? That's something we're less certain about.

But then what do we mean by travel? Why do people do it? Certainly it hasn't always been promoted as a life-enhancing activity. The ancient Greeks and Romans thought of travel as a fall from a golden age. Before they started to travel for business or tourism, so the theory went, people were content to stay where they were born and did not look enviously on other countries. Or as the Latin poet Ovid put it in the *Metamorphoses*, in the golden age: 'Never yet had any pine tree, cut down from its home on the mountains, been launched on ocean's waves, to visit foreign lands; men knew only their own shores.'[1]

Today, of course, that very relativism is what we're after. Travel now responds to one of two contrasting needs: to change circumstances or to confirm them. The motive for change is seen all around us. People travel to Arizona or Florida for their health, or to escape a cold, dreary winter. They travel to take part in a favourite sport, like skiing or scuba-diving. For centuries travellers have gone in search of 'the sublime' – to vast deserts, or waterfalls thundering and spraying off steep mountain gorges – in order to experience a sense of awe and wonder in nature.

Less strong among Americans has been the desire for change in cultural environment. Still, many people around the world feel the need to experience different manners, foods, architectural styles and other conventions. In the late 19th and early 20th centuries, Anglo-Saxon writers and painters fled to Paris in order to escape puritan constraints on art, sex and alcohol in their own countries. Today many travel to Amsterdam to smoke marijuana. Here, even less transgressive differences from home can be inviting. In *The Art of Travel*, English essayist Alain de Botton (not after dope) has written of the simple pleasure he took in a sign in Schiphol Airport, Amsterdam, with its 'Aankomst' and 'Uitgang' for Arrivals and Departures, all done in 'practical modernist fonts, Frutiger or Univers', with a Dutch Calvinist simplicity.[2] Schiphol will also provide the tourist's first taste of real Heineken – not that feeble stuff from the bottle but straight from the tap, at around 6 per cent alcohol.

The need to confirm one's circumstances can be even stronger than the desire to change them. The recent craze for genealogy on the internet shows how keen people are to trace their 'roots'. The urge carries over into physical locations – say, an old home or high school. Beyond the family lies the concern to explore the origins of a shared culture, whether back in Kansas or Massachusetts, or somewhere in Europe, South America or the Orient. Reading the history or seeing pictures of some imagined ancestral territory can sharpen the appetite to go there. Then to see the place itself enlivens its historical or pictorial promise, giving it 'a local habitation and a name' to events shared in this culture.

Americans travel for physical change all the time, only they don't need passports to do so. The country has an astonishing range of topographical features to visit and wonder at, from the Grand Canyon to the Sierra Nevada, the Great Lakes to the Florida

Everglades. 'Hell, living in far west Texas,' wrote one blogger on the subject, 'I can drive 800 miles east and still be in the state of Texas! When I get there, not only will the climate be different, but the culture will be different too.'[3]

'Never need an American look beyond his own country for the sublime and beautiful of natural scenery, but Europe held forth all the charms of storied and poetical association', wrote Washington Irving in 1920, trying to explain to his readers why his collection of essays had as many sketches drawn from European settings as American.[4]

'Association' could turn even unspectacular places into evocative sites of travel. Runnymede, an ordinary meadow bordered by humdrum trees, is made special by the thought that it was there that Magna Carta was signed. Irving thought that America was still too young a country to have a history or a literature associated with specific locales; so the imaginative stimulus of association could not work there.

He was wrong, of course. Even by the 1820s, the United States had acquired places made special by its history, like the otherwise ordinary wooden bridge over the Concord River over which was fired the shot 'heard round the world' that started the American Revolutionary War. But something of Irving's anxiety remains in Americans contemplating the other kind of travel, the one that consolidates the sense of shared culture. It's as though we were a bit overwhelmed by it all, required to know too much history, speak too many languages, before we could set out on our explorations.

This concern is reflected in a website devoted exclusively to the scarcity of passports among the American population. Does this mean we are insular, provincial, indifferent to other cultures – or even to culture itself? Some feel that the whole issue has been 'inflated by those Americans who like to wear their passports like a Boy Scout Badge (i.e., Yes I've been to Europe, I'm so much smarter and cultured than the rest of you.).'[5] An American woman living in the UK, tired of hearing the Brits jeer at American passport statistics, questioned whether 'the mere act of travelling to another country' really did much to increase knowledge and sophistication. While granting that the British travel abroad often, she added: 'many of them just want to go clubbing, stock up on cheap booze or stay in beach resorts populated entirely by other British tourists.'[6]

Anyway, as the blog posters point out, Americans travel abroad less than other nationalities because they get shorter holidays – typically two weeks a year as against four or five in Europe – and in any case are not offered the sort of cheap package tours available to Europeans.

Besides, Americans can get all the European culture they want by staying within the country. 'Many cities have their "Chinatown", "Little Italy" among other ethnic neighborhoods', wrote one blogger. He took a girlfriend who had spent the summer in Italy to the Italian restaurant in Disney World. Though 'very skeptical', 'by the time she got to the cappuccino, she was crying her eyes out because it was just like Italy.'[7]

None of these really work as excuses or compensations. The points about holidays and cheap flights are really just parallel statements of the passport scarcity, not explanations for it. If the demand for foreign travel were there, the market and conditions of employment would have met it by now. As for whether Italy can be recalled in Disney World, sure, just as an Egyptian temple, sphinx and pyramid can be replicated in the Luxor Casino in Las Vegas, or (to take a more upscale example) a Florentine cloister in the Getty Villa in Malibu, California.

Of course there are many Americans for whom foreign travel satisfies a genuine wish for change, who have the curiosity and cultural confidence to encounter the unfamiliar. There are others, though, who sign up to off-the-peg tourism, who allow themselves to be herded into tour groups, lectured at and moved through countries at breakneck speed (if it's Tuesday, it must be Belgium, as the old joke goes). If this bullied and bottled-up experience is foreign travel, then it's not surprising that a majority of Americans decline to shell out the $97 for the necessary permit to undergo it.

Over twice as many Americans claim to go to church as actually do.

An enduring journalistic cliché about the United States is how many people go to church every week. Between 40 and 44 per cent of the population is the figure usually quoted. Of course this proportion falls a long way below the weekly religious attendance quoted for Pakistan (91 per cent), Nigeria (89 per cent), the Philippines (68 per cent) and other devout Third World countries. Nevertheless, apart from Ireland, which weighs in at an impressive 89 per cent, the US famously reports the highest weekly attendance at places of worship in the developed world. This fact is regularly trotted out to fill out profiles of American political affiliations and other social attitudes.

For example, before 1972 Americans who claimed they went to church every week voted the same as those who didn't. By 2000 the third National Survey of Religion and Politics, staged by John C. Green of the University of Akron, was showing a clearly marked 'God gap' between the major political parties. Moreover, this discrepancy widened directly in proportion to the frequency of church attendance.

So those who said they went to church more than once a week divided as 68 per cent voting for Bush in 2000, as against 32 per cent for Gore, while 58 per cent of the once-a-week attendees voted for Bush, as against 42 per cent for Gore. At the other end of the scale, of those who went to church 'a few times a year', 'seldom' or 'never', 40, 39 and 35 per cent respectively voted for Bush, as against 60, 61 and 65 per cent for Gore. The only exceptions to this correlation between frequent attendance and support for the Republicans were Black Protestants, who still come out strongly for the Democrats.[1]

The reasons why the God gap opened in American political affiliation over the last four decades has been neatly summarised by Susan Page, writing in *USA Today*. John Kennedy, to this date the only Roman Catholic to have been elected President, 'didn't have to take a position on abortion', and so could count on the support of nearly 80 per cent of Catholic voters in 1960, while managing to convince conservative Protestants that he wouldn't be taking orders from the Vatican should he be elected President. In 2004, 'the challenge to Kerry, who is Catholic, isn't anti-Catholic feeling by evangelicals', she writes, but 'objections from conservative Catholics that he has failed to follow the dictums of the church closely enough'. In 2004 Bush, a Methodist, won the support of most Catholics who attended mass every week, while Kerry led among those who didn't.[2]

Which is all very interesting, except that the figures for church attendance are notoriously inaccurate. That's because they depend on self-reporting, on people answering questions put to them on the street or more often over the phone. For over half a century, the Gallup Organization has been asking people: 'Did you, yourself, happen to attend church or synagogue in the last seven days?' Repeatedly, between 40 and 44 per cent of respondents answered that they had.

Then in 1993 three researchers decided to count heads. Focusing on Protestant churches in Ashtabula County, Ohio, and eighteen Roman Catholic dioceses around the country, Mark Chaves, Penny Marler and Kirk Hadaway repeatedly numbered the people present in churches and cars in the parking lots week by week. The results? Only 20 per cent of Protestants and 28 per cent of Catholics in the area were actually going to church week by week. They then polled a sample of Ashtabula County residents by telephone, only to be told by 40 per cent of the Protestants and 50 per cent of the Catholics that they had been in church the previous Sunday. Subsequent studies using other samples confirmed these results.

If similar discrepancies lurk in other self-reported surveys, like those of party affiliation and voting intention – not to mention attitudes towards abortion, divorce and gay marriage – then an awful lot of books, articles and journalistic think-pieces are going to need revising. But how to explain the gap between actual and reported church attendance in the first place? The answer is obvious, according to Marler and Hadaway. When asked, 'Americans misrepresent how often they vote, how much they give to charity, and how frequently they use illegal drugs … Men exaggerate their number of sexual partners … Actual attendance at museums, symphonies and operas does not match survey results,' they write. 'We should not expect religious behavior to be immune to such misreporting.'[3]

Since God presumably remains undeceived, the tendency to exaggerate attendance can't be to please Him (or Her). It turned out that some of those questioned after the head count had been carelessly including every time they had shown up at the local church – for choir practice, or a vestry meeting, or for weddings and funerals. One respondent even counted mowing the church lawn on the previous Sunday. But these amounted to only 2 per cent of those cross-questioned. Clearly a much larger number, like those others who exaggerate their charitable giving while under-reporting their use of illegal drugs, were trying to conform to their community's sense of respectability.

And why not? Churches are part of that community. In some places, they *are* the community. Particularly in isolated areas they may amount to the chief social and cultural activities for a highly mobile population. Just as members of fraternal organisations might use the nearest chapter of Kiwanis or the Elks, newly arrived members of a church denomination might go to their local congregation for a welcome and a ready-made social group.

Churches do their best to make it easy for newly arrived adherents to find a local congregation to suit them. The website of the American Presbyterian Church, for example, offers a 'Find a Church' feature. Click on it, and you are offered a choice of inputs under which to search: state, city or other area, ZIP code, or presbytery. Once onto the specific congregation, you can find its vital statistics, like membership numbers (and whether rising or falling), its annual giving (averaging $225,455 per congregation in 2005, but well over $1 million for the larger churches), and 'Christian Education Enrollment'.

Once arrived, the newcomer will find structures of worship and giving alongside Sunday schools, Bible study groups, choirs and Christmas plays, all of which most denominations will supplement with more general social activities like concerts, picnics, 'outreach' programmes in the community, sports programmes and even summer camps. So church attendance can be a way of expressing solidarity with the community, within which it is seen as a meritorious activity.

But there's more to it than that. 'Perhaps counter-intuitively,' writes Andrew Walsh in 'Church, Lies, and Polling Data', 'scholars now suggest that it is the *most committed* believers who overstate their attendance, not those who seldom or never attend services.'[4] Why? Because, as Hadaway and Marler discovered when interviewing the over-reporters, the profile of weekly attendance best fitted their sense of commitment to the church. A woman spoke for this majority: 'Saying yes [to the question, did you attend church within the last seven days] was an affirmation of her involvement in and support of the church. Not attending was atypical, so to count her as a "nonattender" would be inaccurate and misleading.'[5]

So we're left with a lie that's not a lie, a kind of hypocrisy that's the most sincere expression of underlying reality. This apparent contradiction isn't unprecedented in America. Benjamin Franklin, who made himself into the representative of his young country, set the model in this as in so many other forms of American self-advertisement. Explaining why he 'dressed plainly', was never seen at 'Places of idle Diversion', never 'went out a-fishing or shooting', he recalled: 'In order to secure my Credit and Character as a Tradesman, I took care not only to be in *Reality* Industrious and frugal, but to avoid all *Appearances* of the contrary.' He was writing of his business credibility, not his religion, but the general point was the same. There was no point in hiding his hard-won virtue from the public gaze.

Americans spend twice as much on civil litigation as they do on new automobiles – and more than any other industrialised country.

Heard the one about the woman who threw a soft drink over her boyfriend, then when she stalked out, slipped on the wet floor, broke her coccyx, sued the restaurant and was awarded $100,000 in damages? Or the woman who tried to sneak through the window of the ladies' toilet in a nightclub in order to avoid the $3.50 cover charge, slipped, fell, knocked out two front teeth, and sued the club for $12,000 dental expenses? Stories like these make the rounds all over the world as examples of suit-happy America, the litigious society gone off the rails. What are the facts?

As a fraction of gross domestic product, American costs for civil litigation in suits for tort (personal injury) and product liability are three times those in the United Kingdom. The US has 3.3 suits for tort per 1,000 head of population, as against 1.2 per 1,000 in Great Britain. A survey published in 1992 counted 780,000 lawyers in the United States, or 312 for each 100,000 of the population. Comparable figures for England and Wales were 68,067 and 134; for France 27,700 and 49.1.[1]

Why? Well, for one thing, the United States lacks the larger tax-funded social welfare systems found in most European countries. The tort system can function as a longstop remedy for personal injury, forcing negligent defendants to pay for their actions.[2] In turn, the system for funding civil lawsuits adjusts to this difference. In Britain and continental Europe, the loser in a suit has to pay a substantial proportion of the winner's legal fees, while in American law each party pays their own. So in Europe there's a much greater risk in taking a case to court.[3]

Other long-standing cultural differences also play a role. In America much less mystery surrounds the role of lawyers than in Europe. Apart from the judge's simple black robe, no special costume or regalia distinguish the profession in the courtroom. Higher up the scale, judges are subject to the electoral process just as are any other officials in public service. Circuit court judges, appeals court judges, even state supreme court justices are all elected to office.

In America the study of law is almost as much a general education as it is a professional qualification – something like a politics degree in Europe. Many lawyers move into other occupations, like business or politics (to which a law degree serves almost as an apprenticeship). Abraham Lincoln practised law for nearly 25 years in the Illinois courts, dealing with cases at almost all levels of court practice – county, circuit, appellate, and federal, representing clients in a range of civil and criminal actions from debt and divorce to murder.

Feeling more like ordinary citizens than part of a professional elite, American lawyers aren't embarrassed to advertise their services, or to offer potential claimants a no-win, no-fee deal, or to undertake a class action suit on behalf of two or more clients with substantially the same claim.

Along with this demystified status of lawyers goes a strong culture of the citizen's individual rights – not to mention the rights of the consumer in a country where buyers have had the choice of a wide variety of goods and services for generations. When it comes to criminal liability, the Fifth Amendment of the US Constitution defends the citizen against prosecution by the federal government in these terms: 'No person shall be … deprived of life, liberty, or property, without due process of law.' The Fourteenth Amendment applies the same guarantee with respect to the state authorities.

According to popular belief, this comparatively liberal access to the law is supposed to lead to thousands of capricious or even vexatious suits from plaintiffs like the women who fell in the club and restaurant. Doctors are said to be leaving the profession because of the high cost of malpractice insurance. American exports are supposed to have lost their competitive edge because of the cost of the safety features that have to be built into them in order to prevent domestic suits in the field of product liability.

The facts are a little less alarming. For one thing, since 1992, tort lawsuit filings have decreased by 9 per cent nationwide, a figure thrown into even starker relief when set against population growth. In Texas, for example, while the population jumped 23 per cent between 1900 and 2000, tort filings fell from 233 to 164 per 100,000 residents, a 30 per cent decline. In California the rate of filings has dropped by 45 per cent over the same period. And the stories of the two litigious women turned out to be just that – stories, or rather 'whole-cloth fabrications' that had been doing the media gossip rounds for over a year.[4]

According to the American Bar Association, product liability cases are also much exaggerated in the public consciousness, amounting to just 11 per cent of the 248,335 federal civil lawsuits filed in 1995. Moreover, juries award damages to plaintiffs in only 44 per cent of the cases brought, and they tend to shy away from 'punitive' awards even when they do decide for the plaintiff. The impact of such suits on competition between domestic and imported manufactures is negligible. The total risk cost of product liability suits is estimated at less than 1 per cent of sales revenue. Besides, foreign importers, like German and Japanese car-makers, are subject to the same liability laws as American manufacturers.

As for malpractice suits, a General Accounting Office study in August 2003 found that many of the media claims about doctors being forced to leave the profession were false. The direct total cost of the malpractice system is less than 1 per cent of total health-care expenditure, reports the American Bar Association. What's really pushing health-care costs up are high-tech advances in equipment and medication.[5]

Why would the media seek to exaggerate the extent of the 'litigious society' and the damage it's supposedly causing to the American economy? Sometimes it's because magazines, newspapers and broadcasters have their own tracks to cover. According to Stephanie Mencimer, *Newsweek* magazine, one of the biggest media flag-wavers against the litigious society, had a financial interest in seeing lawsuits curtailed. 'Post-Newsweek Stations Inc. has been sued a number of times for employment discrimination and has been hit with an $8.3 million verdict in 1999.'

Powerful lobby groups vulnerable to class action suits also manage to plant misleading statistics and innuendo in the media, according to Mencimer. 'Tobacco companies alone spent $15 million in a single year during the industry's campaign to push the "lawsuit abuse" message.' Republican Party leaders favour the message too, since lawyers represent the second biggest group of donors to the Democrat Party.[6]

For all that, America remains a place where people tend to go to court sooner and oftener than in other countries. If tort suits have declined, and malpractice and product liability cases been shown to be less detrimental to the country's economy than supposed, other kinds of civil lawsuits have increased dramatically. In the decade up to 1994, domestic relations caseloads alone rose in the state courts by 65 per cent.[7] And if the law is more accessible to the ordinary citizen than elsewhere, that stands as one of the country's many strong points.

Thanksgiving is the real American national holiday.

Yes, Thanksgiving, more even than the Fourth of July. Of course the Fourth is the official national holiday, a summer festival with barbecues and fireworks. The Fourth commemorates the day in 1776 when the Founding Fathers signed and published the Declaration of Independence.

In fact the country's independence had already been enacted two days before that. It was on 2 July that a majority of the delegates to the second Continental Congress carried the motion of Richard Henry Lee of Virginia: 'That these United Colonies are, and of right ought to be, free and independent States.' By contrast, the Declaration was not a legal instrument. It was an advertisement that the new country was open and ready for business.

Yet it's Thanksgiving that is the nation's true national holiday. It's the one day in the year when American families, however far apart, try their damnedest to get back together. Remember the movie *Planes, Trains and Automobiles* (1987)? When Steve Martin's flight is cancelled by bad weather, he just has to press on – by train, car, anything (however broken down) – to get home for Thanksgiving. It never occurs to him to give up. All Americans understood that underlying premise of the comic plot. No other motive would have justified his persisting through all those days and nights of delays and frustrations, which included being thrown together with a garrulous shower-ring salesman called Dell. (Yes, the film also took a rare look at class difference in America.)

Thanksgiving celebrates, not the country's independence from Great Britain, but its very foundation, its settlement by the so-called 'Pilgrim Fathers'. The holiday commemorates the settlers' first harvest in Massachusetts, when they sat down to a feast of local wildlife, together with vegetables that they had planted and grown themselves. The first President to suggest a national day of thanks was George Washington in 1789. Since then, others proposed various dates for the holiday. In 1941 Congress finally decided on the fourth Thursday in November.

What actually happened was described by settler Edward Winslow in a letter to 'A loving and old friend' back in England, sent from Plymouth, Massachusetts in the autumn of 1621. 'Our harvest being gotten in,' he wrote, 'our governor sent four men on fowling, that so we might … rejoice together after we had gathered the fruit of our labors.' The 'fowl' were probably wild turkeys. There is no mention of pumpkins. The 'fruit of their labors' amounted to maize or Indian corn and an 'indifferent' crop of barley.

There's an old joke that when the Puritans finally reached America, they first fell on their knees to pray, then fell upon the Indians. Not so. They got on well with the Native Americans at first – not least because of their amazing good luck in attracting the interest of a member of the local tribe. Either kidnapped or traded (the record is unclear), Tisquantum, or Squanto, had done two round trips across the Atlantic: first to England, then back to Newfoundland, then to Spain and finally back to his native Massachusetts. He spoke fluent English and Spanish, as well as his local dialect of the Algonquin language group.

Tisquantum offered to mediate between the settlers and Massasoit, chief of the local tribe, the Wampanoag. He also showed them how to plant corn, by putting a small herring-like fish called an alewife – then in plentiful supply in the North Atlantic – in with each kernel. Since it was this trick, by Winslow's own admission, that made the Puritans' first harvest possible, it comes as no surprise that the Natives were part of that first Thanksgiving. Or as Winslow himself puts it, 'Many of the Indians [came] amongst us, and among the rest their greatest King Massasoit, with some ninety men, whom for three days we entertained and feasted.'[1]

But why should that tiny settlement on the coast of Massachusetts have been chosen as the focus of America's founding holiday? It wasn't the first permanent colony to be established by the British in the New World. Fourteen years before Plymouth, another company had landed at Jamestown, Virginia. Though precarious, the Virginia settlement survived to make Captain John Smith and Pocahontas, his supposed Indian lover, part of American living mythology. And throughout the 17th century nearly three times as many Britons migrated to the Chesapeake Bay region of what is now Virginia and Maryland as did to New England.

Yet it is the New England story, with its Pilgrim Fathers, its first Thanksgiving and its Whig values of self-reliance, self-control and individual enterprise, that forms the American foundation narrative. And ever since then, even as immigrants arrived in much larger numbers from southern and central Europe, the Far East, and the country's Spanish-speaking neighbours to the south, the United States has continued to picture its origins in those steeple-hatted, white English men and women sitting down to celebrate their first harvest. How did so much glamour and prestige come to be attached to this tiny movement of peoples to Massachusetts?

One reason could be that the more northern migrants had chosen freely to make their way into a cold part of the country, whether fleeing religious persecution or investing in a new commercial venture. By contrast, their southern cousins were made up of a few rich families granted large landholdings from the Crown, and a much larger crowd of felons and indentured servants. (Daniel Defoe's Moll Flanders, after all, was transported as a criminal to Virginia, not to Massachusetts.) When searching for founding fathers and mothers, the newly independent democratic republic was hardly likely to choose aristocrats, slaves and pickpockets as national role models.

But there's more to it than that. There is clear evidence that the governor of the first New England settlement constructed the history of Plymouth Plantation so as to place the Pilgrim Fathers at the very heart of America's founding narrative. When they first set foot in Massachusetts in 1620, William Bradford and his friends wrote of their delight in the material wealth of the new-found land, 'all wooded with oaks, pines, sassafras, juniper, birch, holly [and] vines'. After a thirsty morning of exploring on hard cheese and biscuit brought from England, they 'found springs of fresh water … and sat us down and drank our first New England water with as much delight as ever we drank drink in all our lives'. As for the natives, they posed no threat, but instead 'ran away with might and main'.[2]

Yet just ten years later, when Bradford began to write the official history of the colony, he needed something more monumental to leave behind for posterity. So in this later account of their first steps everything is changed. Gone are the concrete details of wood, fruit and spring water. Instead, all is abstract: 'hideous and desolate wilderness.' The winter is 'sharp and violent, and subject to cruel and fierce storms'. The native peoples, far from running away, are 'savage barbarians … readier to fill [the explorers'] sides full of arrows than otherwise'.

Why the change? Clearly Bradford wanted to remake their first encounter with the New World into an ordeal, one that he and his fellow colonists overcame heroically. But there's an additional clue in that word 'wilderness'. Behind the story as he told it lay the model of all migrations, the Israelites in the wilderness, led by Moses to the Promised Land.

And now Bradford was telling the tale as he wanted succeeding generations – the first to be born in America and all those to follow – to remember it. 'May not and ought not the children of these fathers rightly say, "Our fathers were Englishmen which came over this great ocean and were ready to perish in this wilderness; but they cried unto the Lord, and he heard their voice and looked on their adversity."'[3]

By the time he had finished he had slipped into the exact words of Deuteronomy 26:7, where Moses tells the Israelites the story of their national origins. Bradford co-opted the Old Testament story of the Jews wandering in the desert as the American founding narrative.

Why did Bradford's account of America's beginnings prevail over the thousands of other stories that could have been told? Because immigrants arriving in the New World – whatever their national origins, their religion, or lack of it – tend to think of their journey as an upheaval and ordeal to be overcome before attaining the promised land. Though writing about a tiny faction, Bradford spoke to, and for, millions who would follow the Pilgrim Fathers to the New World.

More than 18,000 adults in America die each year because they don't have health insurance.[1]

American healthcare is in crisis. For starters, it's by far the most expensive in the world – weighing in at $2.1 trillion in 2006, 16 per cent of the American gross domestic product, or roughly $7,000 per person. Compare that to the average of just under 9 per cent of GDP for the world's other prosperous democracies.[2]

And what do we get for our money? On the one hand, the most advanced medicine in the world, with Nobel Prize-winning research, new technology, surgical techniques, medication and other forms of treatment being invented and introduced almost daily. The world's rich practically commute to the US for medical care.

That's the good news. The bad is an infant mortality rate of 6.63 deaths per 1,000 live births – and still rising – ranking 36th in the world, just above Croatia. An average life expectancy of 77.43 years, 38th in the world, trailing other first-world countries like Switzerland, Australia, Canada, Italy, France, Spain, the Netherlands and Great Britain.[3]

In between birth and death, the American healthcare system isn't performing all that well either, not for ordinary citizens, anyway. A 2005 survey compared the US with Australia, Canada, Germany, New Zealand and Great Britain under headings relevant to quality of care. On all but two of the indicators, the US came last. 'Patient centeredness' was judged to be dismal, because the system scored so low on 'communication', 'responsiveness to patient preference' and 'choice and continuity'.

Equally poor were 'efficiency' and 'patient safety'. Americans were visiting hospital emergency rooms for conditions that could have been treated by their regular doctor. Only they didn't have one. Medical records went missing, or arrived too late for the appointment. Americans were the most likely to receive the wrong medicine or doses, their lab tests were most likely to have been delayed – even when showing alarming abnormal results – or to be simply incorrect.

Above all, the US scores bottom on the 'equity' of its care. The quality of medical treatment available to Americans depends more on income than in any of the other five countries surveyed.[4] The great divide falls between the insured and the uninsured. The biggest slice of health insurance still comes from employers, who can claim tax relief on the expense. Not only their workers, but also their partners and children are covered.

Lately this has fallen sharply. In 1987 nearly 70 per cent of the American population had some form of occupation-related health insurance. The 2002 report that gave the headline figure of over 18,000 dying because uninsured is already woefully out of date, because by 2006, as more and more businesses withdrew this benefit due to cost, the figure for those insured had dropped to around half the working population. Meanwhile, many firms still including health benefits in their employment package were now offering cheaper options, requiring higher premiums and more 'co-payments' and 'deductibles' chargeable to the claimant when the insurance company pays out.

According to a recent report by two Harvard University researchers, around half of all instances of personal insolvency in the US are now due to medical expenses.[5] Most other bankruptcies, they estimate, result from divorce, but at least with divorce you have a choice.

Of course, people can elect to buy their own health insurance, for which they get no tax relief, but these policies too often contain snags like high deductibles and very limited coverage – if any – for pre-existing conditions. Monthly premiums run between $300 and $400 per month, out of the question for even the hardest-working, most prudent saver on a typical low wage of – say – $1,200 per month.

For the unemployed, or for those on the minimum wage in service or seasonal work, there is Medicaid, a programme for the indigent funded jointly by the federal government and individual states. Those aged over 65 are covered by Medicare, a government funded and administered service, which even those who have been able to afford private healthcare switch to when they reach the qualifying age.

This still leaves 46 million people, like illegal immigrants or those on salaries just above the level qualifying for Medicaid, without any form of health insurance. And their children. That was 15.34 per cent of the population in mid-2006, and the figure is still rising. Of those aged between 25 and 64, around 20 per cent are without cover. For the 18-to-24s, a whopping 30 per cent go without. Race and ethnicity come into it too. Uninsured African Americans amount to 17 per cent of the population, while the figure for Hispanics actually tops that for young adults, at 31.4 per cent.[6]

Without cover, what happens when you get sick or have an accident? To start with, you won't have what the National Center for Health Statistics calls a 'usual place to go' for treatment – a family doctor or a local clinic. Instead, you'll pitch up at the emergency room of the local hospital, where the first treatment you'll undergo will be a 'wallet biopsy' to see whether you have an insurance card. Since you don't, the next question is whether you have the means to pay for treatment. If so, you'll be billed, and if you refuse payment, your salary can be 'garnished', and a lien taken on your home.

So long as the hospital is registered as a non-profit operation, the law requires it to offer (usually good) emergency treatment even to those without money. But this means just what it says. An old man who falls, spraining his wrist and breaking his nose in the process, will have his wrist and nose seen to, but not the brain tumour that caused him to lose his balance in the first place.

Not even a successful biopsy will always preserve you from wallet trauma. This was the main focus of Michael Moore's attack in Sicko! (2007), his latest and so far best documentary film. What he showed is that even the medically insured often get short-changed or denied payment altogether on a technicality, while the insurance worker gets promoted for finding the loophole. Three-quarters of those filing for bankruptcy, to protect their savings and property from medical debt, were insured at the onset of their illness, according to the Harvard report.

Even government coverage has its gaps. Up to 2003, Medicare didn't pay for prescriptions, a heavy cost to the seniors dependent on the programme. Then they agreed to cover (most of) the cost of drugs injected into the patient, or infused via a drip, but not taken as pills, even if the oral version of the drug was safer, easier and cheaper.

This hurt cancer patients whose chemotherapy had to be taken by mouth, not to mention the pills to control nausea and other side-effects of the chemotherapy itself. After a lot of pressure from cancer charities and grass-roots patient groups, this restriction on oral drugs was finally rescinded at the beginning of 2006, but other absurdities remain in the Medicare drug policy. Most notorious of these is the funding 'doughnut hole', which covers the first $2,250 per year of prescription charges, then resumes at $5,100, but excludes the $2,850 in between.

In fact the painstaking business of figuring out who gets what under the various forms of public and private insurance – which hospitals can treat what ailments, what expenses are covered and for how long, at what level the deductibles and co-payments kick in, and hundreds of other variables – absorbs a huge bureaucracy. One estimate is that regulation alone adds $340 billion a year to the cost of American healthcare, or three times what France spends administering health insurance, as a percentage of overall medical spending.[7]

How has the situation been allowed to get this bad for so long? After all, it hardly matches the country's sense of itself. How could such a highly developed consumer culture have wound up with a service that scores so low on 'responsiveness to patient prefer-ence'? Why do its users rank American medicine bottom of the ladder on 'choice and continuity', given how often medical pressure groups mention these benefits as our advantage over national health services in other countries?

In the 1940s Harry Truman proposed a national health service. In 1993 Hillary Clinton suggested the more limited reform that insur-ance companies be mandated to provide healthcare for all. Both were defeated by horror stories about 'socialised medicine'. With four lobbyists for every member of Congress, will the healthcare industry continue to block reform? Do the majority of Americans still believe the propaganda put out so tirelessly by the American Medical Association and the big medical insurance companies?

Maybe not. Healthcare is back on the agenda. In her campaign for the Democratic nomination for President in 2007, Hillary proposed another 'plan'. If you're happy with your insurer, you can stay with them. If not, or uninsured, 'you will have a choice of plans to pick from and that coverage will be affordable'. Tax credits will help 'working families ... to pay their premiums'. Insurance companies won't be allowed to deny protection to clients with pre-existing conditions.[8]

Not exactly universal healthcare from cradle to grave. The insurance companies love it, because it keeps them in business. Maybe that's why Hillary is, according to *Sicko!*, the Senate's second-highest recipient of donations from the healthcare industry.

By 2000 the Great Migration had reversed itself.

Being a land of migrants, America has registered many 'Great Migrations'. The first consisted of about 1,000 Puritans, led by John Winthrop, who settled Boston and its surroundings in 1630. The John Winthrop Society, unsurprisingly, has called this settlement 'the most important and influential single group of Europeans ever to arrive in North America'. Another 'Great Migration' of mainly white settlers moved to Mississippi Territory between 1789 and 1819, and yet another, identically named, saw around 800 settlers move westwards along the Oregon Trail in 1843.

But the truly great migration, involving more people than any other, whether into or within the country, took place between around 1916 and 1970, when 6.5 million African Americans left the old Confederacy of the southern states for cities in the North and West. As late as 1940, as Nicholas Lehmann points out in his study of the movement, '77 per cent of black Americans still lived in the rural South. ... In 1970, when the migration ended, black America was only half southern, and less than a quarter rural; "urban" had become a euphemism for "black".'[1]

Why did they leave? Sharecropping bound most rural blacks to a single crop, cotton, and to a landowner who could cheat the workers at the year-end tally – with impunity, since 'Jim Crow' laws maintained segregation, impeded the black vote and blocked the black cropper's access to the law. Bad as these conditions were, they deteriorated still further when Roosevelt's New Deal passed the Agricultural Adjustment Act of 1933, which sought to control agricultural surpluses by paying farm owners to take land out of production, thus putting tenants, croppers and labourers out of work. The final turn of the screw was the perfection of the cotton-picking machine in 1944. It could do the work of 50 people.

Where did they go? Chicago, for a start, where the African American population reached 100,000 by 1920, 270,000 by 1940 and 813,000 by 1950, rivalling Harlem, New York as the most vibrant black cultural centre in the country.[2] Detroit had 6,000 Afro-

American citizens in 1910, 120,000 in 1930 and around 5½ times that number in 1970 – by then 44 per cent of its population. Demand for labour rose in these and other northern cities when European immigration virtually ceased during the First World War. At first southern blacks took service jobs vacated by white workers moving into the armaments industries or drafted into the armed services.

Later in Chicago the men worked in the stock yards and the Post Office, and the women in the big mail-order retailers, like Montgomery Ward and Sears Roebuck, at wages four to five times what they could get as farm hands in Mississippi. But it was the Second World War, coinciding with New Deal fair-employment practices and affirmative hiring, that brought southern African Americans into industries making tanks and trucks in Detroit and other industrial areas in the North-east, warplanes in southern California and liberty ships and landing craft around San Francisco Bay.

Cities in the North may have offered the newcomers better pay and – on paper, anyway – more civil rights, but they were hardly welcoming. As late as 1949, a black family moving into a Chicago neighbourhood was greeted with a mob of 2,000 whites throwing stones and firebombs. As more and more whites left the city, and public housing projects turned into high-rise ghettos, standards of education and public order began to plummet.

By the time the Great Migration began to subside, with employment increasingly following white flight out of the cities, urban African Americans had become an underclass trapped in ghettos which, to use Nicholas Lehmann's words, their 'self-destructive behavior, … drug use, out-of-wedlock childbearing, dropping out of school' had turned into 'among the worst places to live in the world'.[3]

Back home, meanwhile, the South was crawling painfully into the 20th century, trying by fits and starts to bring itself up to at least the minimum legal and civil-rights standards in the rest of the country. In 1954 the National Association for the Advancement of Colored People took the Topeka, Kansas, Board of Education all the way to the Supreme Court to prove that 'separate' education was not 'equal'. Martin Luther King, Jr, led a decade of marches, boycotts and sit-ins against southern segregation. Teams of liberal students, African American as well as white, led drives for voter registration. By the end of 1965, 250,000 new black voters had been signed up in the South.

Lyndon B. Johnson, America's most actively progressive post-war President, was determined to carry the southern black struggle on to the federal level. Along with reforms like Medicare and Medicaid (see fact 12), the pre-school programme Head Start, and the War on Poverty, which distributed over $1m to local communities in its first year alone, Johnson introduced the fundamentally scene-changing Civil Rights Act of 1964. This outlawed segregation in public places and withheld funding from all federally assisted projects in which any kind of racial discrimination occurred. A year later, his Voting Rights Act swept away the remaining barriers to black voting in the South. As he put it in his characteristic style: 'If they give blacks the vote, ol' Strom Thurmond [the segregationist senator] will be kissing every black ass in South Carolina.'

Urban black communities seemed indifferent to these improvements. A riot in Watts, Los Angeles, killed 34 people and injured over a thousand in 1965. Other uprisings followed in Atlanta, Chicago and – worst of all – Detroit, with 43 deaths and 4,700 federal troops flown in to restore order. Johnson was bitterly disappointed. An influential report by Senator Daniel Moynihan, titled 'The Negro Family. The Case for National Action' (1965), argued that the destruction of the nuclear family might prevent African Americans from ever making their way in civil society. Government officials began to ask whether there was any point 'throwing more money at the problem'. Johnson's successor, Richard Nixon, turned his attention to trying to end the Vietnam War.

Meanwhile, back in the South, as a direct result of legislative gains in the 60s, African Americans began to take their place in southern state legislatures, then as mayors and governors of cities and states in the South as well as the North. They began to move into white-collar employment closed to them up to then, not only in government and other public-service jobs, but also in all kinds of clerical, technical and administrative work – banking, insurance, education and the media. The more money and other benefits the government pumped into the inner cities, the more the better-motivated blacks used it to move out to the suburbs – just as their white neighbours had up to a generation before.

And not just to the northern suburbs. The real shock to all those pessimistic predictions of white opinion-formers came when African Americans began to move back south. Once again, this followed a similar movement by whites. From about 1970 to 2000, Detroit was to lose 37,537 black residents, Chicago 183,014 and New York over half a million. Until 1980, the cities of the west coast seemed immune from this decline, but from 1985, Los Angeles lost 50,546 and San Francisco 37,691. And the gainers? Above all, Atlanta, Georgia, now unofficially the capital of the 'New South', followed by Dallas, Charlotte, North Carolina and Orlando, Florida.[4]

The New South, that is, not the Deep South. The black return is not a simple reversal of the Great Migration. African Americans are not returning in great numbers to Mississippi, for example, and New Orleans is still haemorrhaging its black population – even more so following their treatment after hurricane Katrina. Nor are these back migrants the modern equivalent of those destitute share-croppers who first went north between the wars.

Today's influx is overwhelmingly college-educated and middle-class. In fact, among college graduates, African Americans out-number whites in the migration to the New South. They are coming home, many of them, to old family ties and cultural roots, but above all they are returning for the economic boom, and the consequent demand for high-tech and white-collar jobs in southern cities in Georgia, Alabama, North Carolina, Texas and Florida.

The Great Migration and its sequel wasn't just about African Americans. Like nothing seen before or since, it involved nearly every issue in American domestic politics since the First World War. Without reference to it, the history of the country in the 20th century could not be told.

Of the 239 elected mayors in the state of Oregon, only two draw a salary.[1]

'I wouldn't vote for him for dogcatcher', as the old joke has it against anyone too incompetent, lazy or dishonest to win popular assent for even the most trivial public office. Nowadays, dog-catchers – or animal control officers, to give them their more dignified official title – are usually appointed. But they were once elected, and more than 176,000 other positions across the United States still are. So lying at the heart of that insult is a fact that would be astonishing, even incomprehensible, to residents of most other countries. In America even the humblest public servant must be subject to the public's choice.

Is this an absurdity or the mainstay of the democratic system? Seen from the outside, it could be a bit of both. Americans are highly suspicious of central government. How could we not be, when for over 140 years we were governed by a metropolitan power 3,000 miles and many weeks' sailing away? With contact between London and its American colonies so impeded, Americans got early into the habit of managing most affairs in local assemblies.

Communications didn't get much better after the Revolution. Roads between Massachusetts, Pennsylvania and Virginia were virtually non-existent. More often than not, people had to travel between even these more settled ex-colonies in ships along the Atlantic coast. As people began to move west away from the sea, their new settlements became even more cut off from each other and the mid-Atlantic states.

So the country's official title, the United States of America, means just what it says. America is a federation of 50 states, each of which has a high measure of control over its own affairs. In fact, the first federal constitution, the Articles of Confederation, gave the states such power over the central government that all laws passed by Congress had to be approved by at least nine of the (then) thirteen states. Even then the central government could not force the states to obey them. Congress was also forbidden from raising money through taxes. The Articles were so unworkable that the Founding Fathers had to start all over again. The result was the Constitution as we know it now.

But that didn't end the tension. The most serious struggle between the states and central government was over the issue of slavery. The slave-holding South argued that it was the individual state's right to determine its own social and economic system without interference from Washington. The Civil War (1861–5) settled the question of the slaves, with President Lincoln forcing their emancipation upon the defeated Confederacy of southern states, but the tag-line 'states' rights' survived into the 1950s and 60s as a rallying cry for southern segregationists.

Even today the states retain important control over issues of conscience, like whether or not to punish murder with the death penalty, or to legalise suicide assisted by a doctor. More pro-saically, but arguably more importantly to many people, the states levy their own taxes, and so determine a large segment of public spending. They control their own education and legal systems and a substantial part of their roads and public transport, commission large-scale public works like bridges and dams, manage irrigation and public water supply, and look after many other day-to-day needs.

Unsurprisingly, then, state governments often replicate the federal system of three branches of government checking and balancing each other. The Governor, equivalent to the President, acts as the executive, as against the bicameral legislature, the state equivalent of the federal congress, and the judiciary in the form of the state supreme court. All these are elected, but so are other officials like state treasurers, labour commissioners and the head of the state school system.

But elected office doesn't stop at the state level. There are also counties – over 3,000 of them in the US – and within them over 100,000 elected offices: members of the county fire department and school boards, county commissioners, auditors, often sheriffs. Then there are the cities. Mayors are elected, of course; so are members of the town or city council, whether called selectmen, as in New England, or supervisors in San Francisco.

In parts of the country civic consciousness is so strong that many public servants work for no salary. In Vancouver, Washington, citizen volunteers serve on various boards and commissions dealing with housing, planning, libraries and even 'urban forestry'. 'These officials give countless hours of service simply for the privilege of serving their communities and having a stronger say in how their institutions are run', according to Steve Holgate. 'These positions also serve as a proving ground for those who wish to run for higher office.'[2]

Even more surprisingly, some mayors – among them 237 in the state of Oregon alone – give up their time for the pleasure and prestige of serving their local communities. On a trip to Washington to lobby for the League of Oregon Cities, the amiable Bob Austin, mayor of Estacada, Oregon (population 2,371), seemed bemused to learn that this spirit of altruistic service is far from universal across the country. 'One of the facts that I learned after talking with our counterparts from other states around the country', he commented in the diary he kept on the trip, 'was that they were most all paid for their services to their cities. Most were surprised to hear that only two cities in Oregon have mayors who are paid and only one city where their council/commissioners are also in paid positions.'[3]

But at least they were elected. Nothing illustrates the American appetite for democratic local control more dramatically than the fact that in many parts of the country, members of the judiciary are elected to office. Circuit court judges, appeals court judges – even, in some states, justices on the state supreme court, are all subject to the popular will. The practice is not universal. Each state has its own constitution, which determines what officials get elected and which appointed. And it certainly doesn't happen at the federal level, where appointments to the Supreme Court are in the gift of the President.

Yet even appointments to the Supreme Court involve politics to a degree seldom seen in other countries at the equivalent judicial level. They have to be approved by the Senate, and although that august body generally goes along with the presidential choice, it doesn't always. Out of a total of 132 presidential nominations to the Supreme Court bench, 27 have been turned down, and recently the process has always attracted intense political interest and involvement. Ronald Reagan's nomination of ex-Attorney General Robert Bork to a place on the Court's bench was vigorously opposed in both the Senate and the country, on the grounds of his allegedly backward views on women's and black rights. In the event, the Senate overturned his appointment by 42 to 58.

In most other countries, judges at all levels are selected not by public ballot but by central government – or more likely, by an arcane process deep within the legal profession itself, and inaccessible to the people whose lives will be affected by their judgements. This is quite intentional, of course. The judiciary must be disinterested, always 'above' personal and sectional interest – above all, 'above' politics. Nothing more clearly sets off the American mentality from that of other countries. In America there is nothing above politics. The vote is the ultimate test. The people are the ultimate judges.

Even visitors to the United States have noticed just how invigorating this degree of local control can be. The greater involvement in local government adds not only to a sense of community, but also (more surprisingly, considering how many diverse groups of people have to be accommodated) to its smooth running. All this local commitment depends on local institutions having real power.

The obvious contrast is England, where fewer than 22 per cent of those eligible now vote in local elections because central government has drawn more and more powers to itself. With people in the regions feeling increasingly alienated, fringe groups like the British National Party move in, fastening on these feelings of marginality, while the low polling figures give them increased leverage over the outcome of the ballot.

On other levels and other places, British central government has taken this message to heart. Perhaps impressed by the American example, the Labour government legislated for the (limited) devolution of Scotland and Wales and the introduction of directly elected mayors to the larger English cities. But judging from Tony Blair's attempts to undermine the Welsh choice for First Minister, Rhodri Morgan, and London's obvious preference for Ken Livingstone, the foreign lesson took a while to sink in.

When Bush cut taxes for the rich in 2004, the family that owns Wal-Mart increased their income by $91,500 per hour.

Now they are the richest family in America, worth more than Microsoft's Bill Gates and the hyper-rich investor Warren Buffett put together.[1] In other words, Wal-Mart Stores are big. Big business and big on the ground. Wal-Mart is the world's largest private-sector employer, with 6,600 outlets in fifteen countries. In 2005 it recorded sales of over $300 billion. In two-thirds of the 50 American states it is the largest employer. Over 1.8 million people work for Wal-Mart, of whom 1.5 million are women. At what point does size like this move on from measurements of quantity to something qualitatively different?

Surprisingly, superstores are not an American invention. The first of those out-of-town warehouses surrounded by acres of parking lots, selling everything from food to clothing, hardware and sporting goods under one shed-like roof, opened in France, when Carrefour (French for 'crossroads') gave the world its first hypermarket in 1963.

As so often in France, theory was quick to catch up with practice. During that decade the social philosopher Jean Baudrillard worked out his celebrated hypothesis that consumption had replaced production as the key axis of culture. Along with hypermarkets, it seemed, went hyper-reality. His resulting book, published in 1970, coined the term 'consumer society' in its title.

Yet as with cars, television, penicillin and other European inventions, no country was readier and keener to take up the new retail model than the USA. Why did America prove so receptive to hypermarkets? Because it already had a consumer society – not in Baudrillard's sense but in the form of a long-established tradition, going back at least as far as Benjamin Franklin. It rests on three widely-held ideas – or call them sentiments – that have marked Americans off from their mother country.

The first is that business is an honourable pursuit, not some shameful secret in the family past, to be covered over just as soon as connections and college degrees can open the way into (say) one of the professions. The second is that competition is better for economic well-being than monopoly. And the third is that the customer is always right, because in a competitive field, happy customers will make for happy profits.

As a result, the US had a number of experiments in mass retailing under way by 1926, especially on the west coast, where Skaggs and Seelig Stores merged to form Safeway – still America's second-largest food retailer. Well before the onset of the Second World War, supermarkets like Safeway were offering spacious floor plans with food laid out in easily accessed rows, for customers to compare and choose for themselves.

This was better than having to stand on one side of a counter while the shopkeeper selected something for you that he probably wanted to get rid of anyway. And along with increased choice came volume, which meant lower prices or improved quality – sometimes both. Besides, there was always a place to park outside, and a nice young man or woman to pack your bags at the checkout before carrying them to your car.

Wal-Mart took all these cues – space, choice, convenience – and pushed them to their limits. On top of that, it drove down prices. Back in the 1940s, when he was still running his five-and-dime store in Bentonville, Arkansas, Sam Walton found that if he cut his profit margins, the increased volume of his sales would earn him more than if he stuck to lower volumes at higher mark-ups.

Of course Wal-Mart's founding father wasn't the first retailer to make this discovery, but he was the first to focus on price as the central principle of his business, 'from the utmost frugality of his own office and living habits', as John Lanchester has written, 'to paying everybody involved … as little as possible, [and] exerting the maximum pressure on his suppliers, not just to not-raise their prices, but to lower them, every year'.[2]

It's at this point that quantitative differences began to produce changes in quality. Charles Fishman tells the story of the gallon jar of Vlasic pickles sold at $2.97, a price that bore no relation to the supply of cucumbers or the demand for pickles. Who, apart from a delicatessen owner, could use a jar of pickles so gargantuan that once you had opened it, half the contents would go mouldy before they could be eaten? Yet Wal-Mart was soon selling 200,000 of them. As Fishman points out, it wasn't the market that created the $2.97 gallon of pickles; it was Wal-Mart. They did it 'as a way of making a statement' about low prices.[3] Maybe this was Baudrillard's hyper-reality.

Low prices have their reverberations in the community, of course. Customers love them. Poor customers depend on them. Typically they will spend from 20 to 25 per cent less on groceries bought at Wal-Mart. Yet the downside of the price advantage is the way the retail giant squeezes the system, sucking up local custom from smaller independent business, flattening the local economic and social landscape along with the physical one.

Unions are banned at Wal-Mart. Shop-floor wages average $15,000 a year. That's less than half the $32,300 earned by the average non-supervisory worker on a 40-hour week – and Wal-Mart has often been accused of making its assistants work 'off the clock'. There are no health benefits or pension rights. The stores actually put up posters to inform their workers how to apply for food stamps, Medicaid and other welfare benefits available to the poor. So state and federal taxpayers subsidise Wal-Mart's low-price culture – to the tune of $2,300 per Wal-Mart employee per year, according to most estimates.

In response to criticisms like these, Wal-Mart commissioned a study by the economic analysis and forecasting company Global Insight, which claims that the retail giant saves working families more than $2,300 a year, while creating more than 210,000 jobs in the US. But one assessment is that for every two jobs created by Wal-Mart, three jobs are lost due to many smaller companies going out of business. Stephan Goetz, an economist at Pennsylvania State University, studied Wal-Mart's impact on poverty rates in the US over the decade 1989–99. While poverty declined from 13.1 per cent to 10.7 per cent overall during that period, in counties that had a Wal-Mart the rate fell to only 11 per cent. 'The presence of

Wal-Mart unequivocally raised family poverty rates in US counties during the 1990s', he concluded.[4]

This should come as no surprise, since poverty is a crucial part of Wal-Mart's strategy. Their customers are mainly poor. Though half of them are waged blue-collar workers, 20 per cent are unemployed or elderly. 'Sam Walton's real genius', according to a union organiser for the United Food and Commercial Workers, was that 'he figured out how to make money off of poverty ... The only problem with the business model is that it needs to create more poverty to grow.'[5]

Given their undoubted advantages for at least some of their local populations, should Wal-Mart superstores be resisted? If so, can they be? Forget consumer boycotts, advises the labour journalist Liza Featherstone. 'A worker might call her union and organise a picket', she writes, or 'a citizen might write to her congressman or local newspaper. A consumer makes an isolated, politically slight decision to shop or not shop.' Act as a consumer, and which of us wouldn't be tempted by Wal-Mart's product range and prices? 'The trouble is that choosing not to shop at Wal-Mart for ethical reasons', adds John Lanchester, 'is both a political action and a retreat from politics ... it gives the ethical consumer a nice warm glow, but it also another form of self-expression through consumption, and it is consumption, at root, which is the problem.'[6]

Resistance is growing. Workers in more than 30 states have brought class action suits against Wal-Mart's infringements of wage and hour legislation, while a former Wal-Mart employee called Betty Dukes and 1.6 million other women are suing the store for systematically discriminating against women in pay and promotion prospects.[7]

Meanwhile, cities and countries alike are finding ways to discourage Wal-Mart from building in their locality in the first place. When Wal-Mart wanted to build in Chicago's south side, labour and community groups stopped it by lobbying for a law to force the store to pay a living wage. In 2006 an employment tribunal ordered Asda, Wal-Mart's British branch, to pay £850,000 ($1.63 million) to workers forced to resign from their union. In Germany, which doesn't share the 'customer-always-right' ethos, unions flexed their muscles to the point that Wal-Mart has pulled out of the country altogether. But then who wins?

Maybe, as in H.G. Wells's *The War of the Worlds* (1898), where the monstrous Martian war machines were finally defeated by microbiological infection, Wal-Mart will be humbled by mundane economic forces. Recently the financial press has been full of stories about Wal-Mart's financial woes: its declining sales growth, it flat-lining share price over the last four or five years. The reason most frequently given? Rising American fuel prices. It seems the long drive out to the superstore is beginning to cut into Wal-Mart's price advantage. And with American fuel prices still a long way down the international price scale, there's only one way for them to go.

Network newscasts have declined in viewer numbers by 44 per cent since 1980, and 59 per cent from their peak in 1969.

Goodnight, Edward R. Murrow, and bad luck. In a famous speech to the Radio and Television News Directors convention in 1958, the veteran broadcaster and news presenter told the media to get serious. Television, he said, was leading the country into increasing 'decadence, escapism and insulation from the realities of the world in which we live'. Alongside the soap operas, cowboy adventures and blockbuster quiz and variety shows, he wanted networks and sponsors to find a way of guaranteeing an agreed minimum number of serious news inquiries.

Above all, he wanted news broadcasters not to be afraid of editorialising, so long as they stated their position clearly and admitted their bias. Perhaps 'editorials would not be profitable', he said. In fact, 'if they had a cutting edge, they might even offend'. That is just what Murrow's own newscasts did, when he took on 'the Junior Senator from Wisconsin', Joe McCarthy.[1]

As it turned out, the threat to news broadcasting came not on waves of entertainment from within the network, but from another kind of delivery platform altogether, cable television. In the 1980s, cable news began to supplant the networks as the primary source for breaking news. In 1980, when Cable News Network (CNN) began broadcasting, 52.1 million Americans watched the nightly news broadcasts on the three big established networks. By November 2005, that figure was down to 28.8 million – a 45 per cent slump in 25 years.[2]

Over this time the Columbia Broadcasting System (CBS) suffered the steepest decline in audience share – from 16 ratings points down to 5.5. Many had considered CBS the leader in independent news analysis. This was Murrow's network, and Walter Cronkite's, the news presenter who first came out against the

Vietnam War in February 1968, when he closed a special 'Report from Vietnam' with the opinion that 'This war is unwinnable.'

As for the editorialising, though, Murrow got his way, if not quite how he'd hoped. In 1996, Rupert Murdoch's News Corp launched the cable station Fox News. Though claiming to be 'fair and balanced', and sporting the motto 'We Report. You decide', Fox was designed as a product to fit the 'conservative' niche in the media market. Pro Bush and pro the war in Iraq, with highly opinionated, conservative anchormen and editorial talk-show hosts like Bill O'Reilly, Fox has flummoxed the more 'balanced' cable news service, Time-Warner's CNN. As Jon Fine, media commentator for *Business Week Online*, put it: 'For ... CNN to respond in kind would mean forsaking its serious-news DNA. But ignoring the challenger and focusing on its established bona fides left a market opening that Fox could fly a 747 through.'

Which is just what happened. In early 2002 Fox overtook CNN as the leading cable news station, and still holds that lead. As for the editorial programmes, the audience for Fox News's *The O'Reilly Factor* was more than twice that of CNN's *Larry King Live*.[3]

The film *Goodnight and Good Luck*, much nominated for, but unawarded by the 2006 Oscars, dramatises the good journalist's TV campaign against Senator Joe McCarthy. George Clooney, who acted in, directed and part-wrote the movie, remembers when there were three networks broadcasting news every night; all spanning the full political spectrum. You made up your mind after seeing them, he said. 'Now you go to the station that suits your views, like Fox News for those who believe that Iraq was involved in 9/11.'[4] Part of the film's appeal was to the widespread nostalgic retrospect on the nightly newscast seen by all, bringing the country together as a family.

But it's in the nature of cable to target specific corners of the market. The first American cable station was set up in June 1948, when John Watson, an enterprising TV salesman in the small town of Mahony City, Pennsylvania, set up an antenna on the top of a local mountain, from which he led coaxial cables to the households of people who had bought TV sets from him. That way the locals could receive signals from the Philadelphia stations, up till then blocked by the surrounding mountains. CATV (Community Antenna

Television), as it was then called, went on to be installed in hotels, apartment blocks, and other locations requiring multiple feeds from a single antenna.

From there it was a short step, technically speaking, to pay-as-you-view TV. In 1972, HBO (Home Box Office) first went out over the cable system in Wilkes-Barre, Pennsylvania. Since then HBO has grown to 11.5 million viewers, not least because its present owner, TimeWarner, now distributes the signals by satellite.[5] Whatever the mode of delivery, though, 'cable' TV has retained something of that feeling of a service for subscribers only, aimed at a coterie market of special interests – even when that elite turns into a majority.

Looking back on it all, a symbolic down-turn in the fortunes of network news was Dan Rather's dismissal from CBS in 2004. Rather, Walter Cronkite's successor as anchor for the CBS Evening News, was sacked after heading up a *60 Minutes* report on 8 September of that year, right in the middle of the general election, that President Bush had gone absent without leave from his assignment to the Texas Air National Guard during the Vietnam War of the 1970s.

This was a serious charge. Bush was already under fire for using family influence to get himself posted to the National Guard as a safe alternative to combat in Vietnam. But Rather and CBS seemed to seal the accusation by showing a series of letters and memos from Bush's National Guard commander, Lieutenant Colonel Jerry B. Killian, 'grounding' Bush – that is, withdrawing his flight status – for failure to report for a physical examination, and for other absences from duty.

Within hours, bloggers began to post doubts about the Killian documents shown on *60 Minutes*. Apparently the signature block should have been flush to the left margin, instead of to the right as pictured. The memos showed a letterhead at the top, whereas real memos circulated in the Texas Air National Guard at the time lacked them.

Above all, the body type of the letters and memos themselves could never have been accomplished in the early 1970s. This is because characters mounted on hard-type typewriters used at the time were all fixed to metal blocks of the same width. Thus, on the page an 'i' or an 'l' or a 't' would take up as much space as an 'm' or a 'w'. Furthermore, ordinary typewriters could make no provision for 'kerning', where one letter overlaps another, as in the 'f' and 'l' of 'flight.' The documents shown on *60 Minutes* all had letter spaces of variable widths, with those kerned where appropriate. The conclusion reached was that they had been produced on a word-processor, using Microsoft Word with default settings, some 30 years after their purported dates.

After some huffing and puffing, CBS put out this statement: 'Based on what we now know, CBS News cannot prove that the documents are authentic, which is the only acceptable journalistic standard to justify using them in the report', they said. 'That was a mistake, which we deeply regret.' They set up an independent panel to inquire into where the documents came from and how they came into their hands. Rather apologised too, then lost his job. And all this, as the *Washington Post* commented acidly, 'on the network of Murrow and Cronkite'.[6]

But the story poses another question about the state of the American news media. If network news began to supplant the newspapers from the sixties onwards, and cable news did the same to network from the nineties, is the internet becoming the medium of choice for the new millennium? The tsunami disaster on the day after Christmas 2004 'marked the first time significant numbers of Americans turned to blogs for breaking news', according to 'The State of the News Media, 2005'.[7] If this trend continues, it would mark a far profounder change to news broadcasting than the coming of cable.

And when it comes to websites, the comparative ratings for news outlets perform a surprising somersault. In terms of traffic at the channels' websites, MSNBC (Microsoft/National Broadcasting Company) and CNN streaked ahead of Fox News in December 2005. And people spend more time on these websites, a factor known as 'stickiness' that for advertisers partly compensates for their relatively fewer viewing numbers compared to cable TV.[8]

We used to have to wait even for the best of the old-style anchors to tell us what was happening and what to think about it, or go in search of the cable outlet that suited our pre-formed politics. Now we can all participate in the public debate, putting the record straight, adding our own opinion. Unlike earlier news platforms, blogs provide channels for feedback. They don't just disseminate the news; they democratise it. Now everyone with the time, interest and inclination can be a citizen journalist. How reliably is another matter.

At the millennium, 44 per cent of the adult American population believed that Christ would come again during their lifetime.

That's according to a much-publicised survey by the Pew Research Center, a highly respected, non-partisan think-tank that takes national soundings on public attitudes on everything from religion to the economy, from immigration to foreign policy. But the really striking finding was issued by the same foundation just seven years later. By mid-2006 that figure had fallen to 20 per cent.[1]

That's the power of the millennium on the public imagination. Secular Americans feared it because they thought that computer codes, based on two-digit designations for the year (such as 87 for 1987), would be unable to make the transition from 1999 to 2000, which they would read as 1900. As the programs depending on these codes failed, chaos would descend on the world. Traffic lights would cease to operate, hospital power would shut down, aircraft would collide or fall from the sky altogether, and people wouldn't get their regular social security payments.

The 120 million American Christian evangelicals – that's the 40 per cent of the population who believe in the literal truth of the Bible – expected much the same sort of confusion, but for an entirely different reason. For them the key text was St Paul's first letter to the Thessalonians, Chapter 4, verses 16 and 77, which describes 'the Rapture', when all those who have been called, born again and saved will suddenly be wafted into the sky to meet Jesus descending to receive them.

Walls, ceilings, the roofs of cars, buses and aircraft cockpits would present no barrier. All over the world, planes would fall to earth, cars and trucks would mount the safety barrier to run head-on into oncoming traffic, as their elect guidance was suddenly subtracted from this life. So if the millennium bug didn't get you, the rapture would – either to heaven or left behind among the sinful majority.

'White-trash' sociologist Matt Wray recalls his terror when he woke one April morning in 1973 to find the house cold, his brothers' beds empty, his parents gone. 'I crumpled to the floor and began to cry', he writes. 'The Rapture had occurred while I slept. I felt the crushing weight of my sins, the guilty shame of having abandoned Jesus.' Later he remembered that it was Easter Sunday, and that the family had planned to go to a sunrise service.[2]

The roots of evangelicalism reach down as far as the first quarter of the 16th century, with Martin Luther's attack on the authority of the Roman Catholic Church that sparked the Protestant Reformation. Lutheranism, still called the *evangelische Kirke* in Germany, celebrated the personal experience of Christ's good news (*evangelion* in Greek), denying the power of the Church hierarchy over individual salvation. Salvation was by the believer's faith alone, made possible by the unique sacrifice of Christ on the cross. The Bible, divinely inspired, was the final authority for all matters of faith and doctrine.

Evangelicalism came to America in the form of the 'Great Awakenings' prompted by Jonathan Edwards in the Connecticut Valley in the 1730s and 40s, and the seven missions of the English evangelist George Whitefield between 1737 and 1770. The revival movement was carried on from thousands of Baptist and Methodist camp meetings on the Kentucky and Tennessee frontiers held in the early 19th century, right down to Billy Graham's great crusades during the 1950s. Common to all these movements was a stress on conversion – accepting Christ's call and being born again out of the inherited state of original sin.

With their out-reach to ordinary people, their persuasive powers honed in the pulpit and their organising skills, evangelicals have played a crucial role in American reform movements like women's rights and the abolition of slavery, even though the Bible offered no support for either campaign. In the first half of the 20th century, apart from their pressure for prohibition, evangelicals went quiet on political issues, but for the last 25 years or so they have become politically active again – this time on the other side. Prompted and represented by televangelists like Pat Robertson and the late Jerry

Falwell, they have opposed abortion, gay marriage, secular school-ing and other legislative reforms of the 1960s and 70s.

How the evangelicals shifted, over time, from progressive to reactionary politics is one of the great mysteries of recent American history, but a lot of it has to do with the South, where most of them live. And the South has its own history. From as early as 1845, the southern Baptists split from the northern over the issue of slavery. The Civil War, emancipation and reconstruction – all prosecuted by northern Republicans – turned the South into a voting bloc on which the Democrats could count for the first half of the 20th century. Then came the 1954 Supreme Court ruling against segre-gation in schools, and Lyndon Johnson's Great Society legislative programme of 1964–6, enforcing civil rights, voting rights and equal opportunities, and setting up Medicare and Medicaid for the elderly and poor (see facts 12, 13).

Commonly seen as benefiting African Americans, these measures provided a focus of opposition for those who didn't want to appear racist. In addition, the South was becoming suburban. As Kevin Kruse has shown in his book on Atlanta, the city that boasted it was 'too busy to hate' during the struggle for civil rights, southern whites could side-step the effects of desegregation simply by moving out of the city centres – and opting out of public services like transport and education along the way.[3] Now, instead of serving as a milch cow for Democratic votes, 70 per cent of white southerners vote the other way. Since 1978 no less than 90 per cent of the electoral college votes from the southern states have gone Republican. Without the South, Nixon, Reagan and the Bushes would have been footnotes in history.

So American evangelicals have turned into the 'religious right', notorious for its impact on the neo-conservatives in Washington, led by that self-confessed born-again Christian, George W. Bush. And certainly the evangelicals have made some gains in their agenda. The Defense of Marriage Act (DOMA) reinforces the power of most states to refuse to recognise gay marriages legalised in other states. Executive orders forbid federal funding for stem-cell research, and for organisations that recommend abortion as one method of family planning.

Yet, as so often, things aren't that clear-cut. DOMA was actually signed into law by the Democrat Bill Clinton in 1996. And not all the evangelicals' ambitions have been accomplished – at least not yet. There are no constitutional amendments to restore prayer to public schools, or ban gay marriages, or overturn *Roe v. Wade*, the Supreme Court decision legalising abortion. For these and other reasons, evangelicals have begun to complain that their electoral loyalty isn't paying dividends in federal legislation. One of them has recently claimed that the religious right are used mainly to organise political support for the neo-cons, who then ridiculed their faith-based supporters as 'religious nuts'.[4]

In the run-up to the 2006 mid-term elections, American evangelicals suffered a heavy blow when Ted Haggard, president of the National Association of Evangelicals, was forced to confess to hiring a male prostitute, with whom he had shared sex-enhancing drugs. Needless to say, Haggard had preached fervently against both drugs and gay sex. He resigned, but the scandal is said to have disgusted evangelicals all over the country. Just to add to the confusion, though, despite the Democrats sweeping into majorities in both houses of Congress, the evangelical vote held up, with more than 71 per cent of them voting Republican.

So how heavily do the evangelicals really bear on American politics? After all, 60 per cent of them believe that, given a conflict between what they understand the Bible to mean and the will of the people as expressed in elections, the Bible should prevail. That's 72 million people, or just under a quarter of the American population, who disbelieve in the democratic process. In fact, Matt Wray argues that what their fascination with the last things shows is not their fingers on the public pulse, but an underlying feeling of economic, social and political disenfranchisement. Their 'apocalyptic fears and fantasies of collective death', he thinks, are their way of forming an individual and group identity to ritualise their difference from mainstream American thought and feeling.[5]

Occupational fraud cost the United States $652 billion in 2006.[1]

'Greed is good', said Gordon Gekko, the fictional investment banker in the movie *Wall Street* (1987), as he persuaded the shareholders of an ailing papermaking company to let him take over its assets, prior to stripping them out. 'Greed clarifies, cuts through, and captures the essence of the evolutionary spirit. Greed ... has marked the upward surge of mankind. And greed – you mark my words – will not only save Teldar Paper, but that other malfunctioning corporation called the USA.'

Gekko was meant to be an unattractive character, the villain who gets his comeuppance in the end, symbolising the rise and fall of American corporate greed in the 1980s. But so vivid was Michael Douglas's Oscar-winning performance that he made Wall Street cool. He was 'the inspiration for countless numbers of investment bankers around the world', according to Wikipedia, for whom his 'colorful suspenders, shiny shoulder-padded suits and permanently slicked-back hair became the official look of power and fortune'.[2]

There are many kinds of fraud, of course. Frauds by persuasion target the individual. Even ancient scams still fool people every day, like pyramid selling schemes, or the old 'pigeon drop', in which a 'mark' is persuaded to part with a sum to show 'good faith' against the promise to share a wallet stuffed with money supposedly found in the street. In frauds like these, the victims are almost as guilty as the con artists, since they agree to cut legal corners in order to get something for nothing.

More recent tricks use the internet to extract details of credit cards or bank accounts. An email apparently from the bank will ask account-holders to re-register their accounts, which requires them to enter the branch code and account number in the process. Then there's the evergreen 'Nigerian letter', in which the widow of some foreign potentate offers to split a fortune of millions locked up in a bank account, which she needs only the details of your own account to unlock.

But the really big-time fraud, the one that costs the country $652 billion a year, according to the Association of Certified Fraud Examiners, is the 'occupational' variety. Occupational fraud they define as: 'the use of one's occupation for personal enrichment through the deliberate misuse or misapplication of the employing organization's resources or assets.'[3] Occupational fraud is some-times referred to as a 'white-collar' crime, and popularly – though incorrectly – thought to have no victims apart from a balance sheet.

Most occupational frauds are committed by employees. They may fiddle their expense accounts – an occurrence so common that many don't consider it a fraud at all. Less commonly, an employee might 'skim' the company's receipts, or even dip into the cash till. Buyers of goods or services required by the company may encourage suppliers to offer them 'kickbacks' to secure the order. Ghost suppliers no longer dealing with the company may go on billing it for goods or services, the payments going to an employee who has set up the phoney account. And so on.

Far fewer, yet statistically 3½ times more costly, are the frauds perpetrated by management. Managers can commit all the frauds mentioned above, of course, which their higher-level access to the company's assets will render all the more lucrative. But their real opportunities open up when the company is publicly traded on the stock market. Two rich sources of fraud flow from this fact. The first is that from time to time the price of a firm's stock may be out of step with the value of what the company makes or does. And the second is that managers often take part of their remuneration – say, their bonuses or financing for their retirement – in the form of holdings in the company's stock.

So one trick, especially common during the dot.com boom and bust, is 'pump and dump'. Executives, or their agents, will talk up the value of the company's stock, using supposedly disinterested praise in bogus newsletters or chat-room postings on the internet. When the increased demand inflates the stock price, the executives sell the shares they bought cheaply. In due course, as news of the fraud leaks out and the shares plummet, everyone else loses their money. Small high-tech companies are especially vulnerable to 'pump and dump' schemes. That's because they deal in products as yet not widely understood, and because they're often traded on the 'over-the-counter' market rather than one of the major exchanges, where listing standards are more stringent.

For the big boys trading on New York Stock Exchange (NYSE), or the electronic stock exchange NASDAQ, it's safer to keep the fraud in-house. Insider trading in the company's shares opens all sorts of possibilities, as when managers who know of a development that will raise the price of the company's stock discreetly buy large amounts of the stock at the current lower cost, before going public with the good news. Another fast-growing abuse is illegal stock option manipulation. Executives awarded the option to buy stock in the company can backdate the point of purchase to a period when the company's stock was low, thus making each option more valuable, providing the company's stock is still rising.

But when it's falling, insider trading shifts into a higher gear. That's what happened in the big-ticket headline scandals of the early 2000s, WorldCom and Enron. WorldCom started out in the long-distance discount telephone business. During the 1990s it grew by acquiring and merging with other telecommunications firms, like MCI. At the end of the decade the industry went through a period of relative decline, and WorldCom failed in its proposed merger with Sprint, the internet provider and mobile phone network. WorldCom executives began to juggle their accounts to hide their true financial position, inflating revenues and reporting costs, like interconnecting with other telecommunications firms, as capital assets rather than expenses. By 2003, following a Securities and Exchange Commission (SEC) investigation, it was estimated that the company's assets had been inflated by $11 billion.

At the height of its apparent power in 2000, Enron, the paper and power company based in Houston, Texas, was reporting revenues of $111 billion. Its stock value was $90 per share. The firm was well connected, having contributed heavily to the Republican Party and to G.W. Bush's presidential campaign in the same year. Enron's big accounting advantage was its offshore operations. They had no fewer than 692 subsidiaries in the Cayman Islands, 119 in the Turks and Caicos, 43 in Mauritius and eight in Bermuda.[4] As a result it could move currency around at will, avoiding income tax over four of its last five years of operation and – more to the point – hide its losses.

Enron's executives, who knew that the company's apparent profitability was a trick of accounting smoke and mirrors, began to sell their shares in 2000. In just over a year the stock fell to $15, at which point the company filed for bankruptcy. In the following four years Enron executives were indicted and tried on numerous counts of conspiracy, securities fraud and 'wire fraud', or fraud by electronic communication. Jeffrey Skilling, Chief Executive Officer (CEO) for a few months in 2001, was sentenced to over 24 years in prison. Kenneth Lay, CEO from 1986, was found guilty, but died before he could be sentenced. 5,000 employees lost their jobs.

'Are you consumed by greed?' Jeffrey Skilling was asked on the witness stand. 'No', he answered, pointing out that he had accepted 'just' $21.5 million out of a total of $70 million offered him on becoming Enron CEO.[5] Well, there are degrees of greed, but at least by now, after the two largest bankruptcies and two most notorious cases of corporate fraud in American history, it was less fashionable to pretend that 'greed is good'.

These days, Americans are less dazzled by Wall Street shenanigans. In 2002 Congress passed the Sarbanes-Oxley Act, which introduced tighter regulations around the production of financial reports, including the provision that the company's executives sign and take legal accountability for them. And the SEC is as actively vigilant as ever. In March 2007 they brought charges against thirteen people in what was described as 'the biggest crackdown on alleged insider trading on Wall Street since the 1980s'.[6]

Contrary to popular opinion, all America is not one middle class.

Social class is one of America's best kept secrets. History and national self-identity have convinced Americans that the country is above, or beyond, class. In Europe, South America and most Asian countries, blue-collar and white-collar workers, business and professional people, even those who don't work at all – all have their own socio-economic profiles, lifestyles and group solidarity. By contrast, according to the popular view, all these form segments of one large middle class in America.

There are various reasons for this common opinion. One may be a lingering effect of the psychology of emigration, since all Americans were either emigrants or the descendants of emigrants. Emigration requires investments in time, money and emotions: saving to pay for the passage, parting from friends and family. Then on arrival it demands ingenuity, enterprise, hard work and planning for the future. These are all traits by which sociologists have conventionally identified the middle class. So it may be that emigration either selected or reinforced – probably both – middle-class values in the American population.

A more highfalutin theory was that of Harvard professor Louis Hartz, in *The Founding of New Societies* (1964). America broke off from the mother country, Hartz argued, at that point in British history when bourgeois values were triumphing over the old feudal order. As a result the new nation was founded on middle-class principles like self-reliance and individual enterprise, underpinned by the ownership of private property. Having taken itself out of the European dialectic of history, America no longer had the old feudal system to contend with. More to the point, it would never face the threat of the next phase in the European model, socialist revolution. That's why socialism never caught on in America. Marxism died as an idea, Hartz argued, 'because there is no sense of class, no spirit of revolution, no yearning for the corporate past'.[1]

Not that Americans have ever denied the facts of social stratification. One form of class that we all recognise is the distinction between old and new money. New money has been made in this generation. Old money will have been made by Grandpa or Great Grandpa. It doesn't matter how. Americans have never shared the prejudice of 19th-century British landowners against people in 'trade'.

Old money needs to have been around long enough for at least two generations to have been educated at expensive private schools, gone to an Ivy-League university, got married in the Episcopal Church, belonged to one of the more exclusive clubs, and so on. New money can aspire to these social distinctions, but will achieve them only partially at best, and even then after spending over the odds on them – say, by having to give inordinately to one or more socially approved charities – or trading them in return for a business advantage.

In other words, it all depends on family. You can tell old money by the personal names that proclaim family affiliations. A man will be called So-and-So the 3rd, to emphasise the generations preceding him. More often, a child will be given a 'family name' as a first name, so that she or he will seem to be going about under two surnames, like Davis Coleman, or Courtney Morgan or Tyler Waldorf.

And because they really are surnames by origin, most of these given names are ambiguous as to gender too. 'Courtney' and 'Tyler', for example, could be either a boy or a girl. So if you meet or hear of any Americans whose first and family names can be reversed without sounding any more ridiculous than the 'right' way round, chances are that they are either North-eastern old money or from the South.

So there really are social and economic differences in America, for all to see. The American difference, though, lies in the belief that none of these barriers is impermeable. Abraham Lincoln put it well, while famously drawing the line between slavery and free labour in a speech delivered in 1859. There are some who argue, Lincoln said, that a hired labourer 'is fatally fixed in that condition for life', whereas the truth is that 'capital is the fruit of labor, and could never have existed had not labor *first* existed'. How does labour produce capital?

> The prudent, penniless beginner in the world, labors for
> wages awhile, saves a surplus with which to buy tools or land,
> for himself; then labors on his own account another while,
> and at length hires another new beginner to help him.[2]

This idea worked well enough so long as there were still tracts of virgin land, and hopeful, ambitious settlers to clear them. What about now? In 2005, the *New York Times* ran a series on class, following a widespread survey of current social attitudes. Class, the *Times* decided, could be determined by four parameters: occupation, education, income and wealth.

Education is easily understood – the higher the better. Occupation poses a few surprises. Lawyers and doctors top the list, of course, but professors are down in the second quintile, along with architects, businessmen and managers. Farmers and fishermen are surprisingly near the bottom, just above transport workers, waiters and janitors.

At first sight, even these four criteria of class are very American. In most European and South American countries, for example, they would include birth. But not here, because anyone could attain them – at least theoretically. But practically? Up to a quarter of wealth is inherited. You need a good education for the top jobs, and either wealth or a good parental income to get through college.

'The scramble to scoop up a house in the best school district, channel a child into the right preschool program or land the best medical specialist,' as two *Times* reporters involved in the survey have put it, 'are all part of a quiet contest among social groups that the affluent and educated are winning in a rout.' Even merit is class-based, they suggest. 'Parents with money, education and connections cultivate in their children the habits that the meritocracy rewards.'[3]

Recent evidence supports this pessimistic reading of trends in class mobility. 'There is far less of it than economists once thought', say the *Times* team. A study by the US Bureau of Labor Statistics showed that mobility declined from the 1980s to the 1990s. Another by the Federal Reserve Bank of Boston found that fewer families moved from one quintile of the income ladder to another during the 1980s than the 1970s, and still fewer in the 90s than in the 80s. Even more surprisingly, movement up the class ladder is not much more fluid in the United States than in Great Britain, a hereditary monarchy, and less so than in France, Canada and Denmark.[4]

Yet even as opportunities to get ahead appear to dwindle, Americans are convinced that the class system is freeing up. A recent *New York Times* poll 'found that 40 per cent of Americans believed that the chance of moving up from one class to another had risen over the last 30 years ... [and that] more Americans than 20 years ago believe it is possible to start out poor and become rich.'[5]

How to account for this discrepancy between popular opinion and the facts? The idea that America has no fixed classes is so fundamental to the country's founding ideology and continuing self-identity that it simply outweighs any evidence to the contrary.

And ideas of America are very powerful. In *People of Paradox* (1972), Michael Kammen reminds us that the idea of America came before the fact of it. The idea of Europe took shape only after 'Medieval Europe had become a recognised reality in the political, religious, and economic realms', Kammen says. But the old myth of America as El Dorado or Paradise or Utopia 'surfaced before the fact of America ... and thereby conditioned the form the "facts" would take, and even what people would make of them.'[6] And of course there are no class divisions in Utopia, much less in Paradise.

With 4 per cent of the world's population, the United States produces a quarter of all carbon dioxide emissions.

Will Rogers, the American vaudeville performer, trick lariat-roper, stand-up comedian, actor and newspaper columnist, used to quip: 'All I know is what I read in the papers.' This, his very own tag-line, used to get a laugh every time, because for his audience newspapers were the least reliable source of information. Rogers was pretending to admit to a simpleton's ignorance.

There are two things on which the papers are now unanimous, and challenging them is tantamount to arguing that the earth is flat. The first is that so-called greenhouse gases are causing the world to heat up, with possibly catastrophic effects on global climate. Reporting on 2 February 2007, the UN-sponsored Intergovern-mental Panel on Climate Change, based on the work of hundreds of scientists, made it more or less official. And the second is that America is in the dog house, having first participated in, then refused to ratify, the protocol agreed in Kyoto, Japan in 1997, to curb climate change by reducing the greenhouse gas emissions of industrialised nations to an overall level 5 per cent beneath those of 1990.

Statistics indicting Americans for carbon profligacy continue to roll off the presses – or more accurately, out of the websites. Over 200 million American cars and light trucks use over 200 million gallons of fossil fuel per day. With only 2 per cent of global oil reserves, the US consumes 25 per cent of the world's oil produc-tion. Only 1 per cent of Americans travel on public transport, an eighteenth of that in Japan.[1]

It's not just cars. Fossil fuels burned to generate electricity amounted to two-thirds of the carbon dioxide emissions produced by the US during 2004. Alongside carbon come other chemical emissions – at least 2.4 billion pounds of them released into the atmosphere by US industries every year. The situation is getting

83

worse too. According to Steve Connor, science editor of the London *Independent*, a newspaper particularly hot on the trail of American bad behaviour, 'The United States emitted more greenhouse gases in 2004 than at any time in its history.' This was an increase 'by 1.7 per cent on the previous year, equivalent to a rise of 110 million tons of carbon dioxide.'[2]

The US may be the world's biggest polluter. It's also the world's largest economy, and still one of the fastest-growing, to cite just one context often overlooked in the debate. Although American greenhouse gas emissions are increasing faster than average for the rest of the world, they have begun to lag behind growth. Greenhouse gas emissions per unit of gross domestic product fell by 2.1 per cent in 2004, compared with the year before. 'We should not underestimate the challenge of achieving economic growth whilst reducing emissions and the US is not the only country that is struggling to do this', said Professor Martin Rees, a seriously knowledgeable authority, being president of the Royal Society, Britain's most august and prestigious association of scientists.[3] Meanwhile, in other rapidly expanding industrial economies like China and India, levels increased by 33 and 57 per cent respectively between 1992 and 2002.

For all its impressive statistics, there's something odd about the rhetoric in which this discussion is taking place. For one thing, it's strongly apocalyptic. From their origin in the Book of Revelation, warnings about the end of the world have been punctuated with signs of the last things – from dramatic catastrophes like fires, floods and pestilence to more insidious trends like the perishing of hardwoods. These references gain their power of persuasion by appearing alarming in their own right, yet because quite likely to happen from time to time in the normal course of events, providing a ready supply of apparently significant signs.

So one website warning of global warming cites the thawing permafrost in central Alaska, dying mangroves in Bermuda, 'Stressed Polar Bears' in Canada and cherry trees blossoming 'earlier' – by two days since 1970, as it turns out – in Washington, DC. Also mentioned are a 'Deadly heat wave' in a Texas summer, the 'warmest summer on record' in Edmonton, Canada, the 'Hottest May on record' in Little Rock, Arkansas, a 'Late fall heat wave' from the Rockies to the East Coast, the 'Worst fire season ever' in Mexico and the 'Worst wildfires in 50 years' in Florida. All the last six of these instances occurred in 1998. Was that part of an insidious upward trend in global temperature, or just one of many freak American summers?

Not that the US has been totally inactive on the clean-air front. In March 2005 the Environmental Protection Agency brought in the Clean Air Interstate Rule (CAIR) to reduce ozone and fine particle pollution. States in the eastern US were forced to cut emissions of nitrogen oxides and sulphur dioxide from electricity generating stations.

But most of the action has been on the level of state and city, rather than federal government. From June 2006, eight North-eastern states from Maine down to Delaware agreed the Regional Greenhouse Gas Initiative (RGGI), under which carbon dioxide emissions from 600 power stations would be held at average levels between 2000 and 2004, before being reduced by 10 per cent from 2015 to 2020.

For both CAIR and RGGI the proposed control mechanism would be by 'capping and trading' – that is, setting strict limits, then allowing each individual power plant (or whatever) to buy or sell surplus savings in emissions, with the idea of keeping to target across the region as a whole. This so-called 'carbon trading' started out as an American idea, introduced at Kyoto when the US, under Clinton, was still dealing with the rest of the world on climate change.

Meanwhile, on the west coast at the end of August 2006, California, which has a history of car pollution control going back to the anti-smog laws of 1960, passed the Global Warming Solutions Act. This will reduce the state's greenhouse gas emissions by 25 per cent by 2020, putting California in line with the Kyoto initiative. And cities have followed suit. In January 2007, Seattle's mayor Greg Nikels got the agreement of 369 US cities, from San Francisco and Los Angeles in the west to Philadelphia and New York City on the Atlantic coast, to sign up to the Kyoto Protocol.

And the President's response? G.W. Bush was still in the land of rhetoric – not apocalyptic this time, but quintessentially American. His own solution, as set out in his State of the Union Message to

Congress on 23 January 2007, was to 'reduce gasoline usage in the United States by 20 per cent in the next ten years'. 'When we do that', he added (to applause), 'we will have cut our total imports by the equivalent of three-quarters of all the oil we now import from the Middle East.'

How was this remarkable reduction to be achieved? By increasing investment in hydrogen-cell technology and hybrid vehicles? By improving the fuel efficiency of conventional motors? Nope. Instead Bush proposed to increase domestic oil production – to drill for oil in the Alaskan Arctic National Wildlife Refuge – and vastly expand the production of corn to make the bio-fuel ethanol.

Sad to say, these projects will have no serious effect on greenhouse gases. First of all, cars and light trucks form only one third of carbon dioxide emissions; the rest comes from coal- and gas-fired power stations. Second, ethanol reduces emissions by 13 per cent at best, as compared to petroleum, and the coal required to heat the corn in the process of extracting its sugars would offset even that.

Whatever it lacked in practicality, though, Bush's proposal drew deep on the well-springs of American identity. Isolationism, for a start, the avoidance of 'foreign entanglements', an ancient mainstay of American foreign policy that goes back to the Monroe Doctrine of 1823, which forbade European colonisation in the Americas and undertook to keep the country free of foreign wars. (If only.) And corn! That staple of the American diet, the very nursery plant that kept the Pilgrim Fathers alive in those first cold years in New England (once the natives had shown them how to plant it), would return to save us once again in our last days.

The American population is rising twice as fast as that of the European Union; its fertility rate is higher than that of Brazil, South Korea or China.

On Tuesday 17 October 2006, a significant event passed quietly. Though noted in the daily papers, not a great deal was made of it, because it was only a statistic – minor in itself, if momentous by implication. What happened was that the population of the United States reached and topped 300 million people.

Hidden within that fact, though, a number of other numbers make increasingly amazing reading. One American is born every seven seconds. Over the 20th century the American population increased by 250 per cent, while that of France and Great Britain grew by less than 60 per cent. At present the only factor keeping the population of the European Union from actually falling has been increasing inward migration. In the US, though one immigrant arrives in the country every 31 seconds, two-thirds of the American growth in numbers comes from increase in the native population.

To put all this in perspective, as an *Economist* 'Survey of America' has pointed out, 'America is the only country to have maintained industrial era patterns of demographic growth in a post-industrial age'. Not only that, but apart from the Arab world and 'a handful of middle-income Latin American countries, all the countries with fertility rates higher than America's are very poor.'[1]

There's more. America's population is not only more buoyant than most comparable countries; it's also younger. According to the census of 2000, America's median age – the point at which half the population is younger, half older – was 35.3 years, up from 32.9 years in 1990. At the same time, Italy's was 42, Great Britain's 39. Also, other countries are ageing faster than America. While the American median age will have risen by under six, to 41 by 2050,

Italy's will have reached 52. Meanwhile, 'China will have aged by 15 years, to about 45, and South Korea by a withering 22 years, to 54.'[2]

Why? The best answer lies far back in history, in the American response to a bizarre 18th-century theory advanced by the most learned and prolific zoologist of his time, Georges-Louis Leclerc, Count Buffon. In his 44-volume *Histoire Naturelle* (1749) Buffon argued that species of animals and plants tended to decline in size, number and vitality when transplanted from the Old World to the New. This was, he argued, because in America the process of clearing and cultivation was still in its infancy. The virgin land still consisted mainly of forests and swamps, the transpiration and evaporation from which was said to have produced an atmospheric 'miasma' tending to stunt the growth of plants and animals, and to reduce their will and ability to reproduce.

This effect had supposedly been demonstrated by Buffon and others, through surveys and measurements of specimens of living things transplanted to the New World, all of which began to degenerate on their arrival there. Take the South American tapir, for example, which Buffon rightly identified as a pachyderm, like an elephant, but then wrongly went on to conclude *was* an African elephant reduced to the size of a pig in the humid environment of the New World.

The general rule was extended even to the human natives of America, who, he thought, were smaller and weaker than Europeans. Furthermore, the relative sparseness of pubic and auxiliary hair on their bodies 'proved' that the natives were sexually less active, so likely to produce fewer offspring per couple. And the same would happen to the European migrants then moving to the New World in larger and larger numbers. As generation succeeded generation, the miasma would do for them too. They would become smaller, sexually less vigorous, hence less likely to reproduce.

This dotty notion was taken seriously enough at the time for no less a personage than Thomas Jefferson, author of the Declaration of Independence and third President of the United States, to rebut it in his *Notes on the State of Virginia* (1781–2), with a series of tables comparing American and European animals, side by side in two columns. What Jefferson's statistics showed was that in every case the American example was larger and heavier than its European counterpart. Moreover, the number and variety of American species so outran those of Europe that blank spaces in the European column were left for several pages of the book.

By contrast, the printer, essayist, scientist, inventor and statesman Benjamin Franklin had already refuted Buffon with figures based on human numbers. In his essay, 'Observations Concerning the Increase of Mankind' (1755), Franklin pointed out that the population of his adopted colony, Pennsylvania, had been multiplying by a factor of two every twenty years or so – that is, that each generation was doubling its numbers. Buffon was so struck by this piece of counter-evidence that later he published a retraction to that part of his thesis concerning human transplants from Europe, magnanimously attributing his correction to 'the respectable testimony of the famous Dr Franklin'.

Franklin is sometimes cited as a source for Thomas Robert Malthus, whose *Essay on the Principles of Population* (1798) argued famously that populations increased geometrically – that is, by multiplication – while the food to sustain them could grow only by addition, arithmetically. But Franklin wasn't interested in universal laws of population and food supply. He was focusing on the American colonies, arguing that there people increased in number much more rapidly than in Europe, and venturing reasons why.

Chief among these reasons for American fertility, Franklin argued, was that more Americans than Europeans got married, and earlier in their lives. In crowded European cities, 'where all trades, occupations and offices are full, many delay marrying till they can see how to bear the charges of a family', he wrote. Similarly, in an old country, where all land is owned and cultivated, farmers 'must labour for others that have it' for low wages, and 'by low wages a family is supported with difficulty', and 'this difficulty deters many from marriage'.

But in America land is so plentiful and cheap that any 'labouring man, that understands husbandry, can in a short time save money enough to purchase a piece of new land sufficient for a plantation, whereon he may subsist a family.' So marriage is both earlier and more common in America. Whereas in Europe 'there is but one marriage per annum among 100 persons, perhaps we may here reckon two, and if in Europe they have but 4 births to a marriage (many of their marriages being late), we may reckon 8.' No need to worry about over-population either: 'so vast is the territory of North-America that it will require many ages to settle it fully.'

In other words, America was formed as a settler nation, its population restlessly moving outwards to appropriate, clear and cultivate virgin territory, displacing the Native Americans and irritably brushing aside all legislation from central government, like the British Proclamation of 1763, which sought to check settlement beyond the Appalachian Mountains. In his recent book, *Dangerous Nation*, best-selling historian and *Washington Post* columnist Robert Kagan argues that from the beginning Americans have been expanding and grabbing land like so many imperialists, a habit that has conditioned our foreign policy from far earlier than we like to admit.[3]

Do Franklin's explanations for America's rapid increase in population apply today? At first sight, hardly. There is no longer a vast continent of unsettled land 'chiefly occupied by Indians', as Franklin put it, and the notion that a couple must be married in order to have children now sounds a bit – well, quaint. Yet where the early settler could look forward to developing a farm in the West, the modern American finds hope in a labour market flexible enough to keep the unemployment rate half that of Germany's, and in a mortgage market deep enough to produce a 70 per cent rate of home ownership.

What remains constant between the 18th and 21st centuries is the optimism, the belief in progress. 'Today, two-thirds of Americans think they will achieve the American Dream of self-improvement at some point in their lifetime', says the *Economist* survey. And they are willing to invest their time and effort in that future. 'Americans work harder than almost anyone else – 300 hours a year more than Europeans. They switch jobs more often – about once in every seven years, compared with once every 11 years in Germany and Japan.'[4] And as demographers have repeatedly pointed out, a people's optimism – above all, their faith in the future – is the chief motivator of population growth.

It now takes up to two years to get a visa to study in America.

In March 2006, Manchester's Hallé Orchestra, the UK's longest-established symphony orchestra, had to abandon plans for a concert tour of the US. The reason? The time and money it would take for the 70 musicians, plus a selection of the orchestra's administrative staff, to get temporary work visas to perform in the country. Having filled out the complicated application form and made sure that their face on the passport photo was exactly centred within the two-by-two-inch format, each member of the orchestra would have to be interviewed and fingerprinted at the embassy in London, 185 miles south of Manchester.

Given the long waiting in line and the Consular Section's restricted hours, the applicants would have to stay overnight. Total fees, travel and accommodation would have cost the orchestra £45,000 (then around $83,250), 'a very substantial proportion of what the overall costs [of the tour] were likely to be', according to the orchestra's marketing director, Andy Ryans.[1] Even then, there was the risk that a key player would be refused entry at the last minute. In the end the orchestra gave up on the idea.

The Hallé debacle made the daily news bulletins in both countries, but the problem was not restricted to foreign performers looking to show their talents in the US. What it highlighted was the greatly increased difficulty facing anyone who needed one of the 28 different kinds of non-immigrant visas to visit the US for study or temporary work. Foreign students were especially hard hit.

In their planning emails, the hijacker-assassins of 9/11 referred to their intended targets in code. The Twin Towers were the 'Faculty of Urban Planning', while the Pentagon was the 'Faculty of Fine Arts', and the Capitol Building the 'Faculty of Law'. 'The first term starts in three weeks', ringleader Mohammed Atta emailed his eighteen co-conspirators in late August 2001. 'There are 19 certificates for private studies and four exams.'[2]

That choice of covert terms was packed full of meaning. First, it was a sour joke against all things academic, for being so abstract and reflective, while they were ruthlessly practical and active. Atta himself had 'studied' urban planning as a front while setting up an Al Qaeda sleeper cell in Hamburg. Second, the gallows humour underlying the choice of the disciplines themselves was sardonically appropriate, since neither the rule of law nor the urban landscape of New York would be quite the same after that terrible morning.

Above all, it showed contempt for what had, up to then, been a high degree of intellectual openness in America. So generously had the country welcomed millions of foreign students to its universities that the hijackers judged – correctly, as it turned out – that a certain amount of electronic chatter about departments and faculties would arouse little suspicion, even coming from nineteen young Middle Eastern men constantly on the move. Hani Hanjour, who flew United Airlines Flight 77 into the Pentagon, had entered the US on two different student visas to study English at the Holy Names College in Oakland, California. He failed to turn up for most of his classes.

So it's no wonder that two weeks after 9/11 even a fairly liberal senator like Dianne Feinstein (Democrat, California) was talking about a six-month moratorium on all student visas. That would give the US Immigration and Naturalization Service (INS) time to get a computerised system up and running to track the whereabouts of every foreign student in the country. She quickly backed away from the moratorium idea, following horrified objections from the higher-education lobby, but less than six weeks after the kamikaze attacks President Bush was signing into law the USA Patriot Act.

This attempted to fight terrorism at home by monitoring movements of people in and out of the country in much more detail, and by keeping a closer watch on covert movements at home. Most controversially, the Act boosted the government's powers to tap phones and emails, to seize books, papers, computer hard drives and other media on which business or medical records are kept. Universities would now be required to enter personal and academic details of all its foreign students on a database to be shared with the INS, so that their academic progress and physical movements could be tracked.

Databases require data, of course, so prompted by this higher degree of surveillance, the process of getting a student visa now became more complicated and drawn out. First, the college had to be accredited as a proper academic institution, capable of teaching and supervising postgraduates. Second, foreign applicants were required to pick a specific course of study, and be accepted. At this point they were sent a form showing proof of their offer. Time taken so far, around six weeks.

But the real fun started when they had to go to the nearest US consulate, maybe hundreds of miles away, carrying evidence that they had got a place to study, enough money and sufficient English to follow the course. They also had to prove that they were well enough off in their home countries not to be tempted to overstay their welcome in the US. After being fingerprinted and interviewed, candidates went home to wait for the consular officials to investigate their case. This could take an average of three months. Concern for national security meant that applicants for courses of scientific study, especially if they came from a Muslim country, might have to wait far longer than that.

Then in 2002 things got a lot worse. The Border Security Bill imposed additional importing requirements on the host universities, while requiring intending students to provide their addresses abroad, and the names and addresses of family members. Applicants also had to supply the names of references who could confirm their personal information, as well as stating their past work history, and the names and addresses of their employers. All these informants had to be contacted and their returns checked against known data. Add another three or four months to the process, and this brings us to around nine months in all. For science applicants from the Middle East, double or even triple that total. According to one authoritative study, 'it is now possible for the application process to take up to two years'.[3]

The reason why it takes so long is not just down to slow postal services, or referees delaying their answers, or any other of the usual stumbling blocks along the bureaucratic trail. The real problem is that the Patriot Act now puts the onus on local embassies and consulates to interview the candidates in their home countries, and process the paperwork. Consular officials can now be held legally responsible if a visa-holder commits a terrorist act on US soil. So they are ultra-careful, ultra-deliberate, often checking and re-checking the data and processing the material through sequences of security agencies.

Better late than never, some might say. Surely in the interests of security we could endure a year or two's drop in foreign student numbers, so long as those who finally came through the pipeline were bona fide scholars and researchers, not assassins in disguise? But why would top applicants wait for up to two years, when they can get an answer from universities and governments in Australia, New Zealand, Britain or Canada within three or four weeks? Seventy-nine American universities surveyed reported an 8 per cent drop in the numbers of foreign students (21 per cent in physics) over the academic year 2002–03. In 2003–04 this slid a further 2.4 per cent, and numbers declined a further 1.3 per cent in 2004–05.[4] So if the decline is bottoming out, demand has yet to rebound.

Why do we need foreign students anyway? Well, to start with crude economics, in the last academic year before the restrictions began to squeeze, foreign students and their dependants contributed nearly $12 billion to the economy[5] – not to mention the (literally) incalculable value added by their research. Foreign students account for over 7.9 per cent of all tuition fees received by US universities.[6]

At their peak, foreign postgraduates comprised around a third of postgraduate student numbers. Whole graduate programmes in science and engineering depend on their assistance as researchers. In addition, they often serve as teaching assistants in undergraduate courses, in the larger universities frequently offering the only small-group teaching those students experience.

More broadly, international students are 'our most undervalued foreign-policy asset', as a report by NAFSA, the Association of International Educators has put it.[7] Foreign-policy assets can't be bad in an era when so many foreigners seem to hate us. Above all, we need the variety that foreign students bring – that diversity of languages, religions, outlooks, and ways of living so often lacking in our parochial environment.

German might have been the official language of the United States.

Benjamin Franklin was keen on people emigrating to America. Hard-working European artisans and tenant farmers would work a double benefit, he thought, by freeing themselves from economic and social servitude, while improving the supply and standard of skilled labour in the young country.

When it came to immigrants – that is, emigrants as seen arriving in hordes from the perspective of those already there – Franklin took a very different view. Writing to an English friend in 1753, he expressed his anxiety about the flood of Germans entering Pennsylvania and approaching one third of the colony's population. They were piling up money and influence, increasing in number and making their own laws. Before long, Franklin wrote, we will have lost our advantage in settling here before the Germans. We 'will not … be able to preserve our language, and even our Government will become precarious.'

The German language, above all, became the index of the newcomers' clannishness, their tendency to stick together rather than assimilate to the culture of their adopted country. Later nativist hostility would focus on the German bilingual schools established in parts of the Midwest in the 19th century, and on the common practice of publishing legal notices in the German language in German-American newspapers. During the First World War, when anti-German feeling rose to the absurdity of restaurants renaming hamburger as 'Salisbury steak', midwestern states like Iowa and Nebraska moved to shut down bilingual schools. Most states dropped German from the curriculum. It wasn't until 1923 that the Supreme Court ruled anti-German school laws unconstitutional.[1]

The clue to Franklin's anxiety lay in his mental link between language and government. German seemed to threaten the democratic system itself, because at best it would mean a sizeable majority of recent arrivals who couldn't understand or contribute to the normal discourse of politics. At worst, if Germans should become the majority, the speeches, voting and laws that defined the democratic process might take place in their native language, thus disenfranchising the minority of English-speakers in a particular state or region.

This nervousness, bordering almost on paranoia, lies behind the popular belief that once, in a crucial congressional ballot, German came within one vote of being designated the official language of the USA. It never really happened, though German travel writers to the States, and American teachers of German, never tired of repeating the legend. It was even picked up by the German-American Bund during the 1930s as part of their Nazi propaganda in America.

No such vote took place. The closest the legend came to actuality was when a House of Representatives committee pro-posed that the federal statutes might be published in German as well as English 'for the accommodation of such German citizens of the United States as do not understand the English Language'. After much debate the House moved to adjourn and to consider the proposal later. It was this vote that fell by one vote – 42 to 41 – since the failure to adjourn on this issue was taken as lack of support for the dual-language proposal.

But more generally, language has always been bound up with American national identity. How could this young, progressive, democratic republic hope to make its mark on the world if it continued to speak and do business in the same language of its former oppressor, the monarchical, aristocratic Great Britain? The very words 'monarchical', 'aristocratic' and 'democratic' carried very different overtones on either side of the Atlantic.

The issue went beyond the language of politics; America's cultural independence, too, needed its own vocabulary. 'If we are then asked, why is this country deficient in literature?' wrote the Harvard professor of obstetrics Walter Channing in the *North American Review* in 1815, 'I would answer, in the first place, because it possesses the same language with a nation, totally unlike it in almost every relation.'[2]

One suggestion was that American children should simply be taught another language altogether. But which one? Greek was a possibility, because of its association with learning. Another was French, because the French had sent money and troops to help the colonies in their struggle against Britain. Yet another was Hebrew, because America too considered itself a chosen people. Most hilarious of all these suggestions was Channing's own: the language of the American Indians, whose 'words of description', he thought, were 'very language of poetry'. He didn't say which of the 52 native languages found in North America alone, grouped under 29 families and six phyla, he had in mind.[3]

It was Noah Webster who finally found the compromise between a distinctive American language and what the majority of Americans could actually use. He took the King's English and made it American. First he set to work on the books used to teach children to read. The only schoolbooks the Americans had 'were English schoolbooks, where all the little stories and reading exercises were about how wonderful the King was', as Jill Lapore, professor of history at Harvard has put it.[4]

Webster's *A Grammatical Institute of the English Language* (1783–5) came out in three parts: a spelling book, a grammar and a reader. All the illustrative examples were picked from American experience. The words got a distinctive spelling based on their phonetics. Silent letters like the 'u' in 'parlour' and 'honour' were dropped. 'Plough' became 'plow' and 'centre', 'center'. His first American *Dictionary* (1828) contained 70,000 entries, including words like 'skunk' and 'squash' not found in other English lexicons. Webster's American spellings have lasted to this day, playing their part in defining a distinctive American English.

Now, of course, the anxiety is not over German, but Spanish, the second most common language in the United States after English. Spanish is spoken at home by about 28.1 million people, or 10.5 per cent of the American population. Only about half of these speak English 'very well'. To incorporate linguistic minorities like Hispanics and Koreans into the civic community, Congress re-authorised the Voting Rights Act of 1965 to provide for bilingual and multilingual ballots in 1975. The original VRA abolished the literacy test by which southern states like Mississippi and Alabama prevented African Americans and poor whites from registering to vote. If voters couldn't be excluded by being unable to read, so the argument went ten years later, they shouldn't suffer the same penalty by virtue of the language they spoke.

The recent uproar over illegal migration from Mexico has thrown the whole issue of language back into sharp relief. Congress has recently been debating whether the multilingual ballots requirement should be continued when the VRA comes up for renewal. Conservative pressure groups like the English First Foundation argue that ever since 1905 applicants for American citizenship have been required to learn English. 'Most immigrants are required to demonstrate a knowledge of English before they can achieve citizenship, and thus the right to vote', the Foundation argues. 'But a child born on US soil is automatically a citizen, even if his or her parents arrived on US soil illegally.'[5] The subtext is clear. Legitimate Mexican migrants speak English, and want to. Those who don't are wetbacks.

Immigration has re-emerged as a hot political ticket. It's one of three issues – the other two are his fiscal extravagance and the Iraq war – over which President Bush fell out with his traditional Republican supporters. And language is still at the heart of it. On 10 May 2006, to the dismay of the conservatives, the House Judiciary Committee sent a re-authorisation of the VRA to the floor of the House, upholding multilingual ballots by a large majority. Only nine days later, perhaps to assuage the conservatives' anxieties, the Senate voted to make English the 'national language' of the United States – the first time in history any language has been so assigned. But they were careful not to unpick the existing laws mandating multilingual ballots and other government publications.

Meanwhile, Bush himself was trying to fend off his critics by asking Congress to approve a $1.95 billion allocation to pay for 370 miles of triple-layered fencing on the US–Mexican border, and for National Guard troops and 1,000 additional immigration agents to police it.[6] And when a new Spanish-language version of 'The Star-Spangled Banner' was released in April 2006, Bush reacted by saying: 'I think the national anthem ought to be sung in English, and

I think people who want to be a citizen of this country ought to learn English.'[7]

And this despite the fact that the US State Department website lists four Spanish-language translations of the anthem, the first commissioned by the US government as long ago as 1919. One of these versions Bush himself used to sing at Hispanic festivals when he was running for President back in 2000.

America has some of the worst high schools and most of the best universities in the world.

In the last few years an amazing document has been circulating widely on the internet, passing by email between friends and even appearing in serious newspapers like the *Washington Post* and the *Boston Globe*. So widely has it been noticed that, although genuine, it has already been denounced as an urban myth.[1] Here's how it's usually introduced:

> Remember when grandparents and great-grandparents stated that they only had an 8th-grade education? Well check this out. Could any of us have passed the 8th grade in 1895? This is the 8th-grade final exam from 1895 in Salina, Kansas, USA.

Candidates were allowed five hours in all to answer between eight and ten questions under various headings. 'Give nine rules for use of capital letters', went one. 'What is the cost of a square farm at $15 per acre, the distance of which is 640 rods?' brought Arithmetic home to local conditions, Kansas being famously full of square farms and somewhat square itself. A question in Geography required them to explain: 'What is climate? Upon what does climate depend?' One of eight questions on US History demanded an account of 'the causes and results of the Revolutionary War'. Allowed only 45 minutes for the section as a whole, candidates must have required stamping-press powers of compression even to outline an answer to that one.[2]

This ghostly trace of the past has attracted such attention because Americans are acutely anxious about the current state of secondary education. Is this unease justified? On the basis of international comparisons, yes. The US Department of Education reports that while 4th-graders – that is, eight-year-olds in primary school – score as well or better than most of their peers abroad, 'high school students in the United States are consistently out-performed by those from Asian and some European countries' in mathematics and science.

Fifteen-year-old American students, high school pupils in the 10th grade, 'had lower average scores in mathematics and science literacy compared with most of the same age group in most Organisation for Economic Co-operation and Development member countries'. The OECD is made up of 22 European nations, plus Australia, Canada, Japan, Korea, Mexico, the United States and New Zealand.

And it's getting worse. Performance of American 12th-graders, or high school seniors, actually declined from 1996 to 2005.[3] Attendance fell off too. As education correspondent Tom Vander Ark, Director of the Bill and Melinda Gates Foundation, put it in 2003: 'This coming September about 3.5 million young people in America will begin the 8th grade. Over the succeeding four years more than 1 million of them will drop out – an average of 3,500 each school day.'[4]

On the other hand, according to the widely respected study of world universities undertaken by the Shanghai Jiao Tong University, American institutions of higher learning lead the world. Considering 'every institution that features Nobel Laureates, Fields Medals [for mathematics], highly cited researchers, or articles published in journals, such as *Nature* or *Science*', the investigators found American universities at the top, with seventeen of the best twenty institutions, 51 of the best 100, and so on down to 170 in the top 500.

Britain ranked second, with two – the usual suspects – in the best twenty, eleven in the top 100, and 42 in the best 500. Japan adds the final one to the top twenty, and comes up with five of the best 100 and 36 of the top 500. After that things fall away pretty quickly. Continental Europe has no entries in the top twenty, though Germany has seven entries, and Russia one, in the top 100. The other European countries range from 43 institutions each down to two in the top 500. Apart from China, universities in the Far East, not to mention India and South America, score negligibly.[5] Granted, this ranking is biased heavily towards the sciences, and has nothing to say about how many of those Nobel Laureates actually teach undergraduates face to face.

So how come an American student has only to step over the threshold between high school and college to pass from a failing secondary system to a world-beating university? In England, Wales and Northern Ireland, the answer to this puzzle would be more straightforward. There, students are winnowed while still at school, some staying on beyond the minimum leaving age of sixteen, and most of those going on to specialise in the area of their future study by working to three or four examinations. English universities are selective too, increasingly so towards the upper end of the hierarchy.

But in America the principle of general education for all governs the whole education system, from bottom to top. From 1838, Horace Mann, Secretary of Education for Massachusetts and one of the great education reformers, began to introduce a system of publicly funded 'common schools', which all children were required to attend. The system soon spread, until 72 per cent of American children were attending school by 1910, learning word recognition, reading, comprehension, civics, moral values, history and literature from succeeding volumes of the McGuffey Readers, of which at least 120 million copies were sold between 1836 and 1960. In most states, students are required to attend high school until graduation, or the age of eighteen, whichever comes first.

The same ideal of access for all applies to the universities. Many people outside the US think of American universities in terms of its exclusive 'Ivy League' colleges, a much-misunderstood classification that denotes simply an institution founded before the Revolution. But alongside the Ivy League and other private institutions stand the great state universities, the so-called 'land-grant' colleges established by the Morrill Act of 1862.

Originally conceived to promote agricultural and technical schools, some of which still retain the suffix 'A&M' for agricultural and mechanical, the Act granted to each state a minimum of 90,000 acres of land – the amount increasing with population – to sell or build on in support of as many universities as it wanted. In time, the state universities branched out beyond agriculture and mechanics into the humanities, arts, pure sciences and all the other faculties

and subjects of modern universities, including postgraduate professional schools of law, medicine and business.

In time, what with their scientific research buttressed by defence
spending and enrolments enlarged by the GI Bill of Rights (see fact
26), the land-grant universities grew to rival, and even surpass,
some Ivy League and other private institutions. Of the 124 top
colleges listed in the 2007 *US News and World Report* annual
survey, 65 are public institutions – most of them old land-grant
colleges like the Universities of Illinois, Michigan and Minnesota
and all eight campuses of the University of California.[6]

In America, a problem perceived is often a problem on the way
to a solution. Various public and private bodies, like the National
Governors' Association, chaired by Mark Warner, Governor of
Virginia, and the Bill and Melinda Gates Foundation, have been
exploring ways of reforming American high schools. Ideas so far
have included smaller-sized classes, more rigorous academic programmes and standards, and a greater concentration on research
and study projects, chosen and managed by the individual student.

These suggestions are all about increasing motivation, keeping
those 3,500-a-day high school dropouts to a minimum – above all,
by offering a sharper focus on the world of work, or higher
education to come. In Texas and Arkansas, high school students
are automatically put in the college preparatory stream; they have
to opt out if they don't want it. Here and elsewhere, increased
expectations have improved performance, especially for poor and
minority students. When the San Jose, California, Unified School
District required all students to follow the college preparatory
curriculum required by the University of California, the test scores
of its black 11th-graders increased nearly seven times over other
African American students in the state.[7]

Then, if the school leaver doesn't get into college right away,
there are always community colleges, which can be attended
full- or part-time, maybe while the student is working, and from
which credits can be gained to transfer to the state universities. In
the American university system, excellence does not depend on
exclusivity.

There's one car for every adult in the US.

In America, ask anyone how far away your intended destination is, and they'll tell you how long it will take you to drive there. That's the surest sign that America has a culture of the car.

Think what it takes to underpin this fact. First, near-universal car ownership or availability. Second, a network of roads so good that the time elapsed on them can be predicted more or less without regard to weather, traffic density or other variables that can some-times double travel times in Europe. And speed limits too, of course. They seldom exceed 55 miles per hour, even on four-lane country highways, and 70 on the interstates. Drivers obey them. That adds further to the predictability of journey times.

Americans didn't invent the car, weren't even responsible for most of the technological innovations that made the average car what it is today. The first four-stroke internal combustion engine – the prototype for most car engines to follow – was built by a German, Nikolaus Otto, in 1876. Developing Otto's engine, another German called Gottlieb Daimler produced the world's first four-wheeled automobile in 1886.

The first car-makers to put the engine in front driving wheels at the rear were Panhard-Levassor, a French firm. This design, known as the *système Panhard*, quickly became the standard, because it improved balance and steering. The 1895 Panhard also had the first modern transmission. Disc brakes were invented by the British engineer Frederick Lanchester. The V-8 engine, so often associated with huge American cars, first appeared in France in 1910.[1]

The big American leap forward was in the mode of production that combined the idea of interchangeable parts (itself a French invention dating back to 1790) with the assembly line, first patented by Ransom Eli Olds, who gave his name to the Oldsmobile. Now that it was no longer constructed as a craft object by a few skilled mechanics, each car took much less time to assemble, and hence could be sold more cheaply. In other words, the American contribution to car manufacture was chiefly economic, and hence political. Americans made cars for the people.

It was Henry Ford who perfected this process to manufacture his Model T. First introduced in 1908, the 'Tin Lizzie' entered full mass production in 1913 at Ford's plant in Highland Park, Michigan. There the cars being assembled flowed down a river-like conveyor belt, with tributaries feeding each component into the stream at the exact moment when it would be added to the assembly. Along the line, the workers' jobs were highly specialised. 'The man who puts in a bolt does not put on a nut', as Ford explained. 'The man who puts on the nut does not tighten it.'[2]

By 1914 it took just 93 minutes to assemble a Model T Ford. In all, more than 15 million were made, more than any other model of car for over a century. By the 1920s the price per unit of the Model T had fallen to $300 – about $3,300 in today's money. At the same time competing cars were costing upwards of twice as much.

But cars aren't much use without roads. As cars multiplied, so did pressure on the government to fund road-building schemes. Often these had a rural flavour. 'Get the farmers out of the mud!' was one battle cry. Later projects were built around the theme of 'farm to market'. As early as 1916, Congress passed the Federal-Aid Road Act. After the First World War, the Federal Highway Act of 1921 authorised the Bureau of Public Roads to fund a limited network of two-lane interstate highways.

But the big push came after the Second World War, when President Dwight D. Eisenhower signed the Federal Highway Act of 1956, through which Congress appropriated some $32 billion to construct 41,000 miles of motorway-standard interstate highways criss-crossing the country. Now there are 65 of them in the continental US – not to mention three each in Hawaii and Puerto Rico, and four in Alaska.

Not even the Great Depression of 1929–41 made much of a dent in car ownership or production. New-car sales may have sagged slightly, but motor vehicle registrations were higher in 1935 than at the height of the boom before the crash of 1929; so were fuel consumption and the total of miles travelled. Once again the government acted to promote car use. Franklin Delano Roosevelt's New Deal made road-building a chief focus of various make-work schemes managed by the Works Progress Administration. In all the WPA built 650,000 miles of roads and 78,000 bridges. Many of these were small – some not even paved – but they could make all the difference to an isolated rural community.

In fact the increased leisure forced upon people by the Depression more often than not was channelled into activities around the automobile. From 1935 to 1942 the WPA produced a series of State Guides, carefully researched, attractively written and affordable introductions to the cultural and political history of each state, its social and physical geography, even its customs and folklore. All were built around the assumption that the tourists were travelling by car. The information was organised around projected road tours, giving directions and mileages between points of interest, pinpointing roadhouses offering good meals, and suggesting places to pull in for an overnight stay.

After the Second World War, veterans returning from the conflict craved the peace and quiet of the suburbs. Between 1950 and 1956 the population of the US suburbs increased by 46 per cent, and by 1970 America became the first country in the world to classify more than half its population as suburban. Suburbs meant cars, of course. Shopping, the movies, the ball game were no longer just a walk or a streetcar-ride away. You drove. Drive-in restaurants, drive-in movies, even drive-in banks and churches – all celebrated the anything-goes spirit of suburban driving in the 1950s and 60s. Motels had already sprouted alongside the interstates, and now began to appear in towns too. Gigantic shopping malls would follow.

Sidewalks disappeared. Except in older cities, people stopped walking to the stores, or to go out for a meal. If you wanted a beer or a cup of coffee, you drove to it, even within the same shopping complex. Returning to his native country after over twenty years of living in England, the essayist and travel writer Bill Bryson recalls getting a room in a Heritage Motor Inn outside Carbondale, Illinois, then setting out to find a meal. 'Going for a walk, as I discovered, was a ridiculous and impossible undertaking,' he writes:

> I had to cross parking lots and gas station forecourts, and I kept coming up against little white painted walls marking the boundaries between, say, Long John Silver's Seafood Shoppe and Kentucky Fried Chicken. To get from one to the

other, it was necessary to clamber over the wall, scramble up a grassy embankment and pick your way through a thicket of parked cars.

'That is if you were on foot', he adds. 'What you were supposed to do was to get in your car, drive twelve feet down the street to another parking lot, park the car and get out.'[3]

Of course, this left those people too poor to run a car stranded – not to mention those who live in cities, where cars were of more nuisance than use. By the early 1960s urban public transport had begun to deteriorate, and inter-urban rail services, like Los Angeles' Pacific Electric 'Red Cars', had vanished altogether. Although in time cities would rejig their public transport as rapid transit systems (see fact 30), progress has been decidedly uneven.

In New Orleans, where the old streetcars are now tourist rides,[4] people with cars drove out ahead of Hurricane Katrina in August 2005, most finding refuge with friends or in motels far from the devastation. Meanwhile, the 35 per cent of the city's black population without cars were left marooned as Katrina approached the city. When some of them attempted to walk away from the storm – ironically along the now-deserted interstate highway – they were turned back by a National Guard checkpoint on the on-ramp, and sent instead to overcrowded, unsanitary and downright dangerous refugee collecting points like the Superdome and the New Orleans Convention Center.[5]

America has its own welfare state – the military services.

Do American soldiers, sailors, airmen and marines represent a cross-section of the population, or are they predominantly poor, black and under-educated? Have the country's leaders been sending other people's children to die for them?

Film-writer and critic William Broyles certainly thinks so. Writing in the *New York Times*, he recalled how much he learned and grew after serving in the Marines during the Vietnam War. 'My classmates from high school were in the war; my classmates from college were not.' So he found 'my life ... put into the hands of young men I would otherwise never have met, by and large high-school dropouts'. They 'turned out to be among the finest people I have ever known'.

Even then, as Broyles's memories remind us, it was possible to avoid the draft. For starters, a full-time college course provided a deferment from the call-up. That's how Bill Clinton side-stepped Vietnam. Or if you had connections, you could go right to the head of the queue and join the Air National Guard, learning how to fly while keeping safe at home, away from the action. That's how George W. Bush did it.

But ever since Richard Nixon abolished the draft in 1973, we have had a wholly 'volunteer Army'. This means that idealists like Broyles and film-maker Oliver Stone, whose *Platoon* (1986) dramatised the experience of a white, middle-class volunteer in Vietnam, can join up if they want to, but gives the children of the better off carte blanche to keep out of harm's way.

'We will not have a draft so long as I am President of the United States', Bush said in the run-up to the 2004 general election. You'd better believe it. He knows his constituency. As Broyles points out, 'The are no immediate family members of any of the prime civilian planners of this war serving in it', and 'only one of the 535 members of Congress'. This was later corrected to three, and the total rose again after the 2006 mid-term elections, but the general point still stood.

'The war is being fought by other people's children', wrote Broyles. 'If the children of the nation's elites were facing enemy fire without body armor, ... fighting desperately in an increasingly hostile environment because of arrogant and incompetent civilian leadership, then those problems might well find faster solutions.' Meanwhile, bring back the draft, he suggested – only this time based on 'a strictly impartial lottery, with no deferments'.[1]

While the argument simmers between politicians and their critics of the Vietnam generation, what has actually been happening to the make-up of the American armed forces? Some things remain the same. The military still recruits more African Americans and fewer Hispanics than their proportion of the population. The South continues to provide a larger share of service personnel aged between 18 and 24 – 41 per cent as against 35.6 per cent of the age group in the region. Recruitment from the North-eastern states and from urban areas still tends to lag behind.

In other respects military demographics have been changing – and fast. Women now fight in front-line action, and in the Army more of them are black than white. Class distribution among enlisted personnel has evened out a bit. A recent study comparing social background by postal codes showed that since 9/11 military personnel have tended to reflect the income spread of their civilian contemporaries, with only 20 per cent coming from the poorest quintile of the population. They are also better educated than the Vietnam cohort of enlisted personnel. No more of Broyles's 'high school dropouts'. Now the services require even their most junior recruits to possess a minimum of a high school diploma, a demand which, figures show, has motivated young men and women to complete their secondary schooling in areas returning otherwise poor levels of educational attainment.[2]

So the old cliché that the volunteer forces are made up of uneducated no-hopers who couldn't get a job on civvy street needs some revising. In fact, today's would-be recruits have many options other than military service open to them – which leads on to another question, seldom asked. Why are so many willing to join up in time of war, when there is a good chance of their being blown to pieces?

Well, patriotism, for one thing. Don't underestimate the power of that motive, especially after 9/11. A desire for action, the wish to travel – both all too likely to be satisfied in today's armed forces. A more varied career structure, with better in-service training than in many civilian jobs. But there is another reason too, one that ought to prompt a bitter political debate, but instead is seldom mentioned. The armed forces, though charged with defending American values at home and abroad, run a welfare state as generous and far-reaching in its benefits as any European equivalent.

To be specific, complete medical coverage and free or highly subsidised college-level education, two crucial benefits priced beyond the reach of many civilians, are on offer in the American armed services. How did such progressive benefits, so apparently at odds with the national self-image, come to be provided in such a conservative environment as a military establishment?

The answer lies in the shifting fortunes of American war veterans over time. On being discharged from service in the First World War, soldiers were given $60 and a train ticket home, then left to their own devices. When many failed to find a job or otherwise adjust to civilian life, Congress responded with the World War Compensation Adjusted Act of 1924, offering all veterans a bonus payment depending on how long they had served. There was a catch, though. None of this money would be paid out for twenty years.

When the Great Depression hit the country, putting 13 million people out of work, or one quarter of the work force, 20,000 veterans and their families marched on Washington to ask that their bonuses be paid immediately, rather than in 1944, as provided by the Act. When this 'Bonus Army' didn't get its wish, some stayed behind, camping on the mudflats across the Anacostia River from the Capitol building.

Eventually they were attacked by federal troops under the command of two men who would make their names in the war to come, George S. Patton and Douglas MacArthur. The latter suspected a communist plot. Men, women and children were bayoneted, tear-gassed and slashed by the sabres of Patton's Third Cavalry Regiment. Two veterans and two children were killed, and many others were injured, the campers dispersed and their tents burned.

Ordinary citizens were revolted by this spectacle of the peace-time Army assaulting poor veterans who had risked their lives in a real war. The military and political establishment felt threatened by ex-soldiers, who retained enough of the discipline and organising skills they learned in the services to mobilise in groups of 20,000 to apply pressure virtually anywhere in the country. A mixture of pity and fear lodged the fate of the Bonus Army in the American memory as perhaps the worst single episode of the Depression.

Politicians of all persuasions were determined that it would never happen again. So when servicemen and women were discharged after the Second World War, they found an enlarged and strengthened Veterans Administration behind them, offering not just mustering-out pay and vocational training but medical care and hospitalisation benefits continuing into civilian life.

Then there was the GI Bill of Rights, or the Servicemen's Readjustment Act of 1944, the last great piece of legislation by Franklin Delano Roosevelt's New Deal. Among other benefits, the GI Bill offered low-interest loans for housing, a provision to which historians now attribute the enormous expansion and democratis-ation of the suburbs after the war.

Most famously it provided educational or technical training, covering tuition charges up to $500 per year (in those days enough for even the most prestigious state universities), plus a monthly living allowance. Within seven years of the Bill passing, 2.3 million veterans had gone to college, while another 3.5 million had gone back to high school and 3.4 million got on-the-job training. Many universities doubled or even trebled their numbers, as students arrived from social backgrounds that could never have contem-plated a university education before the war.

As with veterans, so by a process of back-formation, those in active service. The Army, Air Force, Navy and Marines now offer their enlisted personnel full medical and dental coverage and in-service educational training. For those who arrive with a college degree, the services will pay off their student loan in full or in part. For a $100 deduction in monthly pay for just one year, they will finance a college degree up to $36,000 on leaving active service, on the updated GI Bill. Americans look after the men and women in the military, even if it means borrowing clothes from more 'socialised' dispensations and setting up a model welfare state in order to do so.

Americans say more than they need to.

The educational theorist E.D. Hirsch, Jr recalled an experiment conducted in Harvard Square. A researcher with a copy of the *Boston Globe* under his arm asked a passer-by: 'How do you get to Central Square?' The answer shot back: 'Next stop; on the subway.' The next day the same man asked the same question of someone else, only now posing as a tourist: 'I'm from out of town. Can you tell me how to get to Central Square?' This time he was answered in much more detail: how to find the Red Line station in Harvard Square, go down the stairs, buy a token, make sure you wait on the platform marked 'Quincey', then get off at the first stop. 'You'll know that it's Central Square because there's a big sign on the wall. It says, "Central Square".'

This anecdote appeared in Hirsch's best-selling *Cultural Literacy* (1987), as a way of exploring the connection between culture and communication. To explain what his title meant, he produced names of books and authors, people, things, events and ideas that constitute what 'literate Americans' once knew and now don't. The list ran from 'abolitionism' and 'abominable snowman' to 'Zola', 'zoning' and 'Zurich'.

His point was that because of their increasing multiculturalism, Americans were rapidly losing that common culture. As a result they were finding it increasingly difficult to communicate with one another. The young generation of American cultural illiterates, Hirsch argued, are like that tourist. For them every context has to be established cumbersomely before the simplest messages can be transmitted.[1]

Leaving aside such questions as whether it is culturally more 'literate' to identify 'Hoover' as a President, a dam or a vacuum cleaner, Hirsch's concern anticipated similar anxieties in other countries. Long before Europe had to contend with large-scale immigration from Turkey, Pakistan, the West Indies and North Africa, America was building itself out of these and many other European, Asian and South American populations. So it's not surprising that Hirsch's question of how a common culture can be sustained – or built – out of so many diverse peoples goes back a long way in America.

In fact, American concern over the severing of cultural contexts, whether shared with the past or with fellow citizens, probably comes from our origin as immigrants (see fact 2), when all of us, or our parents or earlier forebears, experienced a fundamental rupture with our old homes.

Hirsch's anxiety has surfaced repeatedly in various forms, one of which used to be the nature of American creative writing. This was supposed to suffer from a lack of common experience of past or present to which authors could allude in the hope that readers would pick up their signals. James Fenimore Cooper, Nathaniel Hawthorne, Henry James and T.S. Eliot all came out with their own versions of this lament. Significantly, all four of them had spent a lot of time in Europe, where (they assumed) readers shared a common culture.

As it happened, American literature developed ways of over-coming its readers' supposed lack of a shared culture by making its allusions explicit. Walt Whitman's long poem *Leaves of Grass*, turning its back on the kind of story, argument or theme that would unify an English equivalent like Milton's *Paradise Lost* or Tennyson's *In Memoriam*, picks up materials from contemporary American physical and social geography more or less as it encounters them.

That way the 'background' needed to read the poem is re-created as the foreground of the poem itself. On a different tack of the same voyage, Eliot's *The Waste Land* alludes almost endlessly to the classics of Greek, Latin and English literature, but obligingly (if a bit condescendingly) provides footnotes to help the reader out.

But it's in the American idiom itself that this adjustment to the cultural mix begins. What distinguishes American speech from (say) English is just the sort of redundancy that Hirsch deplored as a sign of cultural decline – that is, redundancy in the technical sense used in information theory. In a noisy environment, like static on the line, a signal must repeat or restate itself to some extent in order to get itself across. Announcements in more conventionally noisy fields do this all the time. 'This is the last call for United

Airlines flight 84 for Los Angeles, loading at gate number 22. Gate 22 for United flight 84 for Los Angeles.'

Studs Terkel's transcriptions of people living and working in Chicago are full of repetitions or restatements, like 'Right in this neighborhood, right across the block', positive and negative reinforcements of the message, like 'What I'm saying is …' and 'Here's what I mean …' or 'I'm not saying …', and by tone markers that signpost irony or its absence, like 'I'm just kidding …' and 'I mean that seriously'.[2]

When American authors finally heard and transcribed the vernacular accurately, we got *Huckleberry Finn* (1884), the short stories of Ring Lardner (various collections from 1916 to 1934), and the plays of Clifford Odets, Arthur Miller, Paddy Chayevsky and David Mamet – not to mention most Hollywood movies, where we have come to take its stylish simplicity for granted, as though anyone could do it. In Ring Lardner's story 'The Love Nest', Lou Gregg, president of Modern Pictures, Inc., tells a visiting journalist what his house means to him:

> 'But no amount of money is too much to spend on home. I mean it's a good investment if it tends to make your family proud and satisfied with their home. I mean every nickel I've spent here is like so much insurance; it insures me of a happy wife and family. And what more can a man ask?'[3]

Later the journalist learns that the wife and family are far from happy, so it may be that Lou's over-emphasis was prompted by anxiety. An even more desperate man is Shelly Levene in David Mamet's play about a cut-throat real estate company in Chicago, *Glengarry Glen Ross* (1984). Aware that his rival, Roma, has already overtaken his sales record, Levene pleads with the boss:

> John … John … John. Okay, John. Look: (*Pause*) The Glengarry Highland's leads, you're sending Roma out. Fine. He's a good man. We know that he is. He's fine. All I'm saying, you look at the *board*. He's throwing … wait, wait, wait, he's throwing them *away*, he's throwing them away. All that I'm saying, things get *set*, I know they do, you get a certain

mindset. ... A guy gets a certain reputation. We know how this
... all I'm saying, put a *closer* on the job ... there's more than
one man for the ... Put a ... wait a second – and you watch
your *dollar* volumes ... you start closing them for *fifty* 'stead of
twenty-five ... you put a closer on the ...[4]

Now there is no more noisy environment than a big city. And an
American city, where ethnicity, class, background, nationality and
levels of education mix more bewilderingly than elsewhere, is the
noisiest setting of all. Like the wannabe script-writers in Robert
Altman's *The Player* (1992), people in everyday life have only a brief
moment in which to make their pitch, and they have to define –
even assert – themselves, without reference to a pre-existing
cultural context. In other words, what E.D. Hirsch took to be a
recent cultural collapse has always been part of the social condition. We Americans have always needed to lay down our own
cultural roadbeds, like tanks or Caterpillar tractors.

Of the ten top-selling vocal artists in 2006, five were country-and-western singers.

Four of the five winners were Carrie Underwood, Tim McGraw, Keith Urban and Rascal Flatts. Flatts alone was America's top-selling musical act in 2006, with almost 5 million albums sold and nearly 4 million digital track sales. The fifth was Johnny Cash, now more of a legend than ever three years after his death, his sales no doubt boosted by the bio-pic, *Walk the Line*.[1] The Dixie Chicks also clocked up five Grammys in February 2007, despite almost no exposure on country radio and the lingering irritation following lead vocalist Natalie Maines's expression of shame over G.W. Bush's invasion of Iraq.

Had Maines been a rapper, a rhythm and blues singer or a folk artist, no one would have noticed. But the politics of country music are – well, patriotic. After 9/11, Toby Keith, the Oklahoma-born singer and songwriter, came out with 'Courtesy of the Red, White and Blue', promising that America would avenge that outrage:

> This big dog will fight
> When you rattle his cage
> And you'll be sorry you messed with
> The US of A.
> 'Cause we'll put a boot in your ass.
> It's the American way.

Despite drawing some of its inspiration from the blues sung around the Mississippi Delta, country music is very white, very Anglo-Saxon, very Protestant. From the beginning, its favourite performers have had British-sounding names like Carter, Wills, Rodgers, Williams, Tillman, Robbins, Gentry, Parton.

Whatever these people have got up to in private, their songs never voiced the 'F' word. The Lord's name was frequently invoked, but never in vain. Alcohol was and remains a topic, but never drugs. Common themes are themes common to us all: family, home, feeling lonely, feeling guilty, above all love: falling in or out of it, being betrayed, getting even, surviving its absence.

Back when it was still called hillbilly, country music drew on a bewildering variety of influences: English and 'Scotch-Irish' ballads, African American blues and work songs, gospel hymns, music from minstrel shows – even Swiss yodels and Hawaiian string bands. To get an idea of country's sources, just think of the numbers in the Coen brothers' film, *O Brother, Where Art Thou?* (2000): the chain gang chanting 'Po' Lazarus'; the gospel singers' lovely harmonies and repeated refrains in 'Down to the River to Pray';[2] the Soggy Bottom Boys singing the old Jimmie Rodgers number, 'In the Jailhouse Now' and the theme tune of the whole movie, 'I am a Man of Constant Sorrow', that expression of alienation so characteristic of country music.

Though much hillbilly music was learned by ear, sheet music from New York City's Tin Pan Alley and the invention of the phonograph soon commercialised its production and distribution. By 1932 radio stations were spreading the message even wider, broadcasting at 50,000 watts, sufficient – since the programmes were carried on long wave – to cover the whole of the south-eastern United States. When movies got wired for sound, cowboys, already popular in the silents, began to sing. With Gene Autry and Roy Rogers, 'country' and 'western' joined forces.

By the end of the thirties, the themes and musical resources of country and western were pretty well set. A survey of songs favoured by Dust Bowl migrants in a government camp in California could be grouped roughly under five themes. First come songs of love lost or betrayed, like 'Frankie and Johnnie', and Jimmie Rodgers's 'Blue Yodel No. 4':

> ... Listen to me mama
> While I sing you this song
> Listen to your daddy
> Sing you this lonesome song
> You've got me worried now
> But I won't be worried long ...

Then there were sentimental songs about the old home left behind – especially poignant for economic migrants – such as 'She's Way up Thar' and 'The Old Spinning Wheel'. Smaller in number but still important were the temperance songs like 'A Drunkard's Child', who dies blessing her father yet imploring others to help him to reform, and 'A Drunkard's Dream', a prophetic vision of the likely outcome if he doesn't mend his ways. In his vision the drunkard sees his wife lying dead, and his children standing around her coffin.

A popular theme, inherited from the British ballads, was the outlaw dying in jail, forsaken by his lover, like Rodgers's 'Blue Yodel No. 2':

> … Write me a letter, send it to me by mail
> Write me a letter, send it to me by mail,
> Just send it to me care of the Birmingham jail.
>
> Well I ain't gonna marry and ain't gonna settle down
> Well I ain't gonna marry and ain't gonna settle down
> I'm gonna be a rounder till the police shoot me down …

But by far the most popular songs were really a variant on the theme of the marginalised outlaw, reflecting the new western emphasis. These were songs by and about cowboys: cowboys missing their gals ('Night Time in Nevada'); cowboys nostalgic for the outdoor life ('Goin' Back to Texas', 'Home on the Range'); cowboys dying, either alone or far from home ('Oh Bury Me Not on the Lone Prairie'), and so on.

Country music has always been associated with rednecks, but that doesn't mean that it's unsophisticated. Religion, for one thing, has offered plenty of complications. Song-writer and recording artist Butch Hancock recalled what it was like to be young on a west Texas cotton farm in the late 1950s. 'In Lubbock we grew up with two main things', he told Nicholas Dawidoff. 'God loves you and he's gonna send you to hell, and … sex is bad and dirty and nasty and awful and you should save it for the one you love.' 'You wonder why we're all crazy', he added.[3]

And along with failure, the marginal status and the loss of and disappointment in love, goes resistance. Jimmie Rodgers's mood ('I won't be worried long') is picked up by Rascal Flatts in 'I'm tired and I'm numb, baby I hate it / I feel bad / That I don't feel bad'. The refrain 'I can get along without you very well' has persisted in country music. 'Redneck' is not the absence of culture, but a culture of its own – conditioned by the rueful acceptance of under-dog status – and country music is its ritual expression. Country music is for those Americans whose ancestors did not step ashore at Plymouth Rock.[4]

Besides, ever since the appearance of *White Trash Cooking* in 1986, a new pride in country manners has been growing, reinforced by a strain of self-deprecating humour that's always been there. Once when Dolly Parton finished a set and was cheered to the roof, someone in the audience shouted out: 'I love you, Dolly.' Quick as a whip she answered back: 'I thought I told you to wait in the van.' OK, so she's done it before and knows all the lines. Still, it was the style of the thing: that comic pretence that she had a man waiting – in a van, note, not a limousine. That's the country way.

It's the women artists who are actively developing the new country style. Sentimental memories of an old home left behind still figure in the repertoire. Carrie Underwood's moving 'Don't Forget to Remember Me' expresses memories of her family voiced by a girl who has moved away to the city. But now the tone of the old message 'I can get along without you very well' is more derisive than defensive – not so much 'Stand by Your Man' as kick him in the nuts. The character in Underwood's 'Before He Cheats' gets her revenge on the man who done her wrong:

> … I dug my key into the side of his pretty little souped up
> 4 wheel drive,
> carved my name into his leather seats …
> I took a Louisville slugger[5] to both head lights,
> slashed a hole in all 4 tires …

But the really brilliant part is her fantasy of what the new lovers are getting up to:

Right now he's probably slow dancing with a bleach blonde
tramp, and she's probably getting frisky …
Right now, he's probably buying her some fruity little drink
cause she can't shoot whiskey …

Right now, she's probably up singing some
white-trash version of Shania karaoke.
Right now, she's probably saying 'I'm drunk'
and he's a thinking that he's gonna get lucky …

There's a subtle distinction here between two kids of country girl:
the real redneck who *can* shoot whiskey and the fake who can only
tolerate a 'fruity little drink', and who gets no closer to Shania
Twain, the Canadian country star, than the karaoke player. Then
there's the false lover who can't tell the difference. That's a more
damaging attack than her assault on his SUV.

Walden Pond has the highest concentration of urine of any lake in New England.[1]

'We had to pay $5 to park in what smelled like a LANDFILL', wrote one outraged blogger after hoping to spend a lazy Sunday walking around the lake in Concord, Massachusetts, not far from Boston, where Henry David Thoreau once famously lived in the woods. 'When we got to the pond ... the water was yellow ... As we followed trails and the people we passed got spookier, we reached the pinnacle of grotesque. LARGE HAIRY SKINNY DIPPERS.' Not only that, but the trails were blocked by people with kids in 'strollers the size of Volkswagens. You can't bring your kids here, unless you want them to see fat old men with ugly no-nos talking about foliage. It was awful.'[2]

Thoreau, the transcendentalist philosopher, peace protester, radical abolitionist and gifted ecologist, lived on and off by the side of Walden Pond from 1845 to 1847, in a rough cabin he built himself out of second-hand lumber. While there, he fished and gathered huckleberries, and planted a field of beans that came to nothing. He watched – and noted, in increasing attention to detail – how the seasons altered the plants and animals, the colours of the trees and sky and lake. And he thought a lot about his country and local community, and about the way we live our lives.

His observations on contemporary institutions, and his more interesting comments on the natural world around him, came out as *Walden; or, Life in the Woods* in 1854, fronted by a sketch showing his little cabin surrounded by pines, with taller trees in the background. The book has become an American classic. In 1991 a survey of professors in the humanities proclaimed *Walden* the single most important work of 19th-century American literature. *Walden* got 45 per cent of their vote, as against 34 per cent for *The Scarlet Letter* by Nathaniel Hawthorne and a mere 29 per cent for Herman Melville's great whaling epic, *Moby-Dick*.

And unlike many books advocated by professors, *Walden* has enjoyed a popular readership to match its recruitment into the canon. Though selling only moderately well at first, it has since gone through nearly 200 editions. It's been especially popular with special-interest groups, from whole-earthers and nudists (those ugly no-nos), through civil-rights marchers and survivalist cults. Above all, the book has appealed to members of the various conservationist and ecology movements, starting with John Muir, the champion of Yosemite Valley in the California Sierra, and an early campaigner for US national parks.

So no doubt all these loyal fans would be profoundly shocked to hear that Walden is now so frequented by hordes of swimmers that its water has the highest concentration of urine in New England. Has it come to this, that the sacred site of Thoreau's rural isolation should be so despoiled by popularity? Well, no, actually. Like everything else about *Walden* and Walden Pond, the reality is very different from what is treasured in the public consciousness.

Take those woods for a start. In Thoreau's day there were hardly any. Most of the trees had been used to make charcoal, for use in the smelting process to extract iron from the underlying bog iron ore. In the late 1840s more trees were cut down to make ties for the railroad then being built from Boston, past the pond, west to Fitchburg. As for solitude – think again. What remained of the woods were squatted in by Irish navvies building the railroad. When the line was complete to Concord, the labourers began to move on, leaving their shanties behind. It was from one of these that Thoreau bought the second-hand lumber to build his own shanty – though of course he didn't call it that.

And Walden became a resort much sooner than the bloggers would have you believe. Just twenty years after Thoreau lived there, the railroad built an excursion park on the pond for day-trippers out from Boston, with children's swings, a dock for boat trips, and even a baseball diamond. In the 1920s the town imported tons of sand to create a beach, and built a bathhouse and an amusement park. It wasn't until the Walden Woods Project, founded in 1990, bought over 150 acres of Walden Woods in Concord and Lincoln that further development was blocked.

If Walden's actuality is unlike its reputation in literature, Thoreau's life there was equally different from what most Americans remember from the book. The time he spent in his cabin was more like kids camping out in the back yard than living in the woods. His mother and sister in Concord, just a mile and a half down the railroad tracks, continued to do his washing and mending. Sunday dinners he would spend with the philosopher and essayist Ralph Waldo Emerson and his family, a mile down Brister's Hill towards Concord.

During the two years he spent at Walden, he was frequently in town, shopping, visiting the post office, reading the newspapers, occasionally giving lectures at the Concord Lyceum. Once he was put in jail briefly for refusing to pay his poll tax in support of the Mexican War, an event that prompted his highly influential essay, 'Civil Disobedience'. Late in the summer of 1846, right in the middle of his stay at Walden, he took two weeks off to go to Maine with his cousin to climb Mt Ktaadn.

To be fair to Thoreau, he never claimed to be a solitary explorer in the primeval woods. Though enormously fond of accounts of frontier travel, like John Charles Frémont's *Report of the Exploring Expedition to the Rocky Mountains* (1845), he preferred to travel more profoundly into the local. Better to 'explore thyself', as he says in the last chapter of *Walden*. 'It is as solitary where I live as on the prairies', he claims in the chapter 'Solitude', while admitting that the cabin was only a mile away from his nearest friend. He even altered the second edition to drop the half-title, 'or, Life in the Woods', so the book wouldn't be confused with others that really were about how to live in the woods, like J.T. Headley's *The Adirondack; or, Life in the Woods* (1849).

Yet so strong is the American appetite for stories that celebrate living beyond the boundaries of civilisation that *Walden* has been commonly read as a guidebook to self-reliance in the wilderness. For reasons connected with the country's history and mythology, the idea of living from time to time on a frontier, hunting, fishing and living off the land, enters easily into the American male imagination.

The irony is that the book really is a lesson in self-reliance, though of another kind. It encourages independent thought, not on a physical frontier but on an economic, social and political one – to the point of subverting many treasured American beliefs.

Take travel and communications. For most 19th-century Americans these meant progress – and still do. But *Walden* probes the deeper 'economy' of such innovations. Shall we catch the new train from Concord to Fitchburg? Or could we walk the 30 miles in less than the time it would take us to earn the fare? 'We are in great haste to construct a magnetic telegraph from Maine to Texas,' he writes in the chapter 'Economy', 'but Maine and Texas, it may be, have nothing to say to each other.'

But *Walden* challenges an even more fundamental American value. For Thomas Jefferson, American enterprise and civic virtue were founded on the economics of farm ownership. But, *Walden* asks, after the farmer has laboured to pay off the interest on his loan and the 'encumbrances' inherited with his land, does he own the farm, or does the farm own him? Black slaves suffer under 'southern overseers', Thoreau writes, but it's far worse 'when you are the slave driver of yourself' ('Economy'). From there, the book goes on to develop a general critique of capital accumulation and the market economy.

So how has *Walden* become so popular among American readers? Perhaps its stress on individual judgement is strong enough to counterbalance its attack on the country's bedrock economics. Maybe the book is read as satire. Or more likely, its attack on middle-class values is read as a new diet published in the newspapers – that is, as a good idea in principle, interesting to read about, which no one can quite being themselves to follow.

For 38 years, San Francisco had a freeway that ended in mid-air.

After the Second World War the government began to lavish shedloads of federal funding on roads. Like the market, or so the theory went, private cars and trucks were going to solve all future problems to do with the circulation of people, goods and wealth. President Eisenhower's Federal Highway Act of 1956 allocated $32 billion to construct 41,000 miles of interstate highways (see page 104).

By this time, American cities had already begun to run their public transport systems down in favour of more and more throughways and flyovers to bring car-commuting suburbanites straight into city centres. In the late 1940s and early 50s, the Brooklyn-Queens Expressway, designed by the tsar of city freeways, Robert Moses, sliced Brooklyn neighbourhoods in two and cut the borough off from its waterfront. Just to prevent backsliding, Los Angeles tore up the tracks of the Pacific Electric, its extensive inter-urban network of heavy electric cars, leaving straight main roads, divided down the middle by acres of ice-plant, where the rails had been.

Meanwhile, people without cars became increasingly stranded. You could see middle-aged ladies, often Hispanic or African American, sitting on benches, waiting patiently for the hourly bus that would take them to domestic work in more affluent parts of town. Forrest Gump, the hero of the 1994 movie, had time to tell most of his life story to one of them.

At first San Francisco was just as keen as other cities to grab state and federal funding to build their own traceries of highways in the sky. Then came the Embarcadero freeway, an elevated road cutting yet another city off from its waterfront. So unpopular was this monstrosity that the local citizenry halted its production, leaving a spur, intended as an approach to the Golden Gate Bridge, unfinished and coming to an abrupt end in mid-air. And there it stayed for 38 years, until weakened by the Loma Pietra earthquake of October 1989. Two years later it was finally torn down, to be replaced by parks and walkways.

There had to be a better solution to urban transport – one that would serve the growing population of the suburbs without giving ground to the environmental damage inflicted on the inner city. There was. From as early as 1946, business and civic leaders in the San Francisco Bay Area had been discussing and even planning the finance for a transport network that would combine urban and inter-urban functions, serving both as a city metro and a rapid link to outlying communities.

From Daly City in the south of San Francisco, the network would run through the city, then via a tunnel under the bay to towns and cities in the East Bay, through Berkeley and Oakland, north to Richmond, east to Pittsburgh and south to Fremont. Trains would be modern, computer-controlled, purpose-built rolling stock. Ample parking would be provided at the outlying stations, so commuters could use their cars where they mattered, keeping them out of the congested city centre.

Technically ahead of its time, BART, or the Bay Area Rapid Transit system, to give its official name, was even more innovative in the way it raised its finance way back in 1946, when those San Francisco civic leaders began to discuss the idea. Of the $1.6 billion invested in BART, only $315 million, or 20.3 per cent of the total, would ever come from the federal government – and that belatedly, after the system was already up and running. 'If BART were being built today,' according to its official online history, '80 per cent of its capital costs could be federal funded under the US Urban Mass Transportation Act of 1974'.[1]

So how did they raise the early money? Locally, that's how. They skimmed $176 million off the tolls paid by drivers to cross the Golden Gate and San Francisco Bay bridges. They allocated $150 million of local sales taxes to the project. In the general election of 1962 they placed a general obligation bond referendum on the ballot. What this said to local voters was, give us permission to issue $792 million-worth of bonds on which your taxes will pay the interest. Remember, this was when public transport was still deeply out of fashion. Besides, the proposal required a 60 per cent majority. Yet still the citizens of the San Francisco Bay Area voted for the measure – just – by 61.2 per cent of the votes cast.

At the time it was being built, BART was the largest civil engineering project in the United States. Contractors had to blast a 3.8-mile tunnel through the hard rock of the Berkeley Hills, and dig out the five-storey stations under Market Street, with separate levels for BART trains and city streetcars, all while keeping the ground water table at bay.

Then there was the Bay itself to keep at bay, while they built the 3.8 miles of underwater tube between Oakland and San Francisco. Fifty-seven giant steel and concrete sections were lowered one by one to the bottom and assembled from within while the bay water was forced out by compressed air, and a specialised medical unit stood by to deal with any casualties. In the event the job was done with one of the best safety records in the history of American heavy construction.

Trains carried their first paying passengers in 1972. Early tickets cost from 30¢ to $1.25, with discounts for seniors and juniors. As passengers arrived at their destination, the exit gate automatically deducted the cost of the journey from the ticket, which could then be recharged as necessary. Now extended to San Francisco airport south of the city, the network comprises 104 miles in total, running 450 modern, air-conditioned cars at an average speed (including 20-second stops) of 30 miles per hour. On open stretches in the East Bay, trains get up to 80.

All this sounds pretty humdrum now, what with mass transit systems popping up all over American cities. Washington, DC's much admired Metro followed the California example in 1976. A near copy of BART, Metrorail is almost exactly as long, connecting the city with communities in Maryland and Virginia. Rolling stock is similarly purpose-built, fast, air-conditioned and comfortable. Tickets are issued and recharged as in the BART system.

Before Metrorail, Washington's transport infrastructure was so weak that you could almost say local people just didn't get around much from one part of the city to another. Now, with 40 per cent of DC residents using the Metro to commute, shop and go out at night, the system has helped to break down barriers of class and colour in the capital, promoting a wider distribution of wealth, consumer awareness and shopping sophistication in an urban area once characterised by President John F. Kennedy as 'a city of Southern efficiency and Northern charm'.

But the city that really took San Francisco's lesson to heart was Portland, Oregon. There too the citizens stopped an elevated freeway in its tracks, another Robert Moses brainchild dubbed the 'Mt Hood Freeway', which would have brought commuters to the east into the city centre, gobbling up downtown business and over 1 per cent of its housing units. There too grass now grows in the parkland that might have been an eight-lane super road. Cars aren't prohibited downtown, but walkways, bike routes, dedicated 'bus-malls' and the Portland Light-Rail System offer tempting alternatives. As a result, the use of public transport has gone up by 65 per cent in the last ten years, and the city has managed to forestall a predicted 40 per cent increase in congestion.[2]

Yet all this, like DC's Metro, came after the National Environmental Policy Act of 1970. This required all federally-funded projects to provide an 'Environmental Impact Statement', which local objectors could use to challenge the proposal in court. Portland residents challenging the Mt Hood Freeway freely acknowledge they couldn't have stopped it without the NEPA. San Francisco had to turn the tables without any such legal machinery, when federal money and near-universal planning opinion favoured the car.

A footnote. Los Angeles is the urban area with the highest density of car population in the world, with 27 freeways gliding commuters around 100 million collective miles per day. Yet it too has got back into the mass transit business, with a new and still growing system that includes a subway, light-rail links and a dedicated busway.

Despite widespread indifference to the game, more American children play soccer than little-league baseball.

Every year the American baseball season culminates in the 'World Series'. Trouble is, almost no one else in the world plays baseball. Meanwhile, the truly global game of association football leaves America cold. Eight out of ten people on the planet watch something of the football World Cup every four years. In the United States the figure is closer to one in ten – and most of those are Hispanic immigrants from countries that do value the game. Imagine only one in ten Brits or Germans or Brazilians watching the World Cup on TV. Not very likely. Sport is one of the most striking expressions of American exceptionalism.

Football in America means American football, the armoured march down the field towards the goalposts, the ball advanced by running and often spectacular forward passing, the game divided neatly into plays, each with its own tactics. That's the football played in high schools and colleges across the country, avidly watched on autumn Saturdays by parents, students and alumni. Then on Saturday and Monday nights, and above all Sundays, come the professional games played in the National Football League, watched by nearly half of American households owning a TV. American football is the most popular spectator sport in the US.

But *association* football, or what Americans call soccer, is another matter. Besides the school kids, women play it – so well that they won the first FIFA[1] women's World Championship in 1991, the first-ever Olympics football team gold medal in 1996, and then again the women's World Cup in 1999. Even men play it, well enough to get to the quarter-finals of the 2002 World Cup, though failing to make much of a mark in 2006.

But no one much at home watched them doing it. Why? 'Provincialism in the American sporting community' is one explanation, the impulse to resist 'a sport imported from overseas'.[2] Another suggestion is that soccer's very success among women and school children gives it a bad name. They play soccer to engage in energetic competitive sport without risking bone and sinew in all the blocking and tackling involved in American football, but Americans love contact sports, consider them manly. 'All of my friends hate [soccer] because "there is not enough contact"', wrote one blogger.[3] Or as film critic Steve Sailer put it, 'If humans were built like horses, soccer would be the perfect sport, but as a game for a species with opposable thumbs, it's played with the wrong set of limbs.'[4]

For Jim Armstrong, writing for AOL News, the fault lies in the fans. 'What is it about a stupid soccer game that makes a freckle-faced kid want to hurl a Molotov cocktail', or taunt an opponent with racist comments, or interrupt a minute's silence to mark the death of Pope John Paul II with boos and jeers in Glasgow? 'Why can't they just sit there, watch the game and take out a second mortgage to pay for beer and hot dogs like we do here in civilization?' Because association football is tribal, that's why. It represents ethnic groups, even (as in Glasgow's Prods and Papists) religions.

Then again, the game itself isn't entirely blameless. 'Maybe soccer is so God-awful boring', writes Armstrong, that 'the only way to keep from falling asleep is to drink heavily and do stupid human tricks.'[5] Why do American spectators find soccer boring? What does it do, or not, that American sports don't or do?

Well, first of all, the scoring rate is painfully slow, compared – say – to basketball (one of the few successful American sport exports, by the way, played and watched by more Chinese than there are *people* in the USA).[6] When scores accumulate rapidly they are statistically more likely to produce suspenseful shifting advantages between opposing teams, not to mention a definitive winner. Slow-scoring soccer is much more likely to produce a draw, a frustrating non-result from the American point of view.

The American quarrel with soccer football may be traced to many sources, but the overriding problem is the game's lack of logical progression to a definitive result. Look at what Americans did with rugby. Rugby is all non-stop action, pausing only for scrums and line-outs. The ball changes hands frequently; play can move suddenly from one end of the field to the other, when a good kicker puts the ball in touch (or out of bounds, to Americans). Seven backs fan out from the scrum, passing to each other along the line, then almost always seem to get stopped by their opponents. All of a sudden the referee awards a penalty, seemingly out of nowhere, and the 'injured' side gets to kick for three points over the crossbar.

This is all too haphazard and unexpected for American spectators. So Americans took rugby and regularised it into American football. Play is divided into four 'downs', each with its own plan decided long before and memorised. The ball changes hands only if intercepted, or if the team in possession can't make at least ten yards in the four downs. It can be run down the field, providing the offensive line (football's equivalent of rugby's forwards) can open a sufficient gap in the opponents' line. Or it can be passed spectacularly, to be caught by a wide receiver. Progress down the field, though intermittent, creates mounting excitement, only occasionally broken if the ball is intercepted or the plays run out.

Compare association football, as seen by the typical American. It's raining. A lot of players run all over the pitch, kicking the ball back and forth. Their opponents run at them, sometimes clouting them on the neck or jumping on their ankles to get the ball away. It's not clear who has the advantage, or where the game is going.

Just occasionally a play seems to develop, as a right midfielder dribbles the ball downfield, deftly avoiding interceptors, then crosses to the centre forward, who strikes for goal – only to have the shot disqualified as mysteriously off-side. Americans have a lot of trouble with the off-side rule. Then, after all this charging up and down, after all these regulations are applied, what's the result? A goal-less draw. Defensive play and rules are all very well, but they do tend to keep things from happening. What Americans want is things happening.

So it's no coincidence, as Michael Mandelbaum, author of *The Meaning of Sports* (2005) points out, that the rules of baseball, basketball and college football actually prohibit draws. When association football really needs a result, as when a match in a knock-out competition remains drawn after extra time, the winner is chosen after a penalty shoot-out. 'Most American sports fans would regard the method ... as absurdly arbitrary, and no more fitting a way to determine a winner than flipping a coin', says Mandelbaum.[7] He's right.

Never mind. At least America was the undisputed world champion in one soccer-related activity: the marketing of brand names to be associated with the tournament, and of food and drink to be sold exclusively in the 2006 World Cup stadiums. Of the fifteen global enterprises who paid between $40 and $50 million to become 'Official Partners' of the 2006 FIFA World Cup, seven were American: Anheuser-Busch breweries, Gillette razors, MasterCard, Avaya Communications, Coca-Cola, McDonald's and the search engine Yahoo. According to the FIFA official website, 'Official Partners receive exclusive marketing opportunities within their designated product category'.

What that meant in practice was that you could buy only one kind of beer in the stadiums or for 100 metres around them. This was Anheuser-Busch's Budweiser – or 'Bud', as they were forced to call it, since the American company had long been in a copyright dispute with the Czech brewers Budvar, who make Bud'jovice (Budweiser in German), a really good lager.

Needless to say, the host country wasn't best pleased at having only American Budweiser to drink at the matches. Germany thinks it invented beer,[8] and it makes some of the best in the world. A quick taste test will confirm this opinion. 'Bud' doesn't even come in under the German 'ancient standard', which stipulates that any beer sold there must be made only of malted barley, hops and spring water. Anheuser-Busch adds rice to the brew. 'It's the worst beer in the world', said Bavarian Social Democrat Franz Maget. Ottmas Riesing, a member of a Bavarian beer club, agreed. 'I wouldn't even wash my car with it.'[9]

The Germans did their best to make amends, though. As English fans arrived at Nuremberg airport for their match with Trinidad and Tobago on 15 June 2006, every one of them got a glass of the local beer, Tucher, as they came through customs. They also got caps advertising the brew, which FIFA officials confiscated as they entered the stadium. The English were lucky. The next day nearly a thousand Dutch fans arrived in Cologne to watch their team play the Ivory Coast. They were wearing shorts advertising a Dutch beer, confusingly called Bavaria. They had to strip down and watch the game in their underpants. That's globalisation.

Huckleberry Finn is the bad boy of American literature.

'All modern American literature comes from one book by Mark Twain called *Huckleberry Finn*', wrote the 20th-century novelist Ernest Hemingway. 'There was nothing before. There has been nothing as good since.' He was thinking about Mark Twain's invention of the American vernacular, the fact that he made his characters talk as people actually did.

Mark Twain himself was very proud of this achievement, and if it had been easy to do, it would have been done by the great authors who came before him, like Nathaniel Hawthorne or Herman Melville or Harriet Beecher Stowe. Before *Huckleberry Finn*, characters in American novels said things like: 'Faith, Sir, I have much inclination to indulge the man, if it should only be to let him behold the firm countenance we maintain.'[1]

Yet Huck's earthy language has prompted a lot of resistance, and from unexpected directions. As soon as it was published, this extended satire on slavery was banned by the Free Public Library in Concord, Massachusetts, of all places. Since Concord had long been a centre of abolitionism (see page 121) and a link on the 'underground railroad' by which fugitive slaves were helped to escape to Canada, it wasn't the book's subject that offended. It was its 'rough, coarse and inelegant' vernacular dialogue, 'more suitable to the slums than to intelligent, respectable people'.[2]

A similar concern for medium over message troubled the National Association for the Advancement of Colored People (NAACP) in 1957, when it denounced *Huckleberry Finn* for its 'racial slurs' and 'belittling racial designations'. That was a polite way of saying that Huck, who tells the story, uses the word 'nigger' over 200 times in the book. In fact this character of limited consciousness, who speaks just as an uneducated adolescent in 1840s Missouri would, comes to reject all judgements based on colour. But Huck's conversion to racial amity has proved of little comfort to African American students forced to read *Huckleberry Finn* as part of their high school diploma.

So little, in fact, that by the 1990s *Huckleberry Finn* had come in as number five of the American Library Association's '100 Most Frequently Challenged Books'.[3] Objections have come from parents of high school students all over the country, most recently in Tempe, Arizona, Enid, Oklahoma, St Louis Park, Minnesota and the Cactus High School, Peoria, Illinois. Now the pressure is not so much to ban the book as to remove it from a list of set texts in high schools, in 70 per cent of which it was once required reading.

This coincides with contemporary critical theory that's sceptical about literary canons anyway, deconstructing them as artefacts of the dominant power. Novelist Jane Smiley takes Huck to task for coming to love Jim the slave, while neglecting actually to set him free. But more widely she quarrels with an academic establishment that has focused on a 'narrow range of white, Protestant, middle-class male authors' whose protagonists mature through confronting or even escaping society, while ignoring women writers, whose characters grow by coping within it.[4]

This is the most important single fact about 'American literature' – not American creative writing in general, but the institution as selected and promoted by American schools and colleges – that it must somehow define American national identity. Otherwise it would just be more literature in English, and there's already plenty of that coming out of other countries, not least the old metropolitan power from which, after all, we declared our independence over two hundred years ago. 'American literature' is a window into how we Americans see ourselves in the world.

Hence certain telltale signs. For one thing, Huck is a loner. Like the novel he inhabits, he is a 'bad boy', a social outcast with no family – apart from a drunken white-trash father who pays him no attention unless he wants something from him – and no place in polite society. He lives in an old sugar-hogshead down at the tanyard. When fostered by the Widow Douglas and her sister, Miss Watson, 'a tolerable slim old maid, with goggles on', Huck finds the restraints of indoor living intolerable:

> Then for an hour it was deadly dull, and I was fidgety. Miss Watson would say, 'Don't put your feet up there, Huckleberry'; and 'Don't scrunch up like that, Huckleberry – set up straight';

and pretty soon she would say, 'Don't gap and stretch like that, Huckleberry – why don't you try to behave?' Then she told me all about the bad place, and I said I wished I was there.

Later, his father finds him and really imprisons him in a log cabin, from which Huck escapes, throwing everyone off the scent by feigning his death.

Stories of captivity start early in American literature, and continue to this day in all those accounts of abductions by aliens (see page 146). They have always been popular. The captives could be white Protestant women kidnapped by Native Americans, as with Mary Rowlandson's story of her *Captivity and Restoration* (1682), which ran through fourteen further editions before the end of the 17th century, or James Fenimore Cooper's *The Last of the Mohicans* (1825). Or it could be Romans enslaving Jews, as in *Ben Hur* (1880). In Susanna Rowson's *Charlotte Temple* (1791), a young American woman is seduced and held an emotional captive by a British officer in the Revolutionary War.

For obvious reasons, fiction set in the South before the Civil War could hardly avoid the theme. Harriet Beecher Stowe's *Uncle Tom's Cabin* (1851–2) is a captivity narrative of sorts. And when black slaves like Frederick Douglass, Henry Bibb and Harriet Jacobs came to tell their own stories, they framed them within the popular convention of captivity, escape and rebirth, thus making them more accessible to the white audience whose attention and sympathies they so needed to arouse.

So it's appropriate, when escaping from his 'Pap' in an ante-bellum slave state, that the outsider Huck Finn should team up with Jim, Miss Watson's slave, who has run away to Jackson's Island in the middle of the Mississippi. When they find a section of an old lumber raft, they decide to head down-river as far as Cairo, Illinois, where they can catch a steamboat up the Ohio River into the free states. In the event they drift right past Cairo in the fog, and head on down the Mississippi, deep into slave territory.

In 'real life', of course, they could simply have crossed the rest of the river from Jackson's Island to be in the free state of Illinois right away. But that would prevent the long river journey that forms the major part of the novel, and another of the book's peculiarly American features. Stories of travel along rivers or roads have long fascinated American readers, starting with Sarah Kemble Knight's account of her five-month round trip on horseback, alone except for a guide, from Boston to New York City (written in 1704–05, published in 1825, many reprints since).

In the movie *Easy Rider* (1969), Dennis Hopper and Peter Fonda play two counterculture bikers on the way from Los Angeles to New Orleans 'in search of America', as the movie posters had it. Most recently, in Cormac McCarthy's *The Road* (2006), a father and son travel across a post-apocalyptic America devastated by some unspecified holocaust – possibly a nuclear war or a collision with an asteroid.

The travel format as a pretext for multiple satires on contemporary life is not an American invention. Cervantes did it with *Don Quixote* as early as 1605. Certainly *Huckleberry Finn* bristles with satire. Huck's naive point of view is a perfect foil for the many episodes of snobbery, gullibility and cruelty he experiences as they drift further and further into the South. Above all, as the two fugitives bond and Huck defies his conscience in helping a 'nigger' to escape, slavery itself is revealed not just as wicked – as most northern abolitionists argued – but as simply illusory when set against deeper human realities.

But the American difference in the road-novel formula is the element of fundamental change. When the captives escape, they 'die' to their old lives and are born again into a new. And as with all rites of passage, there's no going back. At the end, Huck has to 'light out for the Territory ahead of the rest' before he is adopted and 'sivilized' all over again. 'I can't stand it', he says. 'I been there before.' Are there vestiges here of the common American experience, whether first-hand or handed down, of migration – the Old World experienced as confining, the irreversible passage to the New as a traumatic break with the past, and an initiation into a fuller life?

When the massive volcano under Yellowstone Park erupts, it will kill tens of thousands of people and make the loudest noise heard by man for 75,000 years.

America's (and the world's) first national park, Yellowstone is a fabulous region of mountains, waterfalls, wildlife and hot springs up in the north-west corner of Wyoming, just spilling into Montana and Idaho. Millions visit the park every year, camping, hiking, fishing, white-water rafting, skiing, taking pictures and just gawking – at the buffalo, wolves, elk, the black and grizzly bears, the birds and wild flowers, and above all the fumaroles, the boiling mud pots smelling of rotten eggs, the clear scalding pools lined with brilliant blue bacteria, rimmed with bright yellow algae, and the spectacular geysers – the Grand, the Daisy, the Castle, the Great Fountain and Old Faithful, which spouts every 34–120 minutes, depending on how long its former eruption has lasted.

The bad news is that under this spectacular show of nature's rich variety there lurks a dire threat to the western United States, if not the continent or even the planet. Those dancing waters and merrily bubbling kettles of mud are only the tiniest surface manifestations of a vast cauldron of volcanic potential, a huge, swelling reservoir of molten rock that threatens to explode with 2,500 times the force of the volcano that blew the top off Mount St Helens in 1980.

Volcanoes like Mount St Helens build up as a column of molten rock arising from the earth's centre reaches the surface to spew lava and ash out of a central vent, building up a cone-shaped mountain around it. Supervolcanoes like Yellowstone are different. With them the molten rock doesn't surface as lava, but remains as magma, slowly filling vast subterranean caverns, melting the

surrounding rock to form a viscous seal preventing the increasing
pressure of gas from venting.

When they finally blow, super volcanoes really make a difference.
The last one to erupt was Toba in Sumatra, 74,000 years ago. With
10,000 times the force of the Mount St Helens eruption, Toba
produced enough ash and other debris to cover the ground 2,500
miles away over a foot deep. Sunlight was blocked out all over the
world, reducing global temperatures by an average of three to four
degrees centigrade. Black acid rain wiped out three-quarters of all
plants in the northern hemisphere. One theory holds that the human
population was reduced to between one and ten thousand breed-
ing pairs, and that all of us are descended from the few humans
remaining after Toba.

As for the Yellowstone supervolcano, recent scientific findings
suggest that it has erupted on a regular basis every 600,000 years.
The last one happened 640,000 years ago, 'so the next one is
overdue', according to a much-cited BBC *Horizon* programme that
went out in February 2000.[1] Scientific measurements show that in
parts of Yellowstone the ground rose over 2½ feet during the 20th
century.

When the big bang comes, thousands of cubic miles of ash
blown into the atmosphere will coat vast areas of the United States
and Canada, once again, as with Toba, lowering global temperatures and dousing the continent's vegetation in acid rain. The
effects on a settled country would be unimaginable. With an explo-
sive force some 2,500 times that of Mount St Helens, people would
be killed in their tens of thousands within minutes; crops of all kinds
would be destroyed; the economy would almost certainly collapse.

But seriously, now, isn't all this an urban myth, or another out-
growth of that lush American perennial, paranoia? Does the rise in
ground elevation really indicate an increase in magma underneath?
Is the magma really building up to a dangerous level, or just shifting
from one part of the region to another? Does the Yellowstone
supervolcano really erupt with the same regularity as Old Faithful?

Lending weight to the paranoia side of the scale is the fact that
one of the strongest predictions of the impending disaster appears
on 'Armageddon Online', alongside sidebar hyperlinks to 'Meteor
Impacts', 'Biblical Prophecies' and 'Alien Invasion'. Fox News

hedges its bets somewhat. Pointing out that the recent rise in ground level and increased geyser activity 'could be making one of the largest volcanoes on Earth even bigger', they quote a scientist from the US Geological Survey who 'doesn't believe that Yellowstone is ready to erupt'. Still, it makes a good story.

Definitely playing down the scare is Mike Stark, of the *Billings* (Montana) *Gazette*. 'Here is a reason to breathe easier', he writes, citing new research suggesting that the volume of magma under Yellowstone is probably a lot smaller than previously estimated. 'Civilization probably won't be crippled anytime soon by a pulverizing volcanic eruption at Yellowstone National Park.'[2] But then, living where he does, he would say that, wouldn't he? So would 'service scientists with the Yellowstone Volcano Observatory' who 'see no evidence that another such cataclysmic eruption will occur at Yellowstone in the foreseeable future'.[3]

So maybe it is an urban myth after all, like the belief that if you are forced at gun-point to raid your savings through an ATM, entering your PIN number backwards will alert the local police and bring them instantly to your rescue. Or the rumour of an 'invitation virus' lurking within any email headed 'Invitation'. Open it and the virus will 'burn' your entire hard disk, robbing your computer of all its memory. Or the claim that the rising political star and Democratic hopeful, Senator Barack Obama, is an Islamic fanatic in disguise.

No better way to assess the truth value of such stories than to turn to Snopes.com, the great analysts of urban myths. The invitation virus they say is a 'Hoax'. Obama's father was a Muslim from Kenya, they report, but no longer active in the faith by the time he married. Besides, Barack's father and mother split up when he was two, so the boy saw very little of him when growing up. Obama is a Christian, associated with the United Church of Christ since well before he went into politics. Judgement: 'False'. As for the PIN, they explain that yes, an inventor did once devise a system for alerting the authorities through a number entered backwards, but neither the banks nor the police wanted anything to do with the scheme. This one too they label 'False'.

And the Yellowstone supervolcano? Snopes.com recounts the stories of increased height and temperature of the ground, possibly indicating that the magma was swelling beneath. They note the fact that 2003 saw dormant geysers springing back to life and an earthquake of magnitude 4.4 under the park's southern boundary. 'Whether recent events and findings at Yellowstone represent nothing more than a slightly unusual blip in the park's geothermal and seismic history,' they conclude, 'or whether they herald a coming disaster can't be definitely stated.' Their verdict on the Yellowstone supervolcano story? Not 'Hoax', not 'False', but 'Undetermined'.[4]

So not an urban myth, then. The worst outlook may come to pass. And why not? After all, *Horizon* isn't a flaky talk show but serious popular science. So is the National Geographic Channel, which ran a programme on supervolcanoes in their *Naked Science* series, in which they showed 'Schoolchildren from the LaMotte School in Montana participat[ing] in an evacuation drill in the event of a "supereruption" at nearby Yellowstone National Park.' There they were, all lined up in their dark ski goggles and face masks. Not much protection against armageddon there, maybe, but a sign that even the locals are taking the prediction seriously.

As the old joke has it, just because you're paranoid doesn't mean that they're not out to get you. Compared to Europe, anyway, America is a landscape of extremes – in routine climate, let alone 'geothermal and seismic history'. San Franciscans have lived with their earthquakes since early last century; it doesn't impinge much on their day-to-day living. Some things just don't bear thinking about.

With a total audience of over 7.5 million, *Hot Rod* magazine has one of the largest circulations of any car publication in the world.[1]

Hot rods and custom cars are to the Detroit product as jazz is to classical music – improvised variations on a familiar theme. Like jazz, hot rods and custom cars are an expression of American vernacular inventiveness, the individual creativity of ordinary people. They have also served to express American social dynamics since the Second World War.

The first hot rods were stripped-down, souped-up Ford Model T or Model A roadsters rescued from local junkyards. These were open cars seating two or three at the front and possibly another two in a folding down 'rumble seat' at the back. With the addition of dual carburettors, dual exhaust headers and twin exhaust pipes, they were raced on the dry lakes north-east of Los Angeles in the 1920s and 30s.[2]

At the end of the Second World War, the major car manufacturers could stop building tanks and B-24 bombers and return to the peacetime production of automobiles. Workers in wartime industries had been accumulating cash, but hadn't had much to spend it on. As they stripped the showrooms bare, these avid consumers traded in their 1930s models so lovingly nursed along during the war.

So when veterans began to come home, they found a glut of cheap cars on the second-hand market. Among these were the 1932 Ford, the first popular car to be offered with a V-8 engine, and the sleeker 1939, with its more rounded fenders, sloping rear and flush headlights. These two models marked the great split in hot rodding, that between the 'street rod' and the custom car.

To hot rodders it didn't matter that the '32 Ford was already looking old-fashioned. Those wire wheels and sticky-out fenders were going to be discarded anyway. The car was perfect for hotting up. Easy to work on, cheap and plentiful, its frame already adapted for the Ford flathead V-8, the 'deuce' appealed to would-be drag racers who also wanted a tractable car for the street. On the other hand, the '39 – and later the 1951 Mercury – suggested form over function, looks over guts, bodywork over mechanics. These were the preferred cars for customising.

You could tell a street rod from a custom car, because the rods looked as though they were made for speed at the cost of everything else. Lowered at the front and raised at the back, they usually dispensed with hoods (or bonnets) to leave room for all sorts of chromium-plated gizmos – dual carbs or even a super-charger mounted between the cylinder banks – as well as twin exhaust headers and pipes.

Meanwhile, the custom car kept a quieter profile. Lowered at the rear, or sometimes both front and back, its top often 'chopped' to bring the roof line down, it took the stock Detroit car body and smoothed it down even further, often recessing door handles and 'frenching', or fairing in, lights and licence plate-holders.

How you turned a 1932 Ford roadster into a street rod depended on your skill and finances. The object was to improve the car's traction and the engine's 'breathing' – improving intake and exhaust to make the combustion cycle quicker and the engine more powerful. At the lower end of the skill-price scale you could substitute 'glasspack' mufflers – silencers lined on the inside walls with fibreglass, but allowing the exhaust a straight, unbaffled passage through the pipe. They didn't add much power, but at least they made a sexy rumble. Higher up the price range came twin exhaust headers and pipes to go with your glasspacks. And if you really wanted to improve performance, you could slap a supercharger on top of the engine, to force the air and fuel mixture into it.

Custom cars were not so easily modified. Apart from the clamps you could buy to compress the car springs and lower the profile, most customising involved skilled mechanical or body work. The proper way to lower the car was to 'channel' it by cutting notches in the floor pan so that the body would sit lower on the frame, or even by dropping the axle or lowering the frame itself. Lowering, or 'chopping' the top called for access to a body shop, where sections of the stanchions and door posts could be cut out, the ends re-welded and the joins smoothed out with lead brazing, followed by lots of grinding. Lead brazing was also required for 'frenching'. In time, glass-reinforced plastic would largely take over from lead.

Then there was finish. The early dry-lake rodders cared nothing for colour, preferring the car's original paint job, however worn, or a red-lead primer coat to convey that sense of businesslike work in progress. Not so the custom car fans, or even the street rod enthu-siasts. Now the fashion was for colours as unlike Detroit stock as possible: chrome yellows. Deep purples, candy apple red, often finished in a metallic surface or giving the illusion of deep lacquer, were sometimes adorned with motifs like flames or waves. Inside, the upholstery might be pleated black and white leather, the instru-ments set in a dashboard of hammered aluminium, like the skin of a 1930s pursuit plane.

Just as hot rods and custom cars stated their opposition to the mass-produced Detroit product, so their builders and drivers identified themselves as part of a counterculture. The novelist and essayist Tom Wolfe makes much of the 'teenage netherworld' behind the movement. 'Latch key children' of parents who both went out to work during the war, these kids grew up resenting the more settled world of wage-earning suburbia.[3] This 'problem' was both explored and exploited in the film *Rebel Without a Cause* (1955), in which the misunderstood teenagers meet by night for a 'chicken run', driving their cars towards a cliff to see who will be the first to 'chicken out' and jump from the car.

American anxiety over this newly discovered phenomenon of the rebellious teenager began to focus more and more sharply on hot rodding itself. Police began to target drive-in restaurants where the rodders would meet to challenge each other to race.[4] But the teenagers' lifestyle in general was also under attack. To meet this problem, enthusiasts campaigned to institutionalise the sport, arranging hot rod exhibitions, negotiating with the police to set aside designated tracks for drag racing, and generally celebrating the building and driving of hot rods and custom cars as only another hobby. Established in 1948, Robert E. Peterson's *Hot Rod* magazine was selling 300,000 copies by 1950.[5]

As a result, hot rodding began to be absorbed into the economic, if not yet the cultural mainstream. Detroit designers began to court the leading customisers, like George Barris and Ed 'Big Daddy' Roth to find out what shapes and styles the kids were into. Later, Detroit produced cars to appeal to the hot rodders now grown up and more affluent, with 'muscle cars' built around engines of well over 6 litres' cubic capacity, like the Ford 390 and the Chevrolet 396 V-8s. Today Chrysler offers a sleek roadster lowered in front, with pointy nose and retro front fenders sticking out from the car body. It's called the Plymouth Prowler, and it's yours for $55,000.

But the hot rod movement itself went retro long before the turn of the century. A mood of nostalgia had already begun to set in as early as 1973, when the film *American Graffiti* featured kids in the summer before they went off to college, toodling around in rods and customs, then going out for a bit of drag racing on the surrounding county roads. 'Where were you in '62?' asked the movie's posters.

Style has been a crucial aspect of the hot rodding scene almost from the beginning. The first street rods mimicked and reworked the raw dry-lakers, just as the custom cars modified the Detroit originals to give them the illusion of speed. Illusion is the right word. All that streamlining – the chopping, channelling, frenching and smoothing – would be pointless on a vehicle travelling under 200 miles per hour. It was a style. Wolfe calls it the 'streamlined baroque modern'.[6]

But there has always been an element of show – indeed, artistic expression – to hod rods. Visiting George Barris's Kustom City, Tom Wolfe realised he was in a gallery of cars. 'Half of them will never touch the road,' he wrote. 'They're put on trucks and trailers and carted all over the country to be exhibited.'[7] Some designs were never even built full-size, but existed only as plastic model kits to be assembled by kids all over the country who might never see a real hot rod or custom car. But then, what was 'real' in the first place?

2.9 million Americans claim to have been abducted by aliens.

While driving home from a holiday in Canada in September 1961, Betty and Barney Hill saw a star-like light that seemed to track their car. As they sped southwards, they heard a beeping sound, then felt a bump. The next day Barney noticed that his shoes had been badly scuffed, as though he had been dragged through the under-brush. His back hurt. He noticed a ring of warts around his groin. Betty suffered nightmares.

After medical examinations proved inconclusive, the couple were referred to Dr Benjamin Simon, a Boston psychiatrist. Recog-nising the symptoms of what would later be called post-traumatic stress disorder, Dr Simon tried hypnotising the Hills in sessions running from December 1963 to June of the following year, to see if he could uncover the repressed cause of their anxiety. The results were striking. Independently, both Betty and Barney came up with much the same story.

The car had been surrounded by alien beings, vaguely human in shape, but smaller, with receding chins and large, dark eyes that slanted upwards and outwards, partially wrapped around the head. Leading the Hills back to their spaceship, the aliens proceeded to experiment on them separately. Betty had a needle stuck into her abdomen, and Barney had semen extracted by a suction device fitted on a ring affixed to his groin area. On being returned to their car, the Hills were told that they would remember nothing of the alien intervention.

With the benefit of the same kind of psychological retrieval, how many other Americans would claim to have been abducted by aliens? 2.9 million, according to a recent survey by the Roper Organisation, which put to a random sample of the American popu-lation a series of questions known to elicit a psychological profile common to alien abductees.[1]

The story starts with the mania over unidentified flying objects, or UFOs. Not long after the Second World War, people began to see things in the sky that didn't look or perform like any known aircraft. At night they sometimes appeared as lights, sometimes flying in formation. By day, as white or silver objects, often disc-shaped. Most of the sightings were in the American South-west – in Arizona, New Mexico, southern California – though the objects could appear almost everywhere, including Washington, DC, where a formation of lights was seen to accelerate from 100 to an estimated 7,200 miles per hour on the night of 19 July 1952. They were photographed over the Capitol building, and tracked on radar.

'Official' explanations for these phenomena ranged from high-altitude weather balloons to lens-shaped clouds, but after the Freedom of Information Act came into force in 1966, people began to extract clues from the US military as to what was really going on. It turned out that after the Second World War, American and Canadian engineers had been developing German designs for saucer-shaped vertical-takeoff planes. Meanwhile, the US Air Force had been experimenting with radical new airframes, propulsion and guidance systems around its Nellis, Nevada, test range.

Since the universal laws of physics are loaded against the likelihood of any extraterrestrial being getting here in under several thousand years,[2] how did Americans come to believe that these UFOs came from outer space? It all started with an apparent aircraft crash, which was to spawn a rash of alien-invasion stories, from news accounts and scholarly reports, to books, movies and TV science-fiction series – not to mention 21.6 million hits on Google. In July 1947, a rancher came across some odd wreckage on his land about 75 miles north-west of the military air base at Roswell, New Mexico. When called to the site, Air Force intelligence officers thought the debris might have come from a UFO, but quickly changed their story to identify the remains of a weather balloon with a hexagonal radar reflector attached.

After that, stories emerged of a complete 'saucer' being recovered, then hastily hidden by the authorities. More sensational was the rumour that alien bodies had been recovered from the crash, on one of which an autopsy had been performed. The government countered with the statement that a number of high-altitude experiments had involved dummies, to gauge the effect of falls and sudden decompression on the human frame. The darkest and most recent of the Roswell theories is set out in Nick Redfern's *Body Snatchers in the Desert: The Horrible Truth at the Heart of the Roswell Story* (2005), which argues that the 'aliens' had been Japanese prisoners of war on whom the American military were testing the effects of decompression and radiation.

At least the Roswell aliens were harmless victims, whether of gravity or the American military. It was the Hills' story that set the pattern for the alien-abduction narrative, popularised by John Fuller's *The Interrupted Journey* (1966), followed by a made-for-TV movie called *The UFO Incident* (Universal-NBC, 1975). Meanwhile, a steady stream of documentary reports, books and coverage on cable channels like Sci-Fi and Discovery kept the Roswell story alive. So did the fictional spin-offs including TV series like *Dark Skies* (1996–7), *Roswell* (1999–2002) (alien survivors of the crash adopt human form and live as teenagers in Roswell), *Taken* (2002), and the longest-running of them all, *The X-Files* (1993–2002). All these representations of the alien-visitors phenomenon – and more – would play their part in conditioning the response to alien abduction.

For not only did the Hills tell much the same story, independently of each other; so have countless later 'victims' similarly debriefed through hypnosis for stress. Dr John Mack, another Boston psychiatrist, has hypnotised over 200 abductees, eliciting much the same story as told by the Hills. Little people with pointy chins and wrap-around eyes steal the subject away to their spaceship, where they do 'experiments' on them. And now yet a third Boston shrink – this time not a psychiatrist, but a member of the Harvard University Department of Psychology, has come up with similar findings.

But Dr Susan Clancy draws very different conclusions from them. She had got burned when using hypnosis to unlock repressed traumatic memories of childhood sexual abuse. The more she investigated, the less she could believe in the literal truth of what she was hearing. Finally she devised a series of simple tests to tell how much, and how well, her subjects could remember things.

Not well, it turned out. Had the victims unconsciously fabricated their memories of being abused? When in 2000 she published her opinion that many had, she was buried under a 'ton' (her word) of hate mail. But suppose the subjects *had* embroidered, or shaped their experiences into a well-formed narrative. Did that mean they hadn't really been abused at all? There was no way of telling.

So Clancy decided to continue her research into what has come to be called false memory syndrome in a field of events which no one could believe to be literally true – alien abductions. She found a profile common to people who remembered being abducted by aliens: 'new-age' beliefs, a fascination for science fiction, a tendency to believe in ghosts, monsters or witches.

Above all they shared a common experience, 'sleep paralysis', when the sleeper wakes up before a dream disperses, and before the part of the brain that inhibits motor messages fails to disengage. The subject is perplexingly awake, while apparently tied down to the bed and still witnessing hallucinations of (say) ghosts or other spectres left over from the recent dream.

So much for the psychology. But why do the abductees all tell more or less the same story? Well, either it really happened that way, or (as Clancy thinks) they have formed their narratives from the media spin-offs from the Roswell and Hills' stories. When they woke up in a state of sleep paralysis, she told a presenter on National Public Radio recently, they thought: '"Oh my God, what was that?" And then later on in their lives, they read something, or saw something on TV, and they said, "You know, what happened to me that night is a lot like [that]".'[3]

Even assuming she's right, though, how do you explain the first, the prototype of all these captivity narratives, the story told by Betty and Barney Hill? Martin Kottmeyer, the psychologist and expert on UFO stories, thinks he has cracked this one. He points out that it wasn't until their hypnosis session on 22 February 1964 that the Hills came up with their story, when they first described the aliens' wrap-around eyes.

That was just twelve days after an episode called 'The Bellero Shield' appeared on the popular sci-fi TV series, *The Outer Limits*, with the first-ever representation in popular culture of space aliens with wrap-around eyes. More particularly, the alien in the television version tells his captive that though he can't understand her language, he can read her meaning in her eyes. Twelve days later,

Betty Hill told Dr Simon, under hypnosis: 'They won't talk to me. Only the eyes are talking to me. I-I-I-I don't understand that.'[4]

People all over the world claim to have been visited by interstellar aliens. More often than not, however, these are imagined as benign. In the common American version the visitors are hostile. The story is of invasion, kidnapping, experimentation, penetration into the deepest recesses of the body – and near-paranoid distrust of a government that should be shielding us from these horrors, instead of covering them up. America has always been fond of stories of captivity and transformation (see fact 32), starting with Mary Rowlandson's best-seller of how she was abducted by hostile Indians in 17th-century Massachusetts (1682), and how the 'English' army failed to rescue her. The alien-abduction plot is integral to American culture – and not just recent popular culture either.

In America you drive what you are.

As elsewhere in the world, Americans define themselves through their cars, though with this difference: cars in America register not so much the drivers' class as the image they have built around themselves.

So style takes precedence over function. A suburban mom's SUV (sports-utility vehicle with four-wheel drive) is not for strenuous, off-road trekking, but for capacity and family protection as she does her week's shopping in the mall en route to taking the kids to soccer practice. Pick-up trucks can carry furniture or even heavy engineering machinery, and be adapted for camping via an add-on module, but mainly they are driven empty, except for a box of tools, to connote a no-frills, down-to-earth male who can fix things with his hands.

Sports cars and hot rods – well, the overtones are obvious. Even the sedan, which the British – to Americans' amusement – call a 'saloon car', carries a message beyond its utilitarian purpose, depending on where manufactured. Made in Japan, it might suggest a thrifty, practical-minded driver, someone anxious to avoid time and money lost on repairs – in fact, someone not much interested in cars. A car from Germany or Sweden says cosmopolitan, even liberal, with lots of money to spend – unless it's a BMW, in which case it's Black Man's Wheels. An American car probably belongs to one of the dwindling number of people who live in Detroit and still work in the automotive industry – or so the sour joke goes.

But in America the message gets a lot more explicit. The straight-up way to say what you're thinking or feeling is via the bumper sticker. These are fixed on the back bumper of the car, giving out a concise message of support or exhortation. Not just the mark of exhibitionists and proselytisers, they are sported by drivers right across the range of educational and cultural sophistication.

151

Bumper stickers may promote an interest, as with the blunt 'Eat Beef' on the back of a cattleman's Cadillac in Texas. They may proclaim a religious affiliation, as in 'Honk if you love Jesus', or a lifestyle choice: 'Childfree and Loving it!' 'I brake for deer' boasts an empathy with nature, warning the following vehicle of sudden stops on a country road, should Bambi appear in the headlights. It wasn't long before a wit from Maine twisted this into 'I brake for lobsters', expressing an interest sardonically more gustatory than ecological.

Feminism still exerts a strong influence. 'Well-behaved women rarely make history' is popular; there are several versions. The saying is learnedly attributed on the sticker itself to Harvard professor Laurel Thatcher Ulrich, who has done so much to advance knowledge of the role played by ordinary people in American history. 'Eve was framed' is more predictable, 'Real women drive trucks' more assertively butch. But what about the recent 'Women want everything from one man. Men want one thing from every woman'? Whose side are we on here? Here blame seems evenly divided between the genders.

Stickers classified as 'Affirmations' on the internet shopping sites can be divided into exhortations to independence ('Speak your mind, even if your voice shakes'; 'Be yourself. Imitation is suicide'; 'Eagles don't flock') and consolations for when the enterprise seems to be failing. 'The road to success is always under construction' goes one. Another is more thought-provoking: 'Everything will be alright in the end. If it's not, it's not the end.' Others revert to quietist fatalism: 'This too shall pass' and 'Smile and let it go'.[1] As so often, it is liberal New England that subverts such sugar-coated sentiments. A particularly dark sticker in Cambridge, Massachusetts, long ago drew attention to the car as instrument, rather than medium for a message: 'So many pedestrians, so little time'.

But as always in America, it's in the politics that things turn serious – or seriously funny. Bumper stickers increase in complexity when they move on to politics. Though remaining necessarily concise, they can gain impact through allusion. Thus during the 2004 general election, the message 'Re-Defeat George Bush' depended on your knowing that he lost the popular vote for

President four years earlier, squeezing into office only after a protracted, bitter struggle over who won the state of Florida's electoral college votes. The Democrats felt cheated, so of course there was a sticker for them too: 'The Democrats won! – the State of Denial'.

On the other side of the political divide, 'I'd rather go HUNTING with Dick Cheney than DRIVING with Ted Kennedy' came out in February 2006, shortly after the Republican Vice President accidentally winged a local lawyer while shooting quail on a friend's Texas ranch. The comparison, you were supposed to recall, was with the drowning of Mary Jo Kopechne, when Democratic Senator Edward Kennedy, driving her back to her motel, mistakenly drove into a pond off a road on Chappaquiddick Island after a party in July 1969. Tasteless? You bet! Bumper stickers are not bound by canons of decorum.

As might be expected, George W. Bush has come in for a lot of sticker satire. 'Somewhere in Texas there's a village missing an idiot' is fairly typical. Also popular is 'When Clinton lied, nobody died', comparing Clintonian evasion over Monica Lewinsky to Bush's 'weapons of mass destruction', his trumped-up rationale for war. 'Bush didn't plan to fail in Iraq. He just failed to plan', is a neat anastrophe, becoming truer by the day. More topically, alongside his picture another ran the comforting message, 'I fixed Iraq; now I'll fix New Orleans'. The allusion, of course, was to Hurricane Katrina and the subsequent flooding in late August 2005, which Bush 'fixed' by watching the disaster in shock on the evening news, then flying over the city in Air Force One for 35 minutes.

'Make levees, not war' was another post-Katrina contribution. Here the allusion was to the popular slogan of the sixties counter-culture, 'Make love, not war', later enshrined in the last line of John Lennon's song, 'Mind Games' ('I want you to make love, not war, I know you've heard it before'), and to the fact that it was the broken levees, whose repair and replacement had been so ignored by the Bush administration, that did the real damage to New Orleans.

Civil versus military expenditure: the issue cuts into the red meat of political debate. 'Bush spent your social security on his war' alludes to the President's deficit financing to pay for a reckless military adventure, as opposed to his ambition to 'reform' social security – in other words, put an end to it. So far, so good, but wait a minute. What about those telltale personal pronouns, 'your' and 'his'? Weren't a large majority of voters in favour of the invasion of Iraq? It wasn't just his war; it was ours too. Not all bumper stickers play fair. In fact, few do.

Bumper stickers are popular in America because people aren't self-conscious about advertising their affiliations. And what goes on the car goes on the person. Enamel flags on lapels blossomed after 9/11. So did badges of honourable discharge from the armed services. Both these and others backing a particular political party have a long history. At his inauguration as first President of the United States, George Washington's supporters wore brass tags that read 'G.W. – Long Live the President'.

As technology moved on to cheaply stamped tin discs topped with pictures and celluloid, the classic campaign button was born and worn, from the presidential contest between William McKinley and William Jennings Bryan in 1896 down to the present day: Herbert Hoover against Al Smith (for 'American liberty'); Franklin Delano Roosevelt running for his third term in 1940 against Wendell Wilkie, whose slogan was the brave but hopeless 'Win with Wilkie'; then after the war, Harry Truman, Eisenhower ('I like Ike') and John F. Kennedy ('Prosperity for All'); Nixon and Agnew ('A Winning Team'); Ronald Reagan ('Republican Integrity') – and so on down to the re-election of G.W. Bush ('America's Top Gun', shown making the V-for-Victory sign after the 'defeat' of Iraq).

Many of these are collectors' items now, but others come out to take their place. Latterly the message – whatever message – has moved on to T-shirts, with no apparent diminution of button and sticker production. It's all part of the open society.

In 2005 a US federal court established that the teaching of intelligent design in American public schools is unconstitutional.

The origins of human life – whether rooted in Darwinian natural selection or explained through a literal reading of the Book of Genesis – has recently resurfaced as a furious debate between Christian fundamentalists and atheist scientists like Richard Dawkins, author of *The Selfish Gene* (1976) and *The God Delusion* (2006). Unlike other countries in which the issue is not germane to their constitutions (whether written or unwritten), America has a long history of tackling this controversy through the courts.

In 1925 the State of Tennessee took teacher John Thomas Scopes to court for having broken the Butler Act, a law prohibiting the teaching of 'any theory that denies the story of the Divine Creation of man as taught in the Bible'. Scopes had introduced his class to Darwinian natural selection, expressly forbidden by the state law as a theory 'that man has descended from a lower order of animals'.

The so-called 'monkey trial' astonished and amused the nation, not least because each side attracted such illustrious advocates. The prosecution was spearheaded by the fundamentalist preacher and former Democratic presidential candidate on the progressive wing of the party, William Jennings Bryan. Leading the defence was Clarence Darrow, distinguished civil libertarian and America's most brilliant trial lawyer of the time, just fresh from his successful defence of thrill killers Leopold and Loeb.

Darrow and Scopes lost their case, but not before an unprecedented legal manoeuvre in which Darrow called Bryan to the witness stand to answer a number of searching questions into the literal truth of the Bible. For instance, did Joshua really stop the sun in its tracks for a whole day? What would have been the effect on the earth, had he managed it? The Scopes trial inspired the movie

Inherit the Wind (1960), starring Frederick March as Bryan and Spencer Tracy as Darrow.

Scopes lost on appeal to the Tennessee supreme court, but the state repealed the law in the following year. It wasn't until *Epperson v. Arkansas* (1968) that the federal Supreme Court ruled that bans on teaching of evolution were unconstitutional under the Bill of Rights, which protects free speech and prohibits the establishment of religion.

From this followed *Edwards v. Aguillard* (1987), declaring unconstitutional a Louisiana law requiring 'creation science' to be taught in any public school in which evolution was taught. The court held that teaching creationism in public schools is unconstitutional because it attempts to advance a particular religion. The case was notable for the *amicus curiae* brief filed on behalf of the plaintiffs by 72 Nobel Prize-winning scientists and 24 scientific departments and other bodies that described creation science as being freighted with religious tenets – in other words, that the phrase 'creation *science*' was an oxymoron.

Despite the triumphs of evolution in the courts, almost half the American population still doesn't believe in it. A poll taken by the Pew Research Center in 2005 found that 42 per cent still thought that human beings and other forms of life had not 'evolved' but were created by God in more or less their present form when the world began. In the same year Gallup found 45 per cent holding this view.[1]

Creationism is the belief that the Book of Genesis provides the literal history of the origins of life. So God created the world out of nothing in six 24-hour days in 4004 BC, according to a calculation made in 1701 by James Ussher, Archbishop of Armagh, Ireland. In this creation a permanent order of animals and plants was established, over which the first two human beings, Adam and Eve, had dominion. If the stratification of fossils and other geological data seems to suggest that the remains of early life were deposited over a much longer period than 6,000-odd years, that's because Noah's Flood mixed all the animals up and floated them inland, laying them down in layers as it subsided.

In the late 19th century the possibility that species do change over time was so heretical that even Darwin took eight years after his voyage in the *Beagle* to work it out. 'I am almost convinced', he wrote to Sir Joseph Hooker, 'that species are not (it is like confessing a murder) immutable'. It was the *Beagle*'s visit to the Galapagos Islands that held the key to natural selection. Being volcanic, the Galapagos were relatively young, geologically speaking; so the plants and animals to be found there must have migrated from the nearby mainland. Yet their isolation had caused them to diverge from their South American originals, forming new species and even (in the case of the iguanas) separate genera, not to be found anywhere else on earth.

Following *Edwards v. Aguillard*, creationism has resurfaced in a more subtle form known as 'Intelligent Design' (ID), most influentially advanced by Michael J. Behe, a Roman Catholic professor of biochemistry at Lehigh University. Unlike other advocates of Intelligent Design, Behe accepts the common evolution of species.

Out go the 'young-earth hypothesis' and other literal readings of the Bible of the kind that tripped Bryan up. Now the issue was centred on the shortfalls of the evolutionary hypothesis, as revealed in cellular biology, a science not available to Darwin. Taking examples like blood clotting and single-cell bacteria that can move using a kind of propeller called a flagellum, Behe argues in *Darwin's Black Box* that the cellular level of living organisms presents an 'irreducible complexity' of chemical and physical organisation that could never have evolved, but could only have been created by an intelligent designer.[2]

But once again the American courts swung into action. In *Kitzmiller v. the Dover Area School District*, the United States District Court for the Middle District of Pennsylvania heard a case brought in 2005 by eleven parents against a public school authority that required the teaching of ID as an alternative to evolution. Despite expert defence testimony by Behe himself, by historian of science Steve Fuller and others, the court ruled that ID was 'a religious argument', and that 'the writings of leading ID proponents reveal that the designer postulated by their argument is the God of Christianity'. As part of the school curriculum, therefore, ID violated the First Amendment.

It's worth recalling that not all churchmen have reacted to evolutionary theory with horror. In November 1859, the Reverend

Charles Kingsley, later to be celebrated as author of *The Water Babies* (1863), wrote to Darwin to praise *The Origin of Species*, saying that from observing 'the crossing of domesticated animals' he too had ceased to believe in 'the permanence of species'. As for where this left his faith in God, 'it is just as noble a conception of Deity to believe that He created primal forms capable of self development' as to believe that He created them all at once. Or as Frederick Temple, later Archbishop of Canterbury, put it at about the same time: 'God doesn't just make the world; He does something much more wonderful. He makes the world make itself.'

In other words, Biblical creation and evolution are at loggerheads only if you insist on reading the Bible literally. Yet literal reading is itself a product of modern print culture. Medieval theologians could interpret scripture not only as literal history, but also in three separate figurative senses: the allegorical (what it stands for), the moral (what it teaches us), and the anagogical (how it leads us to our destination in heaven). And there are signs that far more Americans than is commonly supposed accept that the opposition between Darwin and Genesis is a category mistake. The same Pew poll that found 42 per cent believing that God created all life in its present form also found that a larger segment of the population – 44 per cent – thought that life had evolved over time, either through 'natural processes' or guided by 'a supreme being'.

Creationists and atheists need each other, not least to advance their lecture fees and book sales. Even the Scopes trial was a publicity stunt. A committee of local businessmen in Dayton, Tennessee, wanted to put their town on the map, so they convinced John Scopes to stand in a case to test the Butler Act. Scopes was the school's football coach, not its science teacher, but had stood in for him while he was ill. He couldn't remember whether he had actually covered evolution on the few days he had taught the class, but told the group: 'If you can prove that I've taught evolution and that I can qualify as a defendant, then I'll be willing to stand trial.'[3]

More than 37 million Americans, or one in eight of the population, live below the official poverty guidelines.

Freda is 33. She has two jobs, one as a cashier and the other as a product demonstrator. She collects food for herself and three sons at Loaves and Fishes, a Christian charity set up originally to provide cooked meals for the destitute and homeless, but lately extended to providing groceries for the poor. Tammy works part-time and her husband full-time. They have two children, yet depend on charity food boxes distributed by the local church.[1]

John earns $6 an hour working full-time driving a Salvation Army truck round to collect second-hand furniture, clothing and other charity discards. He and his wife and two young children pay $400 a month rent for their small bungalow. They don't have a car, a serious deprivation in a country where public transport outside big cities is sketchy at best. Though they get government aid like food stamps, they couldn't get by without the Salvation Army – not just because it provides the family income, but also because it offers goods at a discount, some of the very things collected by John in the first place.[2]

'Poverty guidelines', adjusted for inflation and issued every year by the US Department of Health and Human Services (HHS), represent the annual income below which individuals or families cannot pay for their basics. As of January 2007, an individual needed at least $10,210, a couple $13,690, a couple with one child $17,170, and so on, up to $34,570 for a family of eight. Each additional family member adds $3,480 to the total.[3]

What do these figures mean in practical consequences? Take a typical family of two adults and two children. Their poverty guideline is $20,650 per year. Basic shelter will cost them around $5,550 per year, and utilities $2,500. Food, even with food stamps (not counted in the guidelines, because it's assistance in kind) will add

159

another $4,300 to their annual living costs. If both parents work, they'll need some form of childcare, a minimum of $2,550.

A car will be essential – to go to work, to the store, to take the kids to childcare. A reliable second-hand car, together with fuel, insurance and (likely) repairs, will cost around $5,500. For health and medical expenses, they'll need $2,250 – and that's if at least one of their employers contributes to the family medical insurance. If not, the potential costs are much higher. In all they need $22,650 – or $2,000 over their poverty guideline, just to get by. What will they have to give up?

Poverty in the US is the highest in the developed world. It's higher in the South than in the North-east, higher among Hispanics and African Americans than among whites. And poverty isn't just about the basic life necessities. It bears adversely on healthcare – 46 million Americans have no health insurance (see fact 12) – and it degrades the family diet, since the starchy, fatty junk foods are also the most economical (see fact 40).

The headline news in all this is that American poverty isn't so much about the destitute, the unemployed and handicapped. Every country has its share of those. It's about the working poor – that is, those people who work all the hours God gave them and *still* can't make enough to support their families. In turn there are three facts behind this fact. The first is President Bill Clinton's welfare-to-work legislation. The second is the decline in job quality as more and more low-paid, low-benefit McJobs in the service sector take the place of employment in industry and manufacturing moved overseas in the global labour market. And the third is the abysmal minimum wage, held at $5.15 for a decade, from 1997 to mid-2007.

Following the lead of some states, most famously the 'Wisconsin Works' programme, Clinton's 1996 Personal Responsibility and Work Opportunity Reconciliation Act (PRWORA) replaced welfare as an entitlement with something called 'Temporary Assistance for Needy Families' (TANF). In return the recipient had to be actively looking for work, or undergoing a limited programme of on-the-job training, work experience, community service, or up to twelve months of vocational training.

The Bill offered increased funding for childcare and toughened the rules on child support, helping single mothers claim from absent fathers. After five years of TANF to any individual or family, all government benefits would stop. The federal government devolved the operation to the states, funding it with block grants, and allowed them to tweak the details.

At first the welfare reforms seemed to be producing spectacular results. In the first full year after the Bill became law, the welfare caseload fell by 57 per cent. There has been a 30 per cent increase in single mothers at work. Child poverty rates for African American families dropped more sharply than at any other time since records began. As economic correspondent Will Hutton put it in *The Guardian*: 'The welfare mom has become the working mother.'[4]

You can quibble with these claims. For one thing, the drop in welfare rolls proves nothing. If you offload cases, the caseload will fall. In addition, liberal critics of Clinton's reform have pointed out that the economic boom coinciding with the years immediately following the introduction of TANF accounted for at least some of these positive outcomes. For all these and other objections, though, there does seem to be something of a cultural change taking place among America's poor – from dependency to self-reliance. In itself, this has to be a good thing.

But if the jobs found by this awakened spirit of enterprise are of low value – demanding and imparting little in the way of new skills, poorly paid and bereft of benefits – PWRORA could turn out to be a false hope, and a cruel delusion. And there's evidence that some of the states are becoming a bit too zealous with the sharp end of the carrot-and-stick approach to welfare reform. When the five-year deadline falls due, Wisconsin and New York, for example, now deny food stamps to the claimants, along with temporary assistance allowed under PWRORA. Food stamps are a pre-existing government entitlement, on which welfare-to-work should have no bearing.

Even Clinton had his reservations. Shortly before leaving office in 2001, he identified five issues with PWRORA still to be dealt with. These included offering more help to the 'hard to place' to find work, better job training and more concern with the transportation required to get claimants to jobs that open up. He was glad to be proved right in his claim that 'poor people would rather work than draw a government check for not working', but then added that wages had to be sufficient to support those in their new-found jobs. 'People still have to be able, even on modest wages, to succeed at work and at home', he said, adding that a raise in the national minimum wage was long overdue.[5]

So where does welfare reform leave poverty? Much where it was. Since 2000, when the economy levelled off, 5.4 million more Americans have slid below the poverty guidelines. As for child poverty, there's still more of that than in other developed countries with more generous welfare provisions.

Going to America in the first place required grit, daring, a willingness to take chances. It's part of the country's national self-image that its citizens have an equal chance, that with enterprise and hard work they'll make good. In this mindset, the poor are assumed to be feckless or shiftless, and poverty itself is an embarrassment to be ignored or hidden. It takes a catastrophe, like the 1930s Dust Bowl or Hurricane Katrina in 2005, to attract sympathetic attention to poverty. Then nature takes the blame, not the poor – let alone the system.

As for the minimum wage, a newly elected Democratic Senate made it a priority to put it up, and duly did so on 1 February 2007, by a vote of 93 to 4. After ten years, the national minimum wage was due to be raised from $5.15 per hour to $7.25. But they linked the rise to the Iraqi war spending bill, which President Bush vetoed. So the deal wasn't done until the middle of May that year. By that time, thanks to inflation, it was worth less than it was ten years ago.

As a protest against corruption in City Hall, Rabbit Hash, Kentucky, elected a black Labrador named Junior as its mayor.

Why do allegations of corruption seem to stick so often to the mayors and chief executives of American towns and cities? Why don't we hear more of corruption higher up the administrative chain, among state governors or even presidents? It's partly a simple matter of numbers. There are thousands of mayors across the country, only 50 governors and one President.

As it happens, plenty of governors and one President have got into trouble over the past 30 years, from Alabama's Don Siegelman and Arizona's Fife Symington to Edward D. Petrie, head of the notoriously corrupt state government of Rhode Island. Though not the worst, certainly the governor whose corruption struck the highest national profile over the last 30 years was Spiro T. Agnew of Maryland. As Richard Nixon's running mate, Agnew became the first serving Vice President forced to resign because of corruption. While Governor of Maryland he had accepted bribes and evaded taxes, charges to which he pleaded *nolo contendere* on resigning. He was succeeded by Gerald Ford, who took over from Nixon when *he* was forced to quit following his role in the Watergate burglary and his subsequent attempt to cover up the crime.

But even apart from their numbers, mayors do seem to be especially liable to corruption. This is the downside of an otherwise positive factor in American life, the high degree of autonomy allowed to local government. 'If mayors and city officials have been more corrupt than governors and state officials', says Michael Les Benedict, emeritus professor of history at Ohio State University, and one of the world's leading experts on American politics, 'it probably has to do with the fact that cities and local governments are responsible for so much more of the daily administration of government' than governors and presidents.

'They pay for garbage collection, purchases of police and fire equipment, the care of streets and roads', Benedict adds. 'They control the placement of gas and electric lines. They license TV cable companies to do business in the city. They do the building inspections. They may be in charge of building airports, bus stations, etc. They run the taxi license boards, they issue the liquor licenses, and they do the zoning.'[1] Along with powers like these go corresponding responsibilities and temptations. Quite apart from personal gain, there are so many constituents, friends and political allies to keep happy at the same time.

To this day, William Hale (Big Bill) Thompson is still considered to have been the worst mayor in the history of American big cities. Supported by Al Capone, Thompson was Mayor of Chicago in the late 1920s. Pledged to 'clean up' the city and rid it of organised crime, Big Bill went after the reformers instead. When he left office *The Chicago Tribune* wrote of him: 'He has given the city an international reputation for moronic buffoonery, barbaric crime, triumphant hoodlumism, unchecked graft, and a dejected citizenship. … He made Chicago a byword for the collapse of American civilization.'[2]

In 1931 Thompson was defeated by a Czech immigrant called Anton Cermak, by the largest margin of any mayoral contest to that date in the city. Cermak started out well, launching a highly publicised war on organised crime, shutting down numbers rackets – illegal lotteries called 'policy wheels' – all over the city, and arresting two-thirds of Chicago's largest gambling ring. But it turned out that 'Two-percent Tony', as he came to be called, had merely substituted one set of gangsters for another.

When his old friend and political ally William R. ('Billy the Junkman') Skidmore pledged his support in the fight against the Capone mob, Cermak granted him the city contract to haul scrap iron and used him to collect a weekly 2 per cent on all gambling operations across the city, in return for protection. The only real change had been the party running the city's politics. Thompson's defeat marked the end of Republican power in Chicago. Cermak brought in the Democrat machine, later worked by Richard J. Daley, mayor from 1955 until his death in 1977, and his son Richard M. Daley, who has run the city from 1989 to the present day.

More recent corruption in city hall has been less wholesale, if no less colourful. In December 2002, Vincent ('Buddy') Cianci, former mayor of Providence, Rhode Island, was sent to prison for over five years for racketeering conspiracy, after being acquitted on over a dozen other corruption charges, including bribery and extortion. A federal appeals court upheld the conviction in August 2004.[3]

Across the country in July 2005, a federal jury convicted the acting mayor of San Diego, California, of taking illegal campaign contributions from a strip club owner trying to lift a city ordinance against patrons touching the strippers. The city has also been under federal scrutiny for the large deficit in its pension fund, and for other financial irregularities that have brought it to the verge of bankruptcy.

Back to the Midwest, where Betty Loren-Maltese, mayor of Cicero, Illinois, was sentenced in 2002 to eight years in prison for her part in an insurance scam that siphoned $12 million from the town treasury for her and her associates' personal use. Cicero is the blue-collar – and now largely Hispanic – suburb to the west of Chicago where Al Capone moved his operation to escape the Chicago police.

Meanwhile – to end where we began, in Chicago itself – federal investigators are examining what they suspect to be a city-hall network of fraud in hiring and the distribution of contracts. Though not yet touching Mayor Richard M. Daley, whose five terms in office have led to much improved public schools in the city and a rejuvenated downtown area, the 30 indictments so far have included two senior administrators close to the mayor.

One solution to the problem is to follow the lead of most towns in Oregon, and not pay your mayors at all (see fact 14). Another is to find a species not awfully interested in money anyway, like a goat or a dog. That makes a political point without taxing the town treasury for much more than food scraps and dog biscuit. Goats govern in Anza, California, and Lajitas, Texas. The citizens of Florissant, Colorado, must be happy with Paco Bell, their donkey mayor, because he has just won a second term, narrowly defeating a llama.[4]

And the same must be true of the folk of Rabbit Hash, a small hamlet on the Ohio River at the northernmost point of Kentucky.

Junior is actually the second dog to serve as Mayor of Rabbit Hash. The first was a fifteen-year-old mongrel called Goofy, elected in 1998. Since he was aged fifteen on taking office – that's the equivalent of 73 human years – Goofy didn't live out his term. When he died of testicular cancer in 2001 the town was devastated. As one local resident put it, it was enough to 'make a glass eye cry'.

Come 2004 and Rabbit Hash called for new mayoral elections. This time the field was a lot more crowded. Apart from Junior, candidates included a donkey called Higgins, whose owner ran him as a Republican, Rudy the Brittany spaniel, and Lulu the pig (party affiliation unspecified). Lulu conceded early, but Higgins garnered 712 votes and Rudy a respectable 2,052, only to be smothered by Junior's landslide total of 5,049. Since Rabbit Hash is unincorporated and its borders only vaguely defined, no one knows its true population. Estimates vary from five to 50.

The town is also famous for its traditional store, the oldest in Kentucky, and for a funny slice-of-life movie made in 2004, *Rabbit Hash – Center of the Universe*. It pretends to be just plain mountain folks. Actually it's at the top end of the fertile Bluegrass country, part of metropolitan Cincinnati, Ohio, and just half an hour's drive south from the city centre. River boats run regular tours from the city downriver to this charming but canny slice of retro country living.

And those visitors explain that discrepancy between the town's population and the 7,813 votes cast for its mayor. Like the election that returned Goofy, the ballot was a fundraising event to support the local historical association, with votes priced at a dollar each. Bribery was legal during the election. People from anywhere could vote as often as they wanted, so long as the polls remained open and they could come up with the poll tax. 'It's a true mercenary election', said Terrie Markesbery-Young, who runs the general store.[5] Just like mayoral elections in the Boston of yesteryear: vote early, vote often.

65 per cent of American adults are overweight, 30 per cent are obese, and these proportions are growing.

'I myself am very well in body, mind, spirits, quite stout', an immigrant wrote from Pittsburgh to his brother back in Manchester, England, in 1837. 'I weigh 182lbs so you may think how I am, a man of my sise. Am very corpulent.'[1] Those were the days – when fat was a sign of success and prosperity. What he meant was that he had made it in the New World, and left the lean years in the Old forever.

Nowadays, of course, fatness means something very different. The sight of people waddling through shopping malls, trying to squeeze into a booth in an all-you-can-eat-for-$14.95 restaurant or spreading out across two seats in a crowded bus brings out all kinds of disapproval. We take it as a sign of slovenly living: laziness, lack of exercise, ignorance of proper eating, even a sort of moral collapse.

Like poverty, to which it is related, obesity is a comparative measurement. According to the American Obesity Association, source of these headline figures, anyone with a body-mass index (BMI) of between 25 and 29.9 is overweight. From 30 to 39.9 you are obese, and suffering from a clinical condition. Over 40, you are *severely* obese and probably need a forklift truck to get around. Severe obesity has risen too – from 2.9 per cent of the population in 1988–94 to 4.7 currently.[2]

Obesity is not just a matter of appearance and convenience. The medical effects can be pretty horrendous too. By 2006 it was killing some 400,000 Americans a year, just a shade behind, and rapidly catching up with the total for cigarette smokers, 435,000, as the chief cause of preventable death in the country.[3] Killer diseases associated with obesity include type-2 diabetes, coronary heart disease, high blood pressure and – in postmenopausal women –

breast cancer. Less immediately threatening but still serious are osteoarthritis, decreased fertility in women due to menstrual irregularities, and obstructive sleep apnoea – that is, loud snoring and irregular breathing during deep sleep, causing excessive daytime sleepiness, personality changes, decreased memory, impotence and depression.

Though increasing in many developed countries, obesity is now an acute problem in the US. Why in America specially? The usual explanation is that we eat too much convenience and fast food loaded with fat and carbohydrates, and get too little exercise. Given that many of us would drive our cars to bed if only we could get them up the stairs, there may be something in this simple reasoning. But simple answers won't do for a country so ready to believe in plots hatched by the global food industry and fast-food moguls.

According to the paranoid explanation, what really makes us fat are monosodium glutamate (MSG), hydrolysed vegetable protein and other taste-enhancers added to American convenience foods. These stimulate cravings, leaving us wanting more of the same. As a by-product, they also jolt the pancreas into producing more insulin, which in turn promotes the body to lay down fat.[4] This notion satisfies because it seems to explain so much. MSG or other so-called 'excitotoxins' are in virtually everything Americans eat, from canned soups and frozen prepared meals, to proprietary gravies and salad dressings – not to mention nearly every menu item in fast-food outlets like Burger King, McDonald's, Wendy's and Taco Bell. But then again, so are the fats and carbohydrates that actually do the business.

With obesity so widespread, you'd think we'd at least try to keep it from our children. But fat seems to run in families. According to the American Obesity Association, 'around 30 per cent of children aged from six to nineteen are overweight, and another 15 per cent are obese'. No doubt the chief element in this sorry statistic is the family diet, but in case mothers want to keep their kids from eating badly, the convenience and fast-food producers are making their own end run around the parental line, appealing to the next generation directly via television. With kids now responsible – either directly or through nagging power over parents – for over $500 billion of spending annually, anti fast-food campaigner Eric Schlosser has written: 'American children now see a junk food ad every five minutes while watching TV.'[5] Maybe there's some point to that paranoia after all.

But all this debate over causes and effects ignores another factor connected with overweight Americans. What the usual obesity sources fail to mention is that poverty in America has been increasing at more or less the same rate (though at a lower level) as overweight people. Present levels of American poverty stand at 37 million people, or 12.3 per cent of the population (see fact 38). This figure includes 13.5 million children.[6]

Furthermore, obesity and poverty are linked. This sounds counter-intuitive. We are used to images of poverty in the form of thin-faced children with their ribs showing, staring out of an appeal for African aid. Even the experts seem to have been taken aback by this recent discovery, since they have labelled the phenomenon 'the hunger-obesity paradox'.[7]

The real surprise is why the connection between poverty and obesity should have come as such a surprise. It's obvious that poor households are going to buy the tastiest and most filling foods they can find on a limited budget. That means sugary soft drinks, pizza, doughnuts, hamburgers and salty, starchy snacks like pretzels and potato chips. When whole days go by without enough food, the body stores up fat to tide it over through the 'lean' period. This may be a vestige of our hunter-gatherer metabolism.

In his study 'Does Hunger Cause Obesity?', W.H. Dietz cites the case of a mother on food stamps who for half of every month didn't have enough money to satisfy her daughter's hunger with nutritious food. For the remaining two weeks she would make up the difference with high-fat, high-starch, filling foods. The seven-year-old girl was 220 per cent the normal weight for her age and size.

The writer Fujioka Kim, who quotes this example, points out that a woman and two children driving home from the supermarket could take the edge off their appetites with a 16-ounce bag of potato chips costing $1.99 and a bottle of soda bought on sale for 99¢. For the same money they could have bought three apples and a quart bottle of soy milk. Far fewer calories, more nutrition. Ms Kim offers a few 'easy, inexpensive but healthy recipes' from her own

Japanese-American background. These include 'ninjin salad' – shredded raw carrot with lemon juice squeezed over it – and 'hiya-yakko' – tofu (bean curd) covered with chopped spring onions, ground sesame and a few drops of soy sauce.[8]

Well, maybe sensible eating will catch on even among the poor. But the economic pressure of poverty and the emotional response to it, especially when children come into the equation, form a complex dynamic of motivations which it would be condescending in the better-off to expect to play like an instrument. If poor people don't feed their children well, that isn't necessarily because they are stupid or uninformed about good nutrition. Apart from the economic hurdles in the way of low-calorie, high-nutritional eating, there is what we might call the 'treat factor' to consider. Parents may feel the need to give their kids a treat to make up for things missing elsewhere in their lives.

One place to test the treat factor is in the fast-food market, since it is here that people eat as a break from their routines. Increasingly sensitive to the criticism that they were undermining the nation's health with hamburgers, french fries and sweet drinks, fast-food outlets began to introduce 'healthy options' like fresh fruit and vege-tables to their menus. McDonald's began to add 'fruit 'n' walnut' salads and grilled (instead of deep-fried) chicken to the range offered, later pushing the health-agenda envelope out to carrot sticks and toasted deli sandwiches.

As a result, McDonald's' earnings for January to June 2006 jumped by 17 per cent over the previous half-year. But two months later, after 29 years with the company, Mike Roberts, the chief backer of these innovations, suddenly resigned, leaving seasoned observers of the industry puzzled. Did he know something they didn't know?

Maybe he doubted whether the healthy revolution could last. Already parts of this extremely fast-moving market have turned against healthy eating at the fast-food outlets. 'We listened to con-sumers who said they wanted to eat fresh fruit,' said a spokesman for Wendy's, 'but apparently they lied.'[9] Now hamburgers are meatier, cheesier, thicker than ever, and there's not a blade of lettuce in sight – let alone tofu topped with soy sauce and spring onions. Hardee's now offer a 'Monster Thickburger' consisting of two beef patties, each with cheese and bacon on top. Burger King has gone two better, with their new 'Stacker Quad' – *four* layers of hamburger, and cheese, topped with bacon, packing in as much saturated fat as three Big Macs. And sales are singing.

Thomas A. Edison, who invented recorded sound, thought jazz sounded better played backwards.

Like lots of white, middle-aged Americans in the first quarter of the 20th century, Edison hated jazz. So for all his inventive brilliance, he was pretty conventional in his tastes. Still, since there was no denying its popularity among the young, his company was happy enough to profit from the new craze. Edison Records featured a number of jazz pioneers like pianist Clarence Williams, Fletcher Henderson and his band, blues singer Eva Taylor and Red Nichols on the cornet.

In 1917 the US Navy, anxious to protect its sailors on shore leave in New Orleans, moved to shut down Storyville, the city's red-light district – not so much for the brothels as for the jazz played in and around them. They succeeded only in spreading the contagion around the country.

Following the Great Migration (see fact 13), the pioneers of traditional Dixieland moved north. King Oliver went to Chicago that same year, persuading Louis Armstrong, one of the all-time greats of jazz, to follow him four years later. Their duets fronting the Creole Jazz Band, with Armstrong filling in the counterpoint behind Oliver's lead, attracted new audiences and the beginnings of serious critical attention.

Still, for many figures of authority, jazz remained the devil's music. In the 1930s Henry Ford was so convinced that listening and dancing to jazz was undermining American youth that he built his employees a hall in which they were to engage in the wholesome American practice of square dancing instead. He promoted the activity locally, wrote a book on the subject and persuaded Edison to produce the first square dance records.

Sociologists were worried that the enforced leisure of the Depression would lure the unemployed into dance halls, where the fast rhythms and repetitious beat of jazz would overcome their self-control over time and movement.[1] Even the unborn were at risk. A home for expectant mothers in Cincinnati went to court to prevent the construction of a nearby dance hall where jazz would be played, fearing the music's effect on the foetuses.[2]

Jazz aroused suspicion for at least two reasons. First, there was the extreme hybridity of the form. Unlike square dancing (but like country music), it sprang from many origins, ranging from folk to commercial. As for instruments, the banjo may have started out in Africa, but the cornets, trombones, clarinets and tubas were whatever players could pick up cheap in New Orleans after the Spanish-American War military bands were done with them. The saxophone came later, first in the big swing bands, then perfected by modern soloists like Charlie Parker, John Coltrane and Gerry Mulligan.

The music itself came from a variety of sources. The character-istic jazz dialogue between soloists and the rest of the band may have picked up the shout-and-response pattern of field hollers and other work-related songs. Gospel, blues and popular songs formed the harmonic sequence of early jazz tunes. West African dance and ritual music probably supplied the syncopation, which was picked up by ragtime and set to an insistent 2/4 or 4/4 beat in a rapid tempo. European-derived dance music and marching-band pieces added to the repertoire.

The apparent illegitimacy and marginality of jazz is the second reason for the widespread doubts and fears it aroused. It was marginal, first of all, because it was invented by African Americans. It's easy to forget now, so long after Lyndon B. Johnson's civil rights reforms of the 1960s first brought them into ordinary white-collar jobs like banking, education, administration and the law, just how invisible black Americans could be to the white middle class.

In the first half of the 20th century, 'negroes' swept floors in bus stations and barber shops and worked as maids in private houses. Or else they lived out of sight in the Deep South, or in blue-collar districts of the big northern cities, and worked in factories. What-ever they did for entertainment was their own business, but was widely assumed to be anarchic and extreme. At first, jazz was the culture of the Other.

As such, jazz was associated with drunkenness, drugs and sexual licence (the word 'jazz' – originally 'jass' – was slang for sexual intercourse). It flourished in brothels, honky-tonks – and later, during Prohibition, in speakeasies – and other venues on the edges of respectable settlement or business. As did Shakespearean drama, as it happens, across the Thames, outside the City of London's jurisdiction, which forbade theatres and playhouses as well as brothels and arenas for bull- and bear-baiting.

Another strike against it was that jazz was produced and performed by the musically illiterate – in the literal, neutral sense that most early jazz performers could not read music. So they played by ear. While the classical performer had to pay strict attention to the score, jazz players improvised – not just the melody but ever more ingenious variations on it.

The two activities of reading and spontaneous composition occupy such different parts of the brain that most of the best classical sight-readers can't improvise a note. But soloists improvising their 'breaks' – keeping in time and tune with the rest of the group by following the same chord progression, while inventing their own version of the melody – is the distinguishing feature of jazz. Even the big bands of the 1920s and 30s, though much more scripted than earlier Dixieland or later modern combos, allowed some improvised solo breaks.

It was the big swing bands that eased jazz into the mainstream of American entertainment, especially when led by white band-leaders like Paul Whiteman and Benny Goodman. Radio broadcasts added enormously to audience numbers. Later, as jazz evolved into its bebop phase, it became more of a minority taste.

Venues were now small and out of the way. Chord progressions stuck less to the old popular song repertoire. Solo breaks were fast, their melodic lines complex and chromatic. For many jazz lovers, Charlie Parker, Dizzy Gillespie on trumpet, pianist Thelonious Monk and the amazing Ray Brown on string bass were the high point of jazz originality and musical power, but as with modern poetry and painting, 'bop' left many audiences behind.

By the end of the Second World War, Americans had come to recognise jazz as a central part of the nation's culture – so much so, that it became a weapon in the Cold War. Following a tour of the Soviet Union by Duke Ellington in 1954, the Voice of America began a regular jazz programme for overseas consumption. Featuring jazz as 'the music of freedom', the schedule comprised news, comment and records six nights a week, always beginning with its theme tune, Ellington's own melodically intriguing 'Take the A Train'.

For once propaganda represented the truth. Jazz really was 'the music of freedom', not only in its characteristic improvisation, but also in being denied to Soviet-bloc listeners for whom the music stood for Western decadence. Over 300 million people regularly tuned in from Eastern Europe, and an estimated 300 million worldwide.

Throughout its history, people have found it hard to resist seeing jazz as an example of something or other. Early opponents thought it would incite savage passions destructive to civilised life. Others have admired it for the same reason, as the untutored expression of the primitive breast, or an expression of 'that natural rhythm' of the African American. A good recent book has shown that the blues were 'discovered' by white men and women with 'an emotional attachment to racial difference', who mistook ragtimes and vaudeville songs popular with the black singers they recorded for direct expression of existential angst.[3]

Official disapproval of jazz is now a distant memory. In 1987 the US Congress solemnly declared it 'A National American Treasure'. Not for itself, you understand, but for the 'model' it offers of 'individual expression and democratic cooperation', for its 'uniquely American musical synthesis and culture through the African American experience', and for its 'inspiration in the cultures and most personal experiences of the diverse peoples that constitute our Nation'. Jazz, in other words, is a lesson in the civics of multiculturalism. But it's also wonderful music, the best never written.

American conservatives hate political actors, though happy to back Ronald Reagan as President – not to mention Arnold Schwarzenegger as Governor of California.

At the Academy Awards ceremony on 27 March 1973, Marlon Brando won the Oscar for best leading actor in *The Godfather*. Instead of appearing himself, he sent a young Native American woman, 'Sacheen Littlefeather', to read out a statement refusing his award, because of the film industry's treatment of Indian characters in the movies. Hollywood was outraged at this intrusion of a current political issue into a celebration of artistic achievement. Digging around for background, the media put it about that Littlefeather was really a Mexican-American actress called Maria Cruz, up to then known chiefly as the winner of the 'Miss American Vampire' contest for 1970.

In fact, Ms Cruz/Littlefeather had been born in Salinas, California, of a European mother and a father of mixed Apache, Yaqui and Pueblo blood. She had been a steady campaigner for Indian rights, and continued her activism after her appearance as Brando's stand-in. Of course Oscar ceremonies tend to turn even the sincerest expressions of feeling into kitsch, whether they be of disappointment, gratitude – or concern for Native Americans, come to that. But reaction to the Brando–Littlefeather gesture also showed how edgy the press was at the prospect of actors expressing political opinions.

And always have been. Almost from the beginnings of Hollywood, American politicians and the media – mainly but not exclusively on the right – have been bitterly hostile to movie actors who get involved in politics. Their most notorious attack was the series of investigative hearings held by the House Un-American Activities Committee (HUAC) between 1947 and 1954. Originally formed in 1938 to gather information on communists, fascists and other threats to the American way of life, HUAC turned its attentions exclusively leftwards in response to the Red Scare following the Second World War. Squarely within their sights was the Hollywood film industry.

At first the committee subpoenaed screenwriters like Alvah Bessie, Ring Lardner, Jr, Adrian Scott and Dalton Trumbo. Asked if they were, or ever had been, members of the Communist Party, ten of the witnesses refused to answer, invoking the First Amendment in defence of free speech and the freedom of association.[1] As a result they were formally charged with contempt of Congress and sentenced to a year in prison. These became known as the 'Hollywood Ten'.

To clear themselves of any taint, a number of movie moguls got together in the Waldorf Astoria Hotel in New York to agree that the Hollywood Ten would be fired without compensation, and none would work again in Hollywood. The Waldorf Agreement was followed three years later by a second wave of HUAC hearings, the more comprehensive 'Red Channels' blacklist. This time, actors figured alongside writers and producers – among them, José Ferrer, Sam Jaffe, Zero Mostel and Orson Welles.

Among present-day actors who have come out on political issues are Alan Alda, George Clooney, Richard Dreyfus, Michael J. Fox, Sean Penn, Susan Sarandon and her partner Tim Robbins, Martin Sheen and Barbra Streisand. None of them can be characterised as especially left-wing – let alone communist – but all are certainly liberal, opposing the Iraq war and other points of government policy, not unlike over half the rest of the American population.

Fox, afflicted with Parkinson's disease, has campaigned against Bush's executive order forbidding stem-cell research. For Sarah Jessica Parker, whose active professional career includes the role of Paula in *Failure to Launch* (2006) and Carrie Bradshaw in the TV series *Sex and the City*, it's the budget cuts in social services that rankle. A long-term Democrat who once dated John F. Kennedy, Jr, she claims to be contemplating running for the US Senate.

This time it's not the government attacking the political actors, apart from President Bush's repeated comment, used virtually as a campaign slogan in the run-up to the November 2006 mid-term elections – that a vote against the war was a vote for terrorism. The movie moguls, too, treat their talented actors a lot less harshly these days. 'In the entertainment business, money talks, bullshit walks', as the actress and stand-up comic Janeane Garofalo puts it. 'If you're a woman, the only things you're going to be blacklisted for in Hollywood are body fat and ageing.'[2]

Now the right-wing media do the business – particularly radio shock-jocks and cable TV chat-show hosts like Rush Limbaugh and Fox TV's Bill O'Reilly. O'Reilly, who considers Hollywood actors to be 'far, far left', was laying into them from very early in Bush's first term – in fact, shortly after his dubious 'hanging chad' election victory. When Martin Sheen declared he was behind Jesse Jackson, former associate of Martin Luther King, Jr, and presidential hopeful, O'Reilly riposted in the on-line *Jewish World Review* for April 2001: 'What exactly are you behind, Mr Sheen? Are you behind Jackson's payments to his mistress?'

In the same piece he opined that Barbra Streisand's 'loopy dictums come down from Malibu, Calif.' – as if that was all it took to disqualify them. What he meant, of course, was the la-la land of gated communities inhabited by wealthy actors.[3] O'Reilly's long-standing feud with George Clooney, still running as late as the spring of 2006, started when he alleged (wrongly) that a telethon hosted by the actor in aid of 9/11 failed to distribute all the money raised to victims of the disaster.

But no one plays dirtier than Limbaugh, whose line is that 'What's good for Al Qaeda is good for the Democratic Party in this country today'. After Michael J. Fox appeared in a campaign advert advocating funding for stem-cell research in the run-up to the 2006 mid-term elections, Limbaugh claimed that the actor's Parkinsonian tremors were either the result of his neglecting to take his medication, or a mime he put on to heighten the drama of his appeal. Following a general outcry, Limbaugh said that if he could be proved wrong, he would apologise, but until then he stood by what he said.

Of course a lot of this contention between actors and the media is a phoney war that suits both parties very well. The chat-show hosts need Hollywood glamour to spice up their ratings, and the actors welcome the publicity. The HUAC too sought to liven up its proceedings by moving on from screenwriters whom no one had ever heard of to the celebrities of the 'Red Channels' blacklist. The dramatist Arthur Miller, subpoenaed by the HUAC in 1956 and convicted of contempt when he refused to name names, recalls HUAC chairman Francis E. Walter offering to cancel Miller's subpoena to appear before the committee, provided he could be photographed shaking hands with Miller's new wife Marilyn Monroe.[4]

Why do actors arouse such suspicion when they engage in politics? Are people afraid that their celebrity, not to mention their persuasive powers, will give them an unfair advantage over their opponents in the political debate – in short, as Limbaugh pretended to suspect of Fox, that they will *act*? Maybe there's a vestige here of the old Puritan fear of the stage. The irony is that the only time the movies were used covertly and systematically to interfere in the political process was when the studio bosses made a number of bogus 'documentaries' to tip the electorate against the socialist Upton Sinclair when he ran for California state governor in 1934.

An even more obvious irony is that when right-wing actors go into politics, no one seems to mind. Charlton Heston was president of the very political National Rifle Association from 1998 to 2003. As president of the Screen Actors' Guild, Ronald Reagan double-crossed his own members by supporting moves to blacklist them. Thirteen years later, in a notorious letter to *Playboy* editor Hugh Hefner, he either denied – or more likely forgot – that there had ever been a blacklist. Yet he served for two terms each as Governor of California and President of the United States. Coming up fast on the inside is Arnold Schwarzenegger, who won his second term as California governor as late as November 2006.

Yet the popular memory does not recall these as great conservative victories. Rather, it's as though Reagan and Schwarzenegger were somehow above politics – the former as 'the Great Communicator' and the latter by virtue of a few deft shifts towards a green agenda. Even Bill O'Reilly claims to be politically neutral. 'I'm conservative on some issues, liberal on others, and sane on most', he says on his website.[5]

The internet was an American invention for the military, designed to withstand a nuclear attack.

It all started with Sputnik. On 4 October 1957, the Soviet Union put a tiny satellite in orbit around the earth, setting American teeth on edge every time its little broadcast 'beep, beep, beep' crossed the continent. What Sputnik meant was that the Russians had not just a launch vehicle capable of shooting the thing up and letting it fall again like a Roman candle, but a rocket with sufficient thrust to get its payload high and fast enough so that its velocity would compensate for the earth's gravity. Even more worryingly, they clearly possessed control systems sophisticated enough to guide the rocket's launch and the satellite's insertion into orbit.

Ex-General Dwight D. Eisenhower, just finishing his last term as President, had evidence from still-secret U-2 spy plane photographs that the Sputnik rockets posed no immediate threat to the US. At the same time, as he told the nation in his last presidential broadcast, just three days before he handed over to John F. Kennedy in January 1961, he also feared the accelerating growth in America of 'an immense military establishment and a large arms industry'.

The rest of the country were more worried about the Russian rockets. When just under a month after the first Sputnik, the Soviets launched another, this time carrying a medium-size bitch called Laika, the American military thought it was time for an equivalent show of force. Bolting a four-pound payload onto a three-stage Vanguard rocket, the Naval Research Laboratory decided to show the world that the West too could put a satellite into orbit. The whole thing blew up just a few yards from the ground.

The sovereign people were not best pleased. On 1 October 1958, just under a year after the first Sputnik went into orbit, Congress passed 'An Act to provide for research into the problems of flight within and outside the earth's atmosphere ...', and the

National Aeronautics and Space Agency – better known as NASA – was born. More central to the internet's development, so also was the Advanced Research Projects Agency. Given the task to commission and fund new technologies, ARPA[1] was to report directly to the Department of Defense.

Meanwhile, a big problem loomed. How would America respond to a nuclear strike delivered by one of those superior Russian rockets? Suppose the initial attack knocked out one or more command centres? How would the orders be issued and transmitted to our planes and missiles on their way to the enemy? Step forward, the RAND Corporation, a non-profit think tank originally set up by the Air Force to provide research in space technology. When asked in 1962 to come up with a communications system that would survive a nuclear assault, RAND suggested that the Air Force establish a network based on 'packet switching'.

Packet switching was a new idea then being kicked around by computer scientists at the Massachusetts Institute of Technology (MIT) and Britain's National Physical Laboratory (NPL). They were trying to find ways of getting computers to network and talk to each other more effectively, a process for which point-to-point contact along a dedicated line was proving more restrictive as the amount of data to be transferred increased.

The idea they came up with was to break the message up into 'packets' of data, each one identified as to origin and destination. That way, segments of one message could be shuffled with those of another, or hundreds of others. Different segments of a single message could even travel via different routes, since their individual markers would allow them to be identified and reassembled at their destination. Each packet would be acknowledged; if no confirmation came back to its source within a specified time, the sending computer would transmit another.

But what served to widen the bandwidth along which research computers shared data could also work to circumvent nodes of communication knocked out by a nuclear strike. That's why it was the military use of packet switching that attracted the funding to move the project on. ARPA got involved from 1965, sponsoring design studies and issuing contracts to build an embryo packet-switched network, called ARPANET. In 1969 the first four nodes were connected to each other via ARPANET: the University of California campuses at Los Angeles and Santa Barbara, the Stanford Research Institute and the University of Utah.

At first it was at universities that the internet grew, especially after ARPANET spawned daughter networks dedicated to academic use, like the American National Science Foundation's NSFNET and the British JANET, or Joint Academic Network. Scientists sharing data were the first to benefit, but scholars in the humanities began to be served too. In 1971 Project Gutenberg established the first on-line library of digitised out-of-copyright books. Starting with the Declaration of Independence, the down-loadable titles topped 20,000 by the end of 2006.

Email was another big point of growth. Introduced in 1972, it remained the largest application of the network for over ten years. But as some of the founding fathers point out in their paper on the net's history, the widespread use of email 'was a harbinger of the kind of activity we see on the World Wide Web today, namely, the enormous growth of all kinds of "people-to-people" traffic'.[2]

As for the World Wide Web itself, this was the last piece in the puzzle we know and use as the internet today. Developed around 1990 by Tim Berners-Lee, an Englishman working at CERN, the European particle-physics laboratory just north of Geneva, the World Wide Web set up the protocols of client and server with a standardised address, the formatting codes that organise words and pictures on the page, and above all, 'hypertext', those little underlined words in blue that jump you to another part of the file, or to another file altogether.

To say that the internet has changed our lives would be a banal understatement. It has altered fundamentally the way we buy and sell, relate to one another, learn, satisfy our curiosity, even think. Thanks to the internet, old hierarchies have been shaken, if not broken. Ordinary people, interested and involved in a public issue, can post their opinions on any subject whatever. News, analysis of current affairs, entertainment and education have all become less top-down, less likely to be channelled as one-way communication from elites and experts down to passive recipients of information.

Born in Cold War military anxiety, the internet was quickly opened at a nominal charge, first to universities, and later to the public at large. The growth from four computers with a registered internet address in 1969, to 19.5 million in 1997 and to nearly 400 million by the end of 2006 has a lot to do with openness – not just of the system's architecture, but also of the attitude of those American and British academics who developed it. Lack of hierarchy, sharing and freedom of access have been keynotes throughout the internet's evolution, even at the point when the system went commercial. Now the internet is available to anyone who can afford a modestly-priced PC, a BlackBerry or a third-generation mobile phone.

Yet the apparent freedom of the internet, its levelling openness, has its limits. When bloggers do their homework, check their facts and then engage in public debate, they can change the course of history. But for every one who does, there are a thousand who would rather talk about themselves, an impulse encouraged by the growth of sites like YouTube, which further enfranchises its users' narcissism by adding video technology to the mix. And the internet is only as democratic as the country in which its users live. China, Vietnam, North Korea, Burma, Cuba, Iran, Saudi Arabia, Egypt and a growing roll call of other countries regularly block websites and lock up renegade bloggers.

Meanwhile, another benefit to the civilian world has spun off from that 'immense military establishment' so feared by President Eisenhower. How about those satellites whose signals that anyone with an inexpensive receiver can use to triangulate their position on the globe, within a few feet? Developed by the American military to locate forces and guide missiles, signals from global positioning satellites are also free to everyone else, from the helmsmen of supertankers to taxi drivers in Caracas.

Between 1995 and 2000, almost half the American population moved house; in 2005 alone, one in seven Americans changed their address.[1]

Restless movement is part of American culture. When things get tough, or boring, you can always 'light out' for a more promising land. 'Yonder comes the train, comin' down the track', as the early country artist A.P. Carter used to sing in 1930. 'Carry me away, but it ain't gonna carry me back.'

Nowadays it's done more by road than rail. You can't drive more than a few miles down the highway without coming across a car towing one of those do-it-yourself home-moving devices, the ubiquitous 'U-Haul' trailer – or for the slightly better-off, a truck rented from U-Haul or Ryder – carrying a family to their new destination.

If you're even more affluent and moving a long distance, perhaps subsidised by your employer, you can fly to your new home, have your furniture shipped in the conventional way and your car driven across by a student. There are agencies that arrange that too. Sometimes the expression 'moving house' is taken literally, when wooden frame houses (it really wouldn't work for brick) are jacked up, put on wheels and towed slowly and laboriously to a vacant lot miles away.

The early 19th-century French author and statesman Alexis de Tocqueville noted this incessant movement as early 1835. In his classic study *Democracy in America*, he traced the restlessness of European settlers in the young republic to their experience as emigrants, who had already got into the habit of pulling up stakes whenever things seemed to be going a bit slow for them. Having 'early broke the ties that bound them to their natal earth, ... they have contracted no fresh ones on their way. Emigration ... soon becomes a sort of game of chance, which they pursue for the emotions it excites as much as for the gain it produces.'[2]

As late as the year 1966–7, well over one-fifth of the then population (35,200,000 out of 192,233,000) moved house.[3] Since then, as home ownership has increased, the annual mobility rate has declined to one in seven. But since the population has grown by one-and-a-half times since 1966, that still leaves 40 million Americans (out of over 300 million) moving house every year: equivalent to the population of Spain, and two-thirds that of Italy and the United Kingdom. As the *Economist* sums it up: 'Between 1995 and 2000, almost half of all Americans have changed address, more (often far more) than in any European country.'[4]

Who moves most and who least? The main variables are age and housing tenure. Nearly one-third of people living in rented accommodation move elsewhere, as compared with only one in fourteen of those living in homes they own themselves. Young adults are much more likely to move than their elders. Around one-third of those between 20 and 29 years of age moved during the year 2002–03, more than twice the mobility rate for all ages. Race was a factor too, with Hispanics, blacks and Asians tending to move more frequently (at 18 and 17 per cent of the group), as against 12 per cent of what the US Census Bureau terms 'non-Hispanic whites'. As might be expected, the poor tended to move more often than the better-off, not least because a higher proportion of them lived in rented housing.

More surprisingly, levels of education have little bearing on the tendency to move generally, though those uprooting themselves to move greater distances – to another state or even across the country – are often better-qualified. 'Those with a graduate degree were more likely to have moved 500 miles or more' between 2002 and 2003, according to the Census Report published in 2004, 'while they were also least likely to have moved less than 50 miles, compared with other educational attainment groups.'

So why do Americans change their address? Those moving locally are most likely to be simply trading up to a larger or otherwise more suitable house, or leaving rented for more secure owned accommodation. The movement from the inner cities is still going on, with around 400,000 people a year leaving both Chicago and

Los Angeles since 1999, for outer suburbs like Riverside County, California, which grew from 1.5m to 1.8m, or by 21 per cent, between 2000 and 2004.[5] The inner boroughs of New York City, where the population was increasing until the end of the last century, lost 5.54 per cent of their inhabitants between 2000 and 2005, while the outer ring of the Metropolitan area, which includes counties in New Jersey and Connecticut as well as up along the Hudson River, gained 4.01 per cent in net migration.[6]

But this is not the old 'white flight' of the 1950s and 60s, when those abandoning the inner cities were middle- and upper-middle-class whites trying to get away from poor blacks and Hispanics. Taking the country as a whole, around half of all Asians and Hispanics, and two-fifths of the country's black population, now live in the suburbs. 'If you drive around the San Fernando Valley ("The Valley", supposedly the great white sprawl of Los Angeles),' says the *Economist*, 'you will see Ethiopian, Thai and Korean restaurants, Mexican and Salvadorean grocery stores, Chinese lawyers, and an Armenian cultural centre, all in the space of one block.' In other words, the drain from the inner cities has now become black flight as much as white, as better-educated and more affluent African Americans exercise their own choice of where to live (see fact 13).[7]

Those moving longer distances – say, to the next state or even across the country – divide sharply into two demographic groups: older, often retired couples, and singles and families in their twenties and thirties. The first are looking for a better climate, or to be closer to children and grandchildren already settled at a distance from the old family home. The second are moving for work, either because directed to a different branch of a large corporation for which they already work, or – more common – to improve their prospects with a better employer paying a higher salary.

Like the smaller-scale migration outwards from the city centres, this country-wide movement also follows a pattern. Roughly speaking, the flow is from the North-east to the South-west – from 'rustbelt' to 'sunbelt', from old heavy manufacturing industry to electronics and information technology. Cities losing population have ranged from Buffalo, New York, where manufacturing jobs (mainly in cars and car parts) have dropped by a third since 1990, to Detroit, Michigan, where the unemployment rate more than doubled from 2000 to 2004, from 3.1 to 6.9 per cent, and the population has dropped by 76,000, or 7.5 per cent, during the same period.[8]

Meanwhile, the population of Austin, Texas, has increased by 140 per cent in the last 25 years, and Las Vegas, Nevada, by a staggering 250. Moreover, the cities and states on the winning side of this flow have gained not just raw recruits, but people with graduate and postgraduate degrees attracted by their high-tech and service industries. Cities in Colorado, Arizona and Nevada all saw large gains in their educated populations. 'Las Vegas too, home of Liberace and Celine Dion, saw its graduate population rise by over 20 per cent in the late 1990s, proportionately the largest brain gain of any city.'[9]

Although all this restless movement may not make for settled, traditional communities, it seems to suit nearly everyone. The migrants gain a better climate – both physically and figuratively, in the way of job fit and satisfaction, improved housing, more space around them. The receiving communities gain in community value, in everything from tax base to the increased variety and sophistication of retail services responding to the more cosmopolitan demands of the educated newcomers.

As so often, de Tocqueville saw it coming. In the 1830s too, Americans were moving westwards from the North-east. So many people were leaving Connecticut, he wrote, that 'the population has not been increased by more than one quarter in forty years'. In those days, people were leaving for land. Tired of fighting the tiny parcels of stony farmland in New England, they were off to the richer, more plentiful soil of the Ohio Valley. Who knows, de Tocqueville mused, if they had remained in Connecticut, 'instead of becoming rich landowners, they [might] have remained humble laborers'.[10]

Americans spend upwards of $8 billion every year on self-help programmes and products – four times the profits of the Ford Motor Company in 2005.[1]

In the 1850s the British progressive Samuel Smiles lost all faith in the radical politics and parliamentary reform he had been championing all his life. Short of violent revolution, he decided, the only way forward was through individual reformation. His book arguing this idea, *Self-Help* (1859) gave us the phrase and the Victorians their secular bible. For Smiles, self-help meant just what it said. You got there by your own efforts. And 'effort' was the word. Intelligence, talent, even genius were all very well, but it was work, perseverance and the willingness to pick yourself up and start again after a fall in finance or fortune that produced success.

You would think Samuel Smiles would appeal to us in America, who have set our face against the inherited privilege of class and money, and where people are expected to make their own way, find their own level by their own efforts. As the national narrative has it, self-help is the presiding virtue of the United States – the motor of its success, the very ground of its being. There is a lot of truth in this.

But how is the American to gain access to self-help? Ever since Castiglione's *The Book of the Courtier* (1528, translated into English by Thomas Hoby in 1561), conduct books or manuals of behaviour have been available to ambitious young men and women in times of relative social mobility. The prototype American conduct book was the example set out in Benjamin Franklin's four-part *Autobiography*, written intermittently between 1771 and 1790.

As he tells his story, Franklin, the son of a Boston soap- and candle-maker, left home after quarrelling with his brother and travelled to Philadelphia, where he walked up Market Street with three bread rolls, 'a Dutch dollar and about a shilling in copper' to his name. From these humble beginnings, so common in self-help stories, Franklin made his fortune in publishing, at a time of rapidly expanding print culture. Starting out as an apprentice printer, he secured backing to open his own printing house, then branched out into writing and publishing of newspapers and other periodicals.

Having secured his fortune, he turned to philanthropy, inventing and science, raising funds to found hospitals, the Philadelphia fire department, the nation's first subscription library and an academy that became the University of Pennsylvania. He was a prolific inventor and a leading scientific theorist and experimenter, especially in the field of electromagnetism. Later still, he helped to draft the Declaration of Independence and served as American plenipotentiary in Paris, negotiating treaties of trade and signing the Treaty of Paris, which ended the Revolutionary War between Britain and America. Franklin made himself America's representative man.

How did he make the fortune in the first place? By hard work, of course, perseverance, individual enterprise and self-control – just as Samuel Smiles was later to advise. But also through a canny eye to surface appearances. As noted in fact 9, he 'dressed plainly', was 'seen in no places of idle diversion', never went fishing or shooting, and was self-reliant to the point of carrying his newsprint through the streets on a wheelbarrow. Meanwhile, his rival printer was 'very proud, dress'd like a Gentleman, liv'd expensively, took much Diversion and Pleasure abroad, ran in debt, and neglected his Business, upon which all business left him'.

In all dealings with his fellow citizens, Franklin was concerned as much with appearances as with reality. The *Autobiography* does not hide this motive; it boasts of it. 'In order to secure my Credit and Character as a tradesman,' he confessed, 'I took care not only to be in *Reality* industrious, but to avoid all *Appearances* of the Contrary.' That remark shows a profound understanding of how capitalism works. Credit, and the crucial 'character' on which it depends, are matters of public, external perception, not inner conviction.

If Franklin's self-help wasn't so much the test of his inherent virtues as his lesson in appearing virtuous, nor was it all his own work. The best known of his projects for improvement was his 'junto', a group of young artisans and tradesmen who would meet to discuss issues of the day, and deliver papers for mutual critical analysis.

Both Smiles and the dictionary define 'self-help' as 'the act or an instance of helping or improving oneself without assistance from others'. But Franklin's junto, the prototype of so many reading groups today, was an exercise in communal effort and mutual help. Or as the stand-up comedian George Carlin put it: 'The part I really don't understand is if you're looking for self-help, why would you read a book written by somebody else? That's not self-help, that's help.'[2]

Yet 'help' is just what Americans are currently spending their $8 billion per year on: not just books, but videos, audio tapes, seminars, discussion groups – all invoking and involving other people. A glance at any of the so-called 'self-help clearing houses' on the internet shows hundreds of associations and other bodies poised to assist in any circumstances.

One lists 80 support groups for illnesses – everything from kidney and liver disease, through blindness and deafness, to Parkinson's and epilepsy. Another offers lists of contact numbers for help with ageing, AIDS, and Alzheimer's, through grief and loss, impotence, to stroke, stuttering, substance abuse and (as a separate category) women's health issues. There is 'self-help' for all kinds of personal awareness and development – all those books in airport bookstores – and self-help sites for African Americans and Native Americans, not to mention Alcoholics Anonymous (see page 19).

Does a pattern emerge from these statistics? Obviously they indicate services or benefits from which ordinary people feel excluded, or can't afford. Poor people and some ethnic minorities feel marginal to the socio-economic mainstream. The high concentration of health and psychiatric sites reflects a country in which nearly half of the population has no employment-based health insurance (see page 48). The craze for self-improvement in body and mind may reflect a competitive and socially fluid environment in which there are few objective signposts to success. And so on.

More specifically, the craze may reflect the increasing fragility of social props like lifelong marriage, secure employment and a good pension. In *Self-Help, Inc.: Makeover Culture in America* (2005), sociologist Micki McGee points out that the steepest rise in American sales of self-help books – 96 per cent between 1991 and 1996 – coincided with a period of radical restructuring of the labour market. 'The less predictable and controllable the life course has become,' she writes, 'the more individuals are encouraged to chart their own course and to "master" their destinies. ... In the place of a social safety net, Americans have been offered row upon row of self-help books to boost their spirits and keep them afloat in uncharted economic and social waters.'

But has self-help really helped? McGee has some doubts. 'The promise of self-help can lead workers into a new sort of enslavement,' she warns, 'into a cycle where the self is not improved, but endless[ly] belabored.' Ultimately self-help schemes can't succeed, she argues, because they offer individual or therapeutic solutions to problems that are social and economic in origin.[3] In other words, self-help is a flight from politics into an endless cycle of guilty self-remaking.

America is the land of the make-over. So many people have landed there to make their own way in its classless society. So self-help certainly fits the mould of American national identity. Trouble is, it's neither really 'self' nor 'help'.

In America, charity begins at home, and in states that vote Republican.

When he heard about Hurricane Katrina, Sam Parham, a 260-pound blue-collar worker, took a week off work, threw a chainsaw, a generator, assorted jacks and a large toolbox into the back of his pick-up truck, and headed off on the over 600-mile drive from North Carolina to New Orleans. 'I just can't watch those TV pictures of children stranded and not go down there,' he said, 'and I'm going to do what I can if the country needs me.' On his way he picked up his 50-year-old African American friend, Terry Harper.

Like lots of political conservatives, Sam and Terry aren't exactly conservative in their personal behaviour. They are foulmouthed and sexist. Terry is on a seemingly endless quest for 'pussy'. Sam totes a handgun in the truck. 'If some guy comes to rape my wife, why, this is America: I'm going to put a cap in his ass.' But on the first night of their trip, having paid $78 for a motel, they gave their room to a destitute family from New Orleans who had been promised government aid that the bureaucracy had failed to deliver. Sam gave them bottles of water and money out of his pocket. Then they drove on through the night.

When they got to New Orleans, the army was so busy preventing looting, and the Federal Emergency 'Management' Agency (FEMA) so overwhelmed with the size of the problem, that no one had any idea how to use the volunteers. So they turned back east along the Mississippi coast – to Gulfport and Biloxi. Unable to find a motel room, they slept in the truck.

Next day they went into a Wal-Mart to buy some toys, in case the kids in the washed-out families had lost theirs. On a back road in Gulfport they helped an old man lift a generator down from a truck and got it working for him. Next they loaded up their truck with water and emergency meals for people in Long Beach and Pass Christian, outlying towns cut off from Gulfport. Before they left for home, Sam gave his mobile phone to people who needed to make calls. This is a true story, beautifully told by the novelist and UNICEF envoy Andrew O'Hagan, who accompanied the two rough volunteers throughout their journey.[2] How much does it tell us about America generally?

Generosity is part of the American self-image. After the tsunami on the day after Christmas 2004 killed 230,000 people in Indonesia, Thailand and parts of Malaysia, the American government pledged $15 million, then, under pressure, quickly raised the ante to $35 million, and finally to $350 million. Four days after the event, this stood as the largest sum pledged by any country for the disaster. Senior members of the government were quick with the self-congratulation, Colin Powell, US Secretary of State at the time, told ABC's *Nightline*: 'We are the most generous nation on the face of the earth.'

What he didn't mention was that as a proportion of national wealth, $350 million weighed in as 0.0029 per cent of the Gross Domestic Product (GDP) – not all that impressive, compared to some European countries. As in public, so in private giving. Individually, Americans pledged over $400 million to tsunami relief, surpassing the government's offer, but proportionately this was less than the citizens of most Western European and Scandinavian countries.[3]

And in the field of foreign aid generally, the US has never come close to giving the 0.7 per cent of GDP agreed on by all the developed countries at the UN Conference on Environment and Development in Rio de Janeiro in 1992. At just 0.16 per cent of GDP, 'America's emergency relief in Asia and development aid to poor countries actually ranks near the bottom of the list of developed nations', according to Charles Sennott of the *Boston Globe*.[4]

But when it comes to helping out with catastrophe and hardship at home, Americans really are generous, and much more so than most Europeans, according to Arthur C. Brooks, a professor at Syracuse University. Americans give to local charities three times as much as the British, four times the French and seven times the Germans. The comparisons hold up when it comes to volunteer work. Americans devote twice as much of their time to charitable causes as do the Japanese, three times the Spanish, four times the Italians and five times the Australians.

To put some numbers on these claims, Brooks has worked out that some 70 per cent of American households give an average of $1,800 annually, or 3.5 per cent of their income, while 44 per cent gave up their time to volunteer work, worth an estimated $240 billion per year. A 2001 survey by Independent Sector, a coalition of corporations, foundations and private voluntary organisations, came up with the same figure for volunteers, but offered slightly different numbers for financial donations. They reported that 89 per cent of American households give an annual average of $1,620 to charities and non-profit organisations.[5]

Not surprisingly, the data show a strong correlation between religion and charity. Those going regularly to church were 38 per cent more likely to give money than the seculars and 52 per cent more likely to give up their time. Less expectedly, the denomination or even religion seem not to matter much. Christians (Protestants, Episcopalians, Catholics), Jews, Muslims – all give roughly the same. But the church is neither the main recipient nor the only channel, of all this beneficence. The religious were also more likely to fund and volunteer for secular causes like the local parent–teachers association.

Of course, the long history of American tax relief for charity plays some part in all this. Though many countries provide for covenanted giving to be set against taxable income, the US allows charitable gifts to be deducted from the tax owed. In America, gifts in kind can be counted as well as in cash.

Moreover, Americans can donate money in the form of 'Split-Interest Trusts'. These transfer immediate ownership of the donation to the charity, whether in money, property or valuable goods like antiques and paintings, while allowing the donor both to claim immediate tax relief and also to derive an income from a percentage of their value. All these benefits cost the Internal Revenue Service around $17 billion in forgone tax, another government subsidy that must be factored into any comparison between private and public giving in the US.[229]

Even so, Brooks calculates the effect of tax breaks on American charity at 15 per cent maximum. Besides, using another data set, the General Social Survey of 2002, he has found that formal giving in terms of cash or services is often reinforced by informal generosity. The same people who give annually to charity are also more likely to offer directions to strangers, or give up their place in line to someone in more of a hurry than they, to return a mistake in their favour to a cashier. They are 22 per cent more likely to give up their seat in a bus to someone they don't know, 46 per cent more likely to provide food for a homeless person, and a staggering 124 per cent more prone to give blood.

But the real surprise in all this is the way in which charitable giving is distributed across the country. It's the rednecks in the red states – those voting for George W. Bush in 2000 and 2004 – who are most generous with their time and money. Utah comes first among the givers by far, followed by southern states like Alabama, Mississippi, Tennessee and Arkansas. And the most stingy givers? Why, the blue-bloods in the blue states, of course, led by Rhode Island, Massachusetts, New Hampshire and Vermont.

To put it another way, charitable giving exists in inverse ratio to a belief in the role of effective government. If you think that health-care, famine relief, welfare – you name it – should be left to the government, then you will think of private giving as irrelevant at best – at worst, a distraction from the communal effort. But those who deeply mistrust 'big government' look to their consciences and dig into their pockets when the going gets tough. And judging from what Sam Parham and Terry Harper experienced (and the rest of us saw, heard and read about) of FEMA's lamentable perfor-mance in New Orleans, they are right to do so.

Violent crime in the US has fallen by well over half since its peak in 1993, while it continues to rise in most of Europe.

James Alan Fox is a rare beast in the American jungle – what the British would call a 'media don'. Not only is he a distinguished professor of criminology at Northeastern University in Boston and the author of sixteen scholarly books and countless articles. He also writes a column for the *Boston Herald*, appears regularly on national television and radio programmes, has acted as a consultant for Fox Cable and NBC News, has given expert testimony to Congress, and met with President Clinton and Vice President Gore.

He is an expert in teenage crime, serial killings, and violence in schools and the workplace. He is also a courageous campaigner for the greater control of handguns. So it was no surprise that when Janet Reno, US Attorney General in the Clinton administration, wanted to find out what was happening, and was going to happen, in the field of juvenile violence, she turned to James Alan Fox.

Fox's report, when it was published in 1996, was pretty scary. Things were bad and set to get much worse. Although it had levelled off around 1980, juvenile violent crime had begun to increase from the mid-1980s. Though the overall homicide rate for all age groups declined slightly from 1990 to 1994, murders committed by young adults rose by 2 per cent, while homicides by teenagers aged from fourteen to seventeen rose by 'a tragic 22 per cent'.

Furthermore, all this ruin was accelerating. 'By the year 2005,' Fox predicted, 'the number of teens, ages 14–17, will have increased 20 per cent over its 1994 level.' Violent crime, would, therefore, rise correspondingly; the rise in teen numbers alone would be enough to push juvenile killings from 4,000 a year in 1994 to 5,000 in 2005.

Only it might be even worse than that. 'Given the worsening conditions in which children are being raised, given the breakdown of all our institutions as well as our cultural norms,' Fox warned, 'we will likely have many more than 5,000 teen killers per year.' The report ended with a frightening graph showing the red line of 14–17-year-olds committing under 2,000 homicides a year in 1984 rising to 4,000 in 1994. After that, the line went into dots to warn what will happen 'if [the] recent trend in offending rates persists'. The line of dots reached almost to 9,000.[1]

Well, it was getting near the end of the millennium, and no doubt the seasonal taste for apocalyptic warnings was sharpened by New England's long-standing fondness for jeremiads, those prophetic harangues from the pulpit that used to pack them into Boston's chapels and meeting houses. What actually happened as the millennium approached was that total violent crime (rape, robbery, assault and homicide) began to plummet. By 2005 it had dropped by well over half since its two peaks in 1981 and 1994 – from slightly over 50 occurrences per thousand of population to just 21.[2]

What no one could agree on was why. Various ideas were offered, like the collapse of the crack cocaine market, a stronger economy, more police on the ground, and innovative police strategies like New York Mayor Giuliani's 'broken window' approach: come down hard on minor offences like graffiti and piddling in the street, and serious crime will wither too, in time. But none of these factors seemed to explain more than a fraction of the percentage drop in violent crime, let alone its timing.

Then came a bombshell set off by two further distinguished professors, Steven Levitt, an economist at the University of Chicago, and John Donohue, a specialist in legal economics, then at Stanford. 'The Impact of Legalized Abortion on Crime' soon spread well beyond the sober pages of the *Quarterly Journal of Economics*. According to Levitt and Donohue, it was abortion that brought the crime rate down, after *Roe v. Wade*, the Supreme Court decision that allowed the practice in 1973.[3]

Calculate nineteen or twenty years after this landmark date, the authors argued, and you come up with the exact point at which violent crime figures began to fall. Furthermore, in those five states that legalised abortion in 1970, the fall in violent offences started three years earlier. And the effect was cumulative, as more and more young women who up till then had not been able to afford a safe illegal abortion took advantage of the new law. In the first year after *Roe v. Wade*, around 750,000 women had abortions in the United States – or one abortion for every four live births. By 1980, the number of terminations had reached 1.6 million, or one for every 2.25 live births.

But of course for the theory to work out, the 'right' kind of woman – in other words, the wrong kind – had to be taking advantage of *Roe v. Wade*. 'Very often she was unmarried or in her teens or poor, and sometimes all three', Levitt has written. 'Childhood poverty and a single-parent household … are among the strongest predictors that a child will have a criminal future.'[4]

Needless to say, the thesis aroused huge controversy. In the academic debate, critics suggested that Donohue's and Levitt's connection between abortion and crime was more correlated than causal. Others questioned how their statistics could prove that the hypothetical offspring aborted would have been more likely to commit crimes than those others carried to term. Out in the wider world, the authors were accused of (among other things) a rage for eugenic control.

This last charge, at least, is unfair. Eugenics advocates strong incentives or even coercion. Levitt's more liberal line is that a woman finding herself pregnant is the best judge of how well she will be able to cope – financially, emotionally and socially – with bringing up a child: 'She may be unmarried or in a bad marriage. She may consider herself too poor to raise a child. … She may believe that she is too young or hasn't yet received enough education. … For any of a hundred reasons, she may feel that she cannot provide a home environment that is conducive to raising a healthy and productive child.'[5]

Even so, the authors of 'Impact' admit that *Roe v. Wade* explains at best only about half of the decline in American violent crime since 1994. Other analysts have looked for the answer in the actual micro-communities in which violence either arises or doesn't. For Robert Sampson and his co-workers, it's what they call the 'collective efficacy' of – for example – a city neighbourhood that largely governs the crime rate, rather than large-scale demographic shifts, as variously interpreted by Fox and Levitt.

Collective efficacy is the 'capacity of a group to regulate its members according to desired principles'. This in turn depends on a sense of community built on a degree of 'residential stability'. More important than race, gender or class, they say, is whether people have lived in the neighbourhood long enough to know one another, and thus to take collective action in the face of – say – threatened cuts in public services like garbage collection, police patrols and fire stations, or (less formally) to monitor play groups, deal with truancy and to confront 'persons who are exploiting or disturbing public space'.[6]

What none of these analysts consider are the international comparisons – and for good reasons, since they seem to shoot all the explanations for the American crime decline full of holes. Put the US crime figures alongside those from Australia, Canada, England and Wales, the Netherlands, Scotland and Sweden. Which of these countries do you think had the highest rate of violent robbery in 2000? Surprisingly, it was the Netherlands, at over 15 offences per 1,000 population, followed by Canada at 9 per 1,000.

Meanwhile, the gun-toting, rabble-rousing US of A was bumping along the bottom at 2.4, having nose-dived from peaks of 7.3 and 5.1 in 1982 and 1993 respectively. And apart from Australia and the US, all crime rates in this comparison were accelerating towards the end of the century – that of the Netherlands very steeply.[7]

Robbery is a useful comparison, since it's the only violent crime for which survey rates, as opposed to figures for offences reported to the police, exist for all the countries represented. Still, the data are sufficient to throw into confusion the leading explanation, to date, for the drop in the American violent crime rate. Abortion? Sweden, Great Britain and the Netherlands have had abortion more or less on demand for far longer than the US has.

Just over half of all Americans vote for President, and around one third vote between presidential elections.

Democracy is Greek for 'people power'. In 5th-century BC Athens, where democracy was invented, all those eligible to vote were herded into the assembly area by ushers at either end of a rope dripping with red paint. All citizens with red on their clothes were fined. Later, people were actually paid for attending the assembly, but only the first 6,000 to arrive. By then, the red rope was used to keep the latecomers out.

Some modern democracies have followed the Athenian lead. Voting is compulsory in Australia and Belgium, for example; so these countries regularly clock up voting figures above 95 per cent of the adult population. In continental European democracies where voting is voluntary, over 75 per cent of the adult population regularly participate in elections. Even beleaguered Iraq, its voters threatened by insurgents and suicide bombers, managed a 70 per cent turnout for its two elections in 2005.

Apart from Australians, voters in the English-speaking democracies turn up at much lower rates. Voter participation in Britain and Canada now stands at 60 per cent – having peaked at over 80 per cent in 1974 and 1962 respectively. From its high point in 1960, in the close presidential race between Richard Nixon and John F. Kennedy, American turnout at the polls is now down to around 55 per cent of the adult population. But even that high point was only around 63 per cent.

Americans deplore this low turnout at the polls as a scandal in the world's leading democracy – 'leading', that is, not only through being the most powerful but also the most anxious to set a global example. Newspapers and the internet are full of articles with headlines like 'Why Don't More Americans Vote?' and 'Why Do So

Few People Vote in the US?' Things are generally supposed to be going downhill fast, shoved by distrust of sleazy politicians and negative campaigning.

Of course, things may not be as bad as they seem. The US Census Bureau regularly reports American poll attendance at around ten percentage points above the more widely accepted figure. According to them, 64 per cent of US citizens aged eighteen and over voted in the 2004 presidential election, up from 60 per cent in 2000. But as they warn, these data are taken from the Current Population Survey (CPS), and 'Statistics from surveys are subject to sampling and nonsampling error. The CPS estimate of overall turnout (125.7 million) differs from the "official" turnout, as reported by the Clerk of the House (122.3 million).'[1]

In other words, the Census Bureau figures are based on what people report they have done rather than actually have done, so are no more reliable that those self-reporting data for church attendance (see page 36).

Another palliative is the perspective offered by Samuel L. Popkin and Michael P. McDonald, that the abysmal turnout of American voters is 'an artifact of the way in which it is measured'. The 55 per cent figure for general elections represents the number of all adult Americans who vote. The true base line, they argue, is those *eligible* to vote – that is, adults minus non-citizens, felons, and those not registered. When voters are plotted against the eligible and registered, the turnout comes closer to 70 per cent, which compares favourably with Canada and the UK.[2]

But this won't wash either. Granted the hurdle of registration must be jumped before the finishing line of the polling booth, but ever since the National Voter Registration Act of 1993, the so-called 'voter motor', chances to register have become a part of everyday life. You can register by mail, when applying for a driving licence or enlisting in the armed forces – even when going on welfare. As elections approach, registration booths appear in city squares and out-of-town shopping malls. In some states you can register on the very day you vote. So not to have registered is also a vote – to abstain.

Even worse, when the Voting Rights Act was amended in 1970, lowering the voting age to eighteen, it did very little to encourage the youth to register, let alone vote. While 79 per cent of citizens aged 65 and over registered to vote in the 2004 general election, only 58 per cent of those aged eighteen to 24 managed the task. And of those, only 47 per cent turned up at the polls.[3]

So why is it happening? What is it that puts voters off? Among the causes suggested are the enormous sums needed to mount a political campaign, and the chicanery required to raise them. The recent trend in negative campaigning (see above) may be conveying the sense – especially among younger would-be voters – that politics is a grubby and mean-spirited business, rather than a vision for a future, better society.

It can't be difficulty in getting to the polls. 'Participation, paradox-ically, is highest in states where making it to a polling station can be misery on a wintry day', writes Calvin Woodward. He means places like Minnesota, Alaska, Maine and New Hampshire. These are 'among states that lead the nation in getting voters out, and they put the sunbelt to shame'.[4]

Could it have something to do with political disorientation among the voters? Time was, you knew where you stood with the two main parties. The Democrats started wars and ran up a huge public debt to pay for social programmes, while the Republicans ended wars and balanced the budget. Yet Clinton's Welfare Reform Act of 1996 limited welfare to five years of benefit, after which claimants would have to work, and he ended his terms with the budget balanced.

His Republican successor started a disastrous war and ran up a national debt (as of the end of 2006) of well over $8 trillion, rising by $1.48 billion per day. And where once the Democrats represented working people and the poor for the first half of the 20th century, they seemed more concerned to advance abortion, gay rights and stem cell research at the end of it.

Another possible cause may be the weakening of sub-communities that used to galvanise and reinforce voting, like families, neighbourhoods, factory workforces and labour unions. Robert D. Putnam thinks this erosion of civil engagement has been hastened by television, which has tended to displace spare-time gatherings like bridge clubs and bowling leagues, turning us into passive participants in political campaigns.[5] Because of television, too, parties have spent less time and money on local meetings and door-to-door canvassing to get the vote out, and more on high-impact media campaigns.

Ethnic and class factors seem to be operating too. In California, model of the nation's future when it comes to social mix, 'The majority of likely voters are age 45 and older (62 per cent), have household incomes of $60,000 or more (56 per cent), and have college degrees (53 per cent)', according to Mark Baldassare, Director of Research at California's Public Policy Institute. By contrast, a large majority of non-voters – 76 per cent – are aged 45 or younger, and only 18 per cent have household incomes of over $60,000, while only 17 per cent have college degrees. Again, no fewer than 77 per cent of voters are home-owners, while 66 per cent of non-voters are renters.

'Although no racial or ethnic group constitutes a majority in California', Baldassare writes, 'whites comprise 70 per cent of likely voters, Latinos 14 per cent, blacks 6 per cent, and Asians 5 per cent'. Were California's non-voters to register and vote, he adds, 'we might see more voter support for policies that increased spending for state programs and calls to expand government's role in improving the lives of the less advantaged'.[6]

But if we're looking for specifically American causes of low voter turnout, what about the Electoral College? This archaic system, in which each state 'sends' mythical 'voters' – the number depending on its population – to cast its 'votes' for President, is a vestige of the days when it might take several weeks to ride to Washington from a distant western state. If you're a Democrat supporter in a predominantly Republican state, why vote at all when all the state's electoral votes will go to the other party? And there are times, as in the 2000 general election, when the popular vote goes one way and the electoral another – as mediated by (of all things) the Supreme Court, fulfilling a function for which we never knew it was intended. All those hanging chads brought Florida in for G.W. Bush – and the rest is (not very happy) history.

In 2006 American venture capital investment outstripped European by nearly five to one.

'In the US', says Niklas Zennström, 'if you have a start-up and it doesn't work out, you have gained an experience. In Europe you have made a mistake.' He should know. Along with Janus Friis, Zennström invented Skype, the face-to-face internet telephony program, and the problems they faced trying to raise venture capital in Europe left their scars on the two Swedish inventors.

'We went round Europe trying to raise money for one year to close our first round', Zennström said. 'If we were a Silicon Valley Company, it probably would have taken us one month.'[1]

In 2006 venture capital investment in the USA totalled $25.75 billion, the highest in five years. Europe also finished the year on a venture-capital roll, its highest in four years. But its total invested was €4.12 billion ($5.4 billion), just a whisker under one-fifth the American sum.[2]

The contrast looks even sharper when venture capital investment is set against gross domestic product (GDP). In 2006 the US put 0.2 per cent of its GDP into risk-capital investments. The equivalent fraction for the EU was just one-tenth of that – 0.02 per cent – for start-ups, and 0.09 percent for expansion and modernisation. Within Europe itself there were striking variations, with Sweden and Great Britain well above the European average, and Germany far below it.

Why this disparity? A conference of venture capitalists meeting in Sydney, Australia in June 2006 cited various barriers to risk investment in different regions of the world. 'Singaporeans are good at taking orders, but they don't think outside the box', according to Usha Haley, author of five books on Asian business. South American investment suffers from authoritarian governments. 'All of our countries have vertical decision-making', said

Alberto Garcia Carmona from Buenos Aires, and investment decisions tend to bend to political powers and their wealthy backers.

In Europe, the problem was that old fear again. 'The stigma of failure in Denmark or Germany is extreme', said Björn Christensen, who used to head up the venture branch of Germany's Siemens. 'It's almost like your kids won't talk to you anymore.'[3] David Vickrey agrees. 'In the US failure can be a badge of honor and entrepreneurs will try again, while in Germany failure is often stigmatized.'[4]

But then, how did America get that way? Immigrants take risks to leave home and set up in a new country. As a nation of immigrants and their descendants, America has a head start in the culture of risk capital. For Christensen, who now works in Silicon Valley, the culture of risk investment is in the American DNA. 'It's like generations of people where the gene pool gets better and better.'

In the US, high technology dominates investment in new ventures. The PriceWaterhouse 'Money Tree' report for the year's total, 2006, shows life sciences, biotechnology and medical devices leading the field at $7.2 billion. Internet-specific companies came in second at $4 billion, while the industrial and energy sector garnered $1.6 billion, boosted by lots of new investment in alternative energy.[5]

Venture investors are most active on the east and west coasts, clustered around the Massachusetts Institute of Technology and Silicon Valley, near Stanford University. Moving on from dry statistics, one can get a flavour of what they get up to by Googling them, then clicking on the portfolio of individual companies they have supported.[6]

Thus Flagship Ventures, of Cambridge, Massachusetts, teamed up with professors from Harvard Medical School and MIT to found 'Codon Devices' in the autumn of 2004. The company 'is currently developing its proprietary BioFAB™ production platform that is expected to accurately synthesize kilobase- to megabase-length genetic code', with a view to developing 'comprehensive sets of biological parts for large-scale research projects', and to engineer cells for pharmaceuticals.[7]

Across the country in Santa Clara, California, Intel Capital has invested in Clovis Systems, 'founded to build the System

Infrastructure Software Platform (SISP) that 'allows systems vendors to allocate more resources to their core competencies'. SISP consists of 'Blade Director', 'System Director', and 'Management Director', which are 'used by vendors to accelerate the design and development of a wide range of systems from simple incremental line cards (also called blades) to complex clusters'.[8]

Just up El Camino Real from Santa Clara is Menlo Park, where all sorts of new things are happening. Draper Fisher Juvetson, who funded Skype when Niklas Zennström couldn't find a backer in Europe, have invested in a wide array of medical technology companies, like Aethon, of Pittsburg, Pennsylvania. They have developed a 'robotic delivery system for hospitals, an automated, pilot-less system that hauls materials indoors'. Another DFJ client, Apieron of Menlo Park, makes a 'biosensor device for asthma management'.

In the same town Menlo Ventures are backing a range of communications companies, like Acme Packet ('Products that solve Quality of Service … issues facing current and next generation Voice over IP networks'), Bluesocket ('Wireless gateway to secure and manage 802.11 Wi-Fi wireless LANs, offering encryption and enterprise-level network management features') and Matisse Networks ('Next generation Ethernet switching products'). Not to mention Tablus, a 'developer of outbound enterprise content monitoring'.

It's a whole new language. But then these are new products, or concepts, or – to use a word much favoured by the new projectors – 'applications'. Many of us know already that a LAN is a local computer network like a house or office, served either by the ethernet or a wireless router (WLAN), but it may be awhile before 'BioFABTM' enters the vernacular, or common understanding makes room for the difference between 'kilobase-length' and 'megabase-length' genetic codes. Sooner or later, though, we'll all have an idea of what they mean – in our lives as well as in our vocabularies.

Start-ups are among the most important drivers of intellectual capital creation, and as Jon Dudas pointed out, on being appointed head of the US Patent Office, intellectual property is the single largest sector of the US economy, earning more export dollars than cars, aircraft and agriculture combined.

We don't often think of intellectual property as a product, whether it be a pop song, a movie script or the design for a new life form. It is exactly that, however, and what gives it value is the protection afforded the author by some form of copyright or patent. That's why Dudas also bears the august official title of Under Secretary of Commerce for Intellectual Property.

Dudas was lobbying Congress in March 2004, to ask the government to stop creaming off Patent Office surpluses earned from users' fees, and to use them instead to hire another 2,000 or more patent examiners. With the increased manpower he hoped to clear the backlog of over two years in the time taken to process a patent application. Otherwise, he warned, the delay would grow to the point where venture capitalists will come to 'feel like it's no longer useful to invest in certain technologies because they don't know that they're going to get a … return on their investment'.[9]

Since many patent examiners have to be scientists or engineers, they weren't going to come cheap, but in 2005 the Patent Office began to recruit its additional experts. So the venture capitalists have kept confident. Ideas continue to flow and to find backing.

Not all investment, after all, favours start-ups. Buyouts, for example, can range from 'management buyouts' by executives wanting to gain control of a branch business no longer wanted by its parent company, to the sort of shenanigans that Gordon Gekko got up to in *Wall Street* (1987): hostile take-overs to strip out the assets of a going concern. Buyouts may (or may not) improve business efficiency over all, but in effect they are just recycling money, moving it from one pocket to another. Buyouts do not generate new funds for new ventures. They don't motivate additional employment (usually the opposite, in fact) or add significantly to the stock of intellectual capital.

But investors who raise venture capital risk a lot in backing untried concepts and helping to bring them to the market. Moreover, they remain actively engaged in the projects they sponsor, offering help and providing skills, drawing on the wide range of expertise that their locations along Silicon Valley, or Route

128 around Boston, or any other high-tech part of the country allow them to enlist.

And the statistics of venture investment underpin a general truth – that the United States remains the leading country for enterprise, where people seem more willing than elsewhere to risk all on an idea, and if it fails, to pick themselves up (even out of bankruptcy) and start again.

America's approval rating has dropped to 58 per cent in Britain, 37 per cent in France and 15 per cent in Jordan.

Though the phenomenon of anti-Americanism has intensified world-wide since the 2003 invasion of Iraq,[1] Americans have been living with it and talking about it since before the War of Independence. Throughout its long history, anti-Americanism has flourished in bewildering, sometimes comic variety.

In its earliest, European expression, anti-Americanism was levelled at the physical environment of the New World. In his *Histoire Naturelle* (1749) the French naturalist Georges-Louis Leclerc, Count Buffon, argued that America's 'miasmic' atmosphere caused plants and animals – both native species and those imported from other parts of the world – to decline in weight, size and vitality. This opinion was widely held at the time, and taken seriously enough for Thomas Jefferson and Benjamin Franklin to spend some time and ink in trying to rebut it (see page 87).

After America achieved its independence, the English also deployed imagery drawn from physical nature to express degeneracy of social, political and cultural structures as well. Arriving at the mouth of the Mississippi in December 1827, Frances Trollope, the novelist's mother, saw 'monstrous bulrushes and now and then a crocodile luxuriating in the slime'. Floating downriver was a dislodged tree, 'its roots mocking the heavens; while the dishonoured branches lash[ed] the tide in idle vengeance, ... the fragment of a world in ruins.' Here was the world turned upside down. The tree, personified as a disgraced, and now desperate revolutionary, is America cut loose from its metropolitan centre and degenerated into monstrous disorder as a result.

'In the four corners of the globe,' wrote the English author and preacher Sydney Smith in 1820, 'who reads an American book? or goes to an American play?' Having cut themselves off from their roots, the Americans were destined to mediocrity, he thought. They lacked the social complexity and historical deposits to write poetry or fiction. In science too, Americans remained second-rate. 'What does the world yet owe to American physicians or surgeons? ... What new constellations have been discovered by the telescopes of Americans? What have they done in the mathematics?'[2]

In the mid-19th century, the degeneracy thesis was recast in the form of the 'scientific' racism of another French author, the novelist and diplomat Arthur de Gobineau. His *Essay on the Inequality of the Human Races* (1853–5), posing a hierarchy of races, with the 'Aryans' at the top of the pinnacle, would later be taken up by the Nazis.

Though the 'Aryan' Anglo-Saxons and Scandinavians seemed to be refreshing their stock by colonising the New World, as James W. Ceaser explains, Gobineau thought that 'the universalistic idea of natural equality in America was in fact promoting a democracy of blood, in which the very idea of "race" ... was vanishing. Europe was dumping its "garbage" races into America, and these had already begun to mix with the Anglo-Saxons.'[3]

A quite separate line of attack targeted the disparity between American ideals and practice. For all their fine ideas, weren't Americans mightily hypocritical in owning slaves? Sidney Smith again: 'Finally, under which of the old tyrannical governments of Europe is every sixth man a slave, whom his fellow creatures may buy and sell and torture?' Samuel Johnson had already put it more succinctly in 1775: 'How is it that we hear the loudest yelps for liberty among the drivers of negroes?'[4]

More recently, America has been blamed for its cultural and technological exports: everything from the debilitating and dehumanising effects of mass production and its soulless consumerism, to its dissemination of fast food, violent movies and cheap popular music through a mysterious and little-understood process called 'globalisation'.

Of course, much anti-American sentiment can be dismissed as just plain ignorant, or at best unimaginative. For every person who could identify Sydney Smith today, there are several millions who could give real answers to his rhetorical questions, and all of them in the affirmative.

It's also snobbish. Until recently, at any rate, anti-Americanism has tended to come from the intellectuals of other countries, or from their social and political elites. The English essayist and historian Paul Johnson is good on this, pointing out that while European intellectuals 'must genuflect to democracy as a system, they cannot openly admit ... that a farmer in Kansas, a miner in Pennsylvania or an auto-assembler in Michigan can carry as much social and moral weight as they do'. For people who act on democratic assumptions, Johnson writes, 'the intellectuals have a special derogatory word, "populist".'[5] This is true.

Though originating in foreign countries, anti-Americanism is a fact about America. And all kinds of barriers to understanding are built into the concept itself. Why do we use the term 'anti-Americanism' and seldom or never 'anti-Frenchism' or 'anti-Brazilianism'? One could criticise the Japanese (say, for their covert whaling) without being called 'anti-Japanesist'. Does anti-Americanism somehow transcend the local and specific?

Yes it does, and here's why. From the Pilgrim Fathers of New England to the Founding Fathers of the new republic, America was not just another country in another geographical place. It set out to be a unique society based, first, on a covenant between God and his chosen people, then on the universal values of equality, liberty and government by public consent. Attack those, and you're up against nothing less than what the Declaration of Independence called 'the laws of nature and of nature's God'.

What this means is that anti-Americanism is – partly, at least – an American creation, a by-product of our feeling that we are so special as a nation. As a result, justified criticisms of American policy abroad are frequently dismissed as mere justifications for deep-seated, even hidden and unacknowledged prejudices against the divine and natural order of things that make up the American way.

So in introducing his new book on the subject, Andrei S. Markovits asserts that 'the European animus against things American has little to do with the politics and policies of the Bush administration – or any other administration, for that matter'.[6] Similarly, Josef Joffe, author of *Überpower: The Imperial Temptation of America* (2006), says that 'America will always rile the soul [of the foreigner] because it is the steamroller of modernization'.[7]

Even more breathtaking is Barry Rubin's claim that 'Arab and Muslim rage at the United States has had very little to do with actual US policies … promoting anti-Americanism is simply the best way Muslim leaders have found to distract their publics from the real problem: internal mismanagement. New US policies or a PR campaign will not change matters.'[8]

What, Muslim hostility has *nothing* to do with Guantánamo Bay, the invasion of Iraq, American support for Israel? We may debate – even justify – these policies and actions, but it's pretty far-fetched to claim that they have no impact on Muslim opinion around the world. It's like saying that criticism of Israel's treatment of the Palestinians comes not from objections to its current policies, but from deep-seated anti-Semitism.

And this isn't just a casual comparison. Markovits has a whole chapter on anti-Semitism, because he thinks it has 'consistently been … an integral part of anti-Americanism'.[9] Why? Because of the same tendency to read the attack on the country's actions as an assault on the country itself. In his discussion of anti-Americanism, Joffe puts the Israeli parallel succinctly. When asked whether criticism of Israel was tantamount to anti-Semitism, he answered: 'If you're anti-Israel, what are you against? You are against the right of the Jewish people to their own state.'[10]

So the snobbery, ignorance and fear of modernity that have informed traditional anti-Americanism cannot wholly explain its recent increase. In January 2007, the parents of 24,000 children in northern Pakistan refused to allow them to be vaccinated against polio, because extremist clerics told them that inoculation was an American plot to sterilise innocent Muslim children. We don't need to take this kind of anti-American sentiment – or call it hysteria – to heart. But maybe in other aspects of Bush's foreign policy America has given the rest of the world plenty of grounds for complaint.

Notes

Americans aren't born; they are made.

1 Walt Whitman, Preface to *Leaves of Grass* (1855).
2 Cited in Seymour Martin Lipset, *American Exceptionalism, A Double-Edged Sword* (New York and London: W.W. Norton, 1996).
3 Dennis Barker and Christopher Sylvester, 'The Grasshopper' (obituary of Robert Maxwell), *The Guardian*, 6 November 1991.
4 Anthony Delano, 'The Man Who Never Understood England', *Daily Mail*, 6 November 1991, p. 6; Laurence Marks, 'The Man Who Invented Robert Maxwell', *The Observer*, 10 November 1991, p. 21; Daniel McGrory, '"God's obituary would be shorter"', *Daily Express*, 6 November 1991, p. 4.

Throughout history, around one-third of all migrants to America have returned home.

1 Wilbur Shepperson, *Emigration and Disenchantment: Portraits of Englishmen Repatriated from the United States* (Norman, OK: University of Oklahoma Press, 1965), pp. 4, 5–6.
2 Charlotte Erickson, *Invisible Immigrants: The Adaptation of English and Scottish Immigrants in Nineteenth-Century America* (Leicester: Leicester University Press, 1972), pp. 219, 372.
3 Ibid., p. 118.
4 Ibid., p. 152.
5 See the Pew Research Center report on 'The French-Muslim Connection', http://pewresearch.org/obdeck/?ObDeck1D=50, 17 August 2006, p. 2.
6 Zogby Worldwide, 'Hearts and Minds', http://www.zogbyworldwide.com/sb/Readsb.cfm?ID=669, 19 August 2006.
7 Neil MacFarquhar, 'Pakistanis Find US an Easier Fit Than Britain', *New York Times* online, 21 August 2006, http://www.nytimes.com/2006/08/21/us/21devon.html?hp&ex=1156219200&en=23246a9dcf15f108&ei=5094&partner=

America is a country with 50 capital cities. Few Americans can name them.

1 All these are US Census figures for the core cities, not their surrounding urban areas.

The US Supreme Court has ruled that burning the American flag is a legitimate expression of free speech.

1   Norman Mailer, *Why Are We at War?* (New York: Random House, 2003).
2   'US Flag Laws and Regulations', http://www.wi.net/flag.html; see this source for a full list of laws and conventions regarding the use of the flag.

Nine per cent of US adults report having attended at least one Alcoholics Anonymous meeting in their lifetime.

1   Robin Room, 'Alcoholics Anonymous as a Social Movement', in Barbara S. McCrady and William Miller, eds, *Research on Alcoholics Anonymous: Opportunities and Alternatives* (New Brunswick, NJ: Rutgers Center of Alcohol Studies, 1993), pp. 167–87, 3, http://www.bks.no/alcoanon.htm
2   Peterborough, New Hampshire, *Monadnock Ledger*, 22 June 2006, http://www.mledger.com/index/mlcalendar.shtml
3   John Sutherland, *Last Drink to LA* (London: Short Books, 2001), p. 100.
4   These and other guiding principles are set out in 'The Twelve Traditions' of Alcoholics Anonymous, widely available on the web.
5   Room, op. cit., p. 11. Room's essay is among the most illuminating short studies of Alcoholics Anonymous.

65 million Americans own handguns, and use them to kill 35,000 other Americans every year.

1   Niccolò Machiavelli, *The Prince*, trans. and ed. George Bull (Harmondsworth: Penguin, 1961), p. 79.
2   Emma Hartley, *50 Facts You Need to Know: Europe* (Cambridge: Icon Books, 2006), p. 24.
3   Figures from 'International Homicide Comparisons', GunCite–Gun Control–International Homicide Comparisons, http://www.guncite.com/gun_control_gcgvinco.himl
4   See Reuters, 'House Passes Gun Lawsuit Shield Legislation', http://www.csgv.org/news/headlines/reuters_immunity.cfm
5   Martin Killias, 'International Correlations Between Gun Ownership and Rate of Homicide and Suicide', *Canadian Medical Association Journal*, 148 (1993), pp. 1721–5.
6   Cited in 'International Violent Death Rates', http://guncite.com/gun_control_gcgvintl.html#intl
7   Gary Kleck, *Targeting Guns: Firearms and Their Control* (New York: Walter de Gryter Inc., 1997), p. 253.

8 Brad Edmunds, 'Gun Control Around the World', LewRockwell.com, http://lewrockwell.com/edmunds/edmunds39.html
9 'Some Facts About Guns', Gun Control Network, http://www.gun-control-network.org/GF01.htm

At least once a week, 42 per cent of Americans eat out while they are en route to somewhere else.
1 Eric Schlosser, 'Stuff the Kids', *The Guardian*, 24 April 2006, G2, p. 9.
2 Schlosser, op. cit., pp. 10–11.
3 'Senate Downs Minimum Wage Increase', http://usgovinfo.about.com/b/a/217280.htm Following the mid-term elections later that year, Congress, with Democratic majorities in both houses, finally raised the minimum wage to $7.15 in May 2007, by which time inflation had reduced it to below 1997 values.
4 'McDonald's anger over McJob entry', BBC News, 9 November 2003, http://news.bbc.co.uk/2/hi/americas/3255883.stm
5 Bill Bryson, *I'm a Stranger Here Myself: Notes on Returning to America After Twenty Years Away* (New York: Broadway Books, 1999), pp. 214–15.

Only 18 per cent of American adults own a passport.
1 Publius Ovidius Naso (Ovid), *Metamorphoses*, Book I, trans. Mary M. Innes (Harmondsworth: Penguin Classics, 1955).
2 Alain de Botton, *The Art of Travel* (London: Hamish Hamilton, 2002), p. 70.
3 Richard at 25 September 2005, 8:47pm, Permalink, http://www.gyford.com/phil/writing/2003/01/31/how_many_america.php
4 Washington Irving, 'The Author's Account of Himself', in *The Sketch Book of Geoffrey Crayon, Gent.*, in *Washington Irving, History, Tales and Sketches*, ed. James W. Tuttleton (New York: Library of America, 1983).
5 David at 7 July 2003, 7:41pm, Permalink, as above.
6 Laura Brown at 1 February 2003, 1:05pm, Permalink, as above.
7 Chuck at 12 April 2004, 1:44pm, Permalink, as above.

Over twice as many Americans claim to go to church as actually do.
1 Ruy Teixeira, 'Keepin' the Faith', The Century Foundation, 4 June 2004, http://www.tcf.org/list.asp?type=NC&pubid=584; Pew Forum on Religion and Public Life, 'American Religious Landscapes and Public Life', Fourth National Survey of Religion and Politics, 9 September 2004, http://pewforum.org/docs/index.php?DocID=55
2 Susan Page, 'Churchgoing Closely Tied to Voting Patterns', *USA*

Today, 2 May 2004, http://www.usatoday.com/news/nation/2004-06-02-religion-gap_x.htm

3 Kirk Hadaway and P.L. Marler, 'Did You Really Go To Church This Week? Behind the Poll Data', *The Christian Century*, 6 May 1998, pp. 472–5, Religion Online, http://www.religion-online.org/showarticle. asp?title=237

4 Andrew Walsh, 'Church, Lies and Polling Data', *Religion in the News*, Vol. 1, No. 2 (Fall 1998), http://www.trincoll.edu/depts/csrpl/RIN%20 Vol.1No.2/Church_lies_polling.htm

5 Hadaway and Marler, op. cit.

Americans spend twice as much on civil litigation as they do on new automobiles – and more than any other industrialised country.

1 'The Rule of Lawyers', 'Order in the Tort', *The Economist Survey*, 18 July 1992.

2 American Bar Association, 'Facts About the American Civil Justice System – Questions', http://www.abanet.org/media/factbooks/acjquest. html and http://www.abanet.org/media/factbooks/acjquest2.html

3 Michael Braye, Don Kovenock and Caspar de Vries, 'Comparative Analysis of Litigation Systems: An Auction-theoretic Approach', *Economic Journal*, July 2005.

4 Stephanie Mencimer, 'The Fake Crisis over Lawsuits: Who's Paying to Keep the Myths Alive?', http:www.aliciapatterson.org/APF2102/Menci mer/Mencimer.html ibid

5 American Bar Association, op. cit.

6 Mencimer, op. cit.

7 American Bar Association, op. cit.

Thanksgiving is the real American national holiday.

1 Edward Winslow, 'A Letter Sent From New England to a friend in these parts [i.e. England]', *Mourt's Relation: A Journal of the Pilgrims at Plymouth, 1622*, Part VI, http://etext.lib.virginia.edu/users/deetz/Plymouth/ mourt6.html

2 [William Bradford and Edward Winslow], *Mourt's Relation: A Journal of the Pilgrims at Plymouth, 1622*, Part I, http://etext.lib.virginia.edu/users/ deetz/Plymouth/mourt1.html

3 William Bradford, *Of Plymouth Plantation*, c. 1630–50, Chapter 9, http:// members.aol.com/calebj/bradford_journal9.html

More than 18,000 adults in America die each year because they don't have health insurance.

1 Figure from 'Care Without Coverage: Too Little, Too Late', Institute of Medicine of the National Academies, 21 May 2002, http://www.iom.edu/CMS/3809/4660/4333.aspx

2 Figures from Andrew Stephen, 'Sick: The great American con trick', *New Statesman*, 4 October 2007, http://www.newstatesman.com/200710040028

3 Figures from GeographyIQ, http//www.geographyiq.com/ranking/ranking_Infant_Mortality_Rate_aall.htm, and http://www.geographyiq.com/ranking/ranking_Life_expectancy_at_birth_dall.htm

4 The Commonwealth Fund, 'Mirror, Mirror on the Wall: An Update on the Quality of American Health Care Through the Patient's Lens', http://www.cmwf.org/Publications/Publications_show.htm?doc_id

5 Elizabeth Warren and David Himmelstein, as reported in Karen Springern, 'Health Hazards: How mounting medical costs are plunging more families into debilitating debt and why insurance doesn't always keep them out of bankruptcy', *Newsweek* Web Exclusive, 26 August 2006, http://www.msnbc.msn.com/id/14470912/site/newsweek/

6 Figures from the National Center for Health Statistics, 'Lack of health insurance coverage and type of coverage', Early Release of Selected Estimates Based on Data From the January–March 2006 National Health Interview Survey, http://www.cdc.gov/nchs/about/major/nhis/released200609.htm#1

7 Tom Zwillich, 'Poor Report Card for US Healthcare', CBS News Healthwatch, 20 September 2006, http://www.cbsnews.com/stories/2006/09/20/health/webmd/main2027945.shtml

8 'American Health Choices Plan', *Hillary for President*, http://www.hillaryclinton.com/feature/healthcareplan/

By 2000 the Great Migration had reversed itself.

1 Nicholas Lehmann, *The Promised Land: The Great Black Migration and How it Changed America* (London: Macmillan, 1991), p. 6.

2 See the essay on 'African Americans' in the online 'Encyclopedia of Chicago', from which these population figures come: http://www.encyclopedia.chicagohistory.org/pages/27.html

3 Lehmann, op. cit., p. 353.

4 Figures are from William H. Frey, 'The New Great Migration: Black Americans' Return to the South, 1965–2000', The Brookings Institute Center of Urban and Metropolitan Policy, http://www.brookings.edu/urban/publications/20040524_frey.htm

Of the 239 elected mayors in the state of Oregon, only two draw a salary.

1 Figures from Steve Holgate, 'US Voters Elect Officials from "Dog-catcher" to President', http://usinfo.state.gov/dhr/Archive/2004/Sep/01 -433605.html
2 Ibid.
3 'Mayor Austin Goes to Washington', *Estacada News*, 29 March 2006.

When Bush cut taxes for the rich in 2004, the family that owns Wal-Mart increased their income by $91,500 per hour.

1 Jeffrey Goldberg, 'Annals of Spin. Selling Wal-Mart: Can the Company Co-opt Liberals?', *The New Yorker*, 2 April 2007, p. 32.
2 John Lanchester, 'The Price of Pickles', *London Review of Books*, Vol. 28, 12 June 2006, p. 3.
3 Charles Fishman, *The Wal-Mart Effect: How an Out-of Town Superstore Became a Superpower* (London: Allen Lane, 2006).
4 Quoted in Lanchester, op. cit., p. 6.
5 Liza Featherstone, 'Wal-Mart's Women – employees and customers in unhealthy relationship', *Seattle Post Intelligencer*, 2 January 2005.
6 Lanchester, op. cit., p. 6.
7 Featherstone, op. cit.

Network newscasts have declined in viewer numbers by 44 per cent since 1980, and 59 per cent from their peak in 1969.

1 The Association of Electronic Journalists, 'Keynote Speeches: Edward R. Murrow', RTNDA Convention, Chicago, 15 October 1958, http://www.rtnda.org/resources/speeches/murrow.shtml
2 'The State of the News Media, 2005: An Annual Report on American Journalism', http://www.stateofthemedia.org/2005/narrative_networktv _audience.asp?cat=3&media=4
3 Jon Fine, 'How Fox was Outfoxed', *Business Week Online*, 13 February 2006, http://businessweek.com/magazine/content/06_07/b3971033. htm
4 BBC Television, *Newsnight*, 24 February 2006.
5 K-State Telecom, 'Cable Television: History of Cable TV', http://www. telecom.ksu.edu/cable/history.html
6 Howard Kurtz, 'Media Notes: After Blogs Got Hits, CBS Got a Black Eye', *Washington Post*, 20 September 2004, http://www.washing tonpost.com/wp-dyn/articles/A34153-2004Sep
7 'The State of the News Media, 2005', op. cit.
8 Fine, 'How Fox was Outfoxed', op. cit.

At the millennium, 44 per cent of the adult American population believed that Christ would come again during their lifetime.

1 Sources: Pew Research Center for the People and the Press, 'Americans Look to the 21st Century', October 1999; Pew Forum on Religion and Public Life, 'Many Americans Uneasy with Mix of Religion and Politics', 24 August 2006, pp. 17–18.
2 Matt Wray, 'White Trash Religion', in Matt Wray and Annalee Newitz, eds, *White Trash: Race and Class in America* (New York and London: Routledge, 1997).
3 See Kevin Kruse, *White Flight: Atlanta and the Making of Modern Conservatism* (Princeton: Princeton University Press, 2005).
4 David Kuo, *Tempting Faith: An Inside Story of Political Seduction* (The Free Press, 2006).
5 Wray, op. cit., p. 194.

Occupational fraud cost the United States $652 billion in 2006.

1 James D. Ratley, CFE, 'ACFE Report to the Nation on Occupational Fraud and Abuse', p. 4, http://www.acfe.com/documents/2006-rttn.pdf
2 'Gordon Gekko', Wikipedia, http://en.wikipedia.org/wiki/Gordon_Gekko
3 Joseph T. Wells, 'Occupational Fraud: The Audit as Deterrent', *Journal of Accountancy Online*, April 2002, http://www.aicpa.org/pubs/jofa/apr2002/wells.htm
4 David Cay Johnston, 'How Offshore Havens Helped Enron Escape Taxes', *New York Times* News Service, http://www.uni-muenster.de/PeaCon/global-texte/sem-notes/enron-offshore.htm
5 Andrew Clark, 'I'm Not a Greedy Man, Says Enron Chief', *The Guardian*, 12 April 2006.
6 Larry Elliott, 'US Watchdog Charges 13 With Insider Trading', *The Guardian*, 2 March 2007, p. 28.

Contrary to popular opinion, all America is not one middle class.

1 Louis Hartz and others, *The Founding of New Societies: Studies in the History of the United States, Latin America, South Africa, Canada and Australia* (New York: Harcourt, Brace and World, 1964), p. 7.
2 Abraham Lincoln, 'Address before the Wisconsin State Agricultural Society', Milwaukee, WI, 30 September 1859, http://showcase.netins.net/web/creative/lincoln/speeches/fair.htm
3 Janny Scott and David Leonhardt, 'Class in America: Shadowy Lines That Still Divide', *New York Times*, 15 May 2005.

4 *New York Times*, 'Class Matters: How Class Works, Country by Country', http://www.nytimes.com/packages/html/national/20050515_CLASS_GRAPHIC/index_03.html
5 Scott and Leonhardt, op. cit.
6 Machael Kammen, *People of Paradox: An Inquiry Concerning the Origins of American Civilization* (New York, Knopf, 1972), p. 9.

With 4 per cent of the world's population, the United States produces a quarter of all carbon dioxide emissions.

1 Marie Woolf and Colin Brown, 'Global Warming: The US Contribution in Figures', *The Independent*, 13 June 2005, http://www.commondreams.org/headlines05/0613-02.htm
2 Steve Connor, 'Scientists Condemn US as Emissions of Greenhouse Gases Hit Record Level', *The Independent*, 19 April 2006, http://news.independent.co.uk/world/science_technology/article358583.ece
3 Shaoni Bhattacharya, 'Greenhouse Gas Emissions by the US Reached Their Highest Annual Total on Record in 2004', *New Scientist*, 21 December 2005, http://www.newscientist.com/article.ns?id=dn8495

The American population is rising twice as fast as that of the European Union; its fertility rate is higher than that of Brazil, South Korea or China.

1 'Centrifugal Forces', 'Survey of America', *The Economist*, 14 July 2005.
2 Ibid.
3 Robert Kagan, *Dangerous Nation: America's Place in the World from its Earliest Days to the Dawn of the 20th Century* (New York: Knopf, 2006).
4 Figures from 'Centrifugal Forces', op. cit.

It now takes up to two years to get a visa to study in America.

1 BBC News, 'Red Tape Silences Orchestra Tour', 20 March 2006, http://news.bbc.co.uk/2/hi/entertainment/4860392.stm
2 Giles Tremlett, 'Al-Qaida Leaders Say Nuclear Power Stations Were Original Targets', *Guardian Unlimited*, 9 September 2002, http://www.guardian.co.uk/afghanistan/story/0,1284,788431,00.html
3 Adrian Arroyo, 'The USA Patriot Act and the Enhanced Border Security and Visa Entry Reform Act: Negatively Impacting Academic Institutions by Deterring Foreign Students from Studying in the United States', *Transnational Lawyer*, 16 (Spring 2003), p. 428.
4 Arroyo, pp. 430–1; 'US Schools Desperate to Fill Foreign Student Quotas', Workpermit.com, 10 August 2006, http://www.workpermit.com/news/2006_08_10/us/decline_foreign_students.htm

5 Megan Rooney, 'More Effort Urged on Foreign Students', The Chronicle of Higher Education, 31 January 2003, http://www.utwatch.org/oldnews/chronhighered_intl_1_31_03.html

6 Arroyo, p. 432.

7 Cited in Rooney, op. cit.

German might have been the official language of the United States.

1 Dennis Barron, 'The Legendary English-Only Vote of 1795', http://www.waltzmann.net/scg/german%2Dby%2Done%2Dvote.html

2 Walter Channing, 'American Literature', *North American Review*, I, 1815, pp. 307–14, pp. 307–08.

3 Ibid., pp. 313–14; to get an idea of just how diverse Native American languages are, consider that a phylum is a very large category, like Indo-European, and Austronesian, while families include divisions like Teutonic/Germanic and Malayo-Polynesian. Thus English is a Teutonic/Germanic language within the Indo-European phylum.

4 Jill Lapore, 'English in Early America', on Voice of America's *Wordmaster*, 3 July 2003; http://manythings.org/voa/wm/wm215.html

5 The English First Foundation, 'Bilingual Ballots: Fairness or Fraud?', http://www.englishfirst.org/eff/efbb.htm

6 Jonathan Weisman and Jim VandeHei, 'Senate Votes English as National Language', *Washington Post*, 19 May 2006.

7 You can hear it, beautifully rendered by a vocal combo, on the National Public Radio website, at http://npr.org/templates/story.story.php?storyId=5369517. In fact, it's more of a re-working than a translation, since the final verse of 'Nuestro Himno', as it's called, speaks of brotherhood and a continuing struggle towards liberty, while the equivalent stanza of 'The Star-Spangled Banner' is all about the preservation of the nation in its time of trial.

America has some of the worst high schools and most of the best universities in the world.

1 By Snopes.com, not challenging its authenticity but questioning whether the comparison with today's 8th-graders really casts such a gloomy shadow over today's education system. See http://www.snopes.com/language/document/1895exam.htm

2 The whole examination can be seen at http://people.moreheadstate.edu/fs/w.willis/eighthgrade.html and at many other sites.

3 US Department of Education, 'Report on the State of American Schools Shows High Schools Challenged by Math and Science', 1 June 2006, http://www.ed.gov/news/pressreleases/2006/06/06012006.html.

These findings are based on a heavyweight survey by the Institute of Educational Sciences (IES), the Department of Education and the National Center for Educational Statistics (NCES), and on the OECD Programme for International Students Assessment (PISA), which assesses students at the end of their compulsory education.

4   Tom Vander Ark, 'America's High-School Crisis: Policy Reform That Will Make a Difference', *Education Week*, 2 April 2003, http://www. gatesfoundation.org/nr/downloads/ed/educationarticles/edweekapril 2003.pdf

5   Nian Cai Liu and Ying Chen, 'The Academic Ranking of World Universities', *Higher Education in Europe*, Vol. 30 (2005), pp. 127–36, p. 131.

6   *US News and World Report*, 'Rankings: America's Best Colleges', 19 March 2007, http://www.usnews.com/sections/rankings

7   National Education Summit on High Schools, 2005, 'Restore Value to the High School Diploma', http://www.achieve.org/en_US/agenda/ expectations.html

There's one car for every adult in the US.

1   'Inventors: The History of the Automobile', http://inventors.about.com/ library/weekly/aacarsgasa.htm, and http://inventors.about.com/library/ weekly/aacarsassemblya.htm

2   'Greatest Engineering Achievements: Automobile History, Part 2 – Assembly Line', http://www.Greatachievements.org/?id=3873

3   Bill Bryson, *The Lost Continent: Travels in Small-town America* (London: Martin Secker & Warburg, 1989; Black Swan Books, 1999), p. 63.

4   Not, however, No. 952, running to 'Desire'. This is now running on San Francisco's Municipal Railway.

5   See Randall O'Toole, 'Vanishing Automobile update #55', http://www. ti.org/vaupdate55.html. As it happens, O'Toole was defending car ownership in cities, claiming that more care would have saved more lives New Orleans.

America has its own welfare state – the military services.

1   William Broyles, Jr, 'A War for Us, Fought by Them', *New York Times*, 4 May 2004, Late Edition, Final, Section A, p. 29.

2   Tim Kane, 'Who Bears the Burden? Demographic Characteristics of US Military Recruits Before and After 9/11', Heritage Foundation, Center for Data Analysis Report #05-08, 7 November 2005, http://www. heritage.org/Research/NationalSecurity/cda05-08.cfm#_ftn1

Americans say more than they need to.

1 E.D. Hirsch, Jr, *Cultural Literacy: What Every American Needs to Know* (New York: Houghton Mifflin, 1987), pp. 3–4.

2 Studs Terkel, *Division Street: America* (New York: Pantheon Books, 1966).

3 Ring Lardner, 'The Love Nest', in *The Love Nest and Other Stories* (New York: Scribner's, 1925).

4 David Mamet, *Glengarry Glen Ross, A Play in Two Acts* (London: Methuen, 1984).

Of the ten top-selling vocal artists in 2006, five were country-and-western singers.

1 Associated Press, 'Album Sales Continue to Fall, Downloads Climb', MSNBC, http://www.msnbc.msn.com/id/16474850/

2 The traditional version of the song had 'down in the valley' for 'down to the river'.

3 Nicholas Dawidoff, *In the Country of Country* (London: Faber and Faber, 1997), p. 299.

4 Not that the Puritans did this either; see fact 11.

5 For non-American readers, a make of baseball bat.

Walden Pond has the highest concentration of urine of any lake in New England.

1 Austin Meredith, 'A History of the Uses of Walden Pond', American Transcendentalism Web, http://www.vcu.edu/engweb/transcendental ism/authors/thoreau/walden/pondhistory.html

2 David D., 'NASTIEST SKINNY DIPPERS EVER!!', posted 9 October 2006, 'Walden Pond State Reservation – Concord – Yelp', http://www.yelp. com/biz/L5fXhXQgcUHKHuS6bHT6Fg

For 38 years, San Francisco had a freeway that ended in mid-air.

1 'The Project is Rescued', http://www.bart.gov/about/history/history_ 5.asp

2 Sayeeda Warsi, 'Where the Car is Not King', BBC *Newsnight*, 15 August 2006, http://news.bbc.co.uk/2/hi/programmes/newsnight/4777801.stm. See also Clarence Eckerson, Jr, 'Portland Transport: The Road (Freeway) Not Taken', 7 June 2006, http://portlandtransport.com/ archives/2006/06/the_road_freewa.html

Despite widespread indifference to the game, more American children play soccer than little-league baseball.

1   FIFA: Fédération Internationale de Football Association.

2   Steve Holgate, 'Americans Take Soccer to Heart', US Department of State, 'US Society, Values and Politics', http://usinfo.state.gov/usa/ a071103.htm

3   'Big Soccer', 'Why Do Americans Hate Soccer?', http://www.bigsoccer. com/forum/showthread.php?t=12484

4   *Bend it like Beckham* reviewed by Steve Sailor', *The American Conservative*, 21 April 2003, http://www.isteve.com/Film_Bend_It_ Like_Beckham.htm

5   Jim Armstrong, 'It's No Wonder America Can't Stand Soccer: The Game is Bad, but the Fans Are Worse', *AOL Sports News*, 14 March 2005, http://articles.news.aol.com/sports/_a/its-no-wonder-america- cant-stand-soccer/20050414145609990014

6   According to 'China Through a Lens', a state-sponsored website, basketball in China has '100 million fans. Today the number of spectators who attend CBA games is over 800,000 and over 600 million watch them on TV.' http://www.china.org.cn/english/features/2004- 2005cba/118962.htm. The population of the US is 298.4 million.

7   Michael Mandelbaum, 'Why America Hates Fotootball', http://observer. guardian.co.uk/osm/story/0.6903.1270849.00.html

8   Actually it didn't. Beer was first brewed in ancient Egypt.

9   Roger Boyes, 'German Beer Lovers Can Already Taste Defeat', TimesOnline, 20 May 2006, http://www.timesonline.co.uk/article/0,, 13509-2188537,00.html; Thom J. Rose, 'Germans Balk at Budweiser for World Cup', *Washington Times*, 22 April 2004, http://www.wash times.com/upi-breaking/20040421-063135-3943r.htm

Huckleberry Finn is the bad boy of American literature.

1   Colonel Munro in Chapter 16 of James Fenimore Cooper, *The Last of the Mohicans* (1825).

2   *The Boston Transcript*, 17 March 1885.

3   Alvin Powell, 'Fight over Huck Finn Continues: Ed School Professor Wages Battle for Twain Classic', *The Harvard University Gazette*, 28 September 2000, http://www.hno.harvard.edu/gazette/2000/09.28/ huckfinn.htm

4   Jane Smiley, 'Say It Ain't So, Huck: Second Thoughts on Mark Twain's "Masterpiece"', *Harper's Magazine*, December 1995.

When the massive volcano under Yellowstone Park erupts, it will kill tens of thousands of people and make the loudest noise heard by man for 75,000 years.

1 'Supervolcanoes', BBC2 *Horizon*, 3 February 2000, 9:30pm, http://www.bbc.co.uk/science/horizon/1999/supervolcanoes.shtml
2 Mike Stark, 'Yellowstone Park Unlikely to Blow Up Anytime Soon: No Signs of Cataclysmic Eruption', *Billings Gazette*, 28 April 2004, http://www.billingsgazette.com/newdex.php?display=rednews/2004
3 'Super Volcano in Yellowstone National Park', Solcomhouse, http://www.solcomhouse.com/yellowstone.htm
4 Barbara Mikkelson, 'Unmellow Yellow', Urban Reference Pages: Science, Snopes.com, http://www.snopes.com/science/volcano/asp

With a total audience of over 7.5 million, *Hot Rod* magazine has one of the largest circulations of any car publication in the world.

1 Figures from *Hot Rod* media kit information, http://ads.primedia automotive.com/SR/HRmedia.htm. Audience figures based on overall circulation of 706,000, multiplied by 11.19, the estimated number of readers per copy.
2 MSN Autos, John Warde, 'A Short History of Hot Rods', p. 1, http://autos.msn.com/Advice/Article.aspx?contentid=9226
3 Tom Wolfe, *The Kandy-Colored, Tangerine-Flake Streamline Baby* (New York: Pocket Books, 1966), pp. 64–5.
4 Ibid., pp. 72–3.
5 Warde, op. cit., p. 2.
6 Wolfe, op. cit., p. 81.
7 Ibid., p. 68.

2.9 million Americans claim to have been abducted by aliens.

1 For the Roper poll and its methods, see http://www.ufoevidence.org/documents/doc989.htm
2 Einstein's most famous equation tells us that as an object approaches the speed of light, its mass also approaches infinity. Even at the more modest rate of 1 million miles an hour, 25 times faster than our current space vehicles, it would take more than 2,500 years to reach our nearest star, Alpha Centauri.
3 Susan Clancy, interview on National Public Radio, *Day to Day*, 9 November 2005, http://www.nuforc.org/npr.html
4 Martin Kottmeyer, 'The Eyes that Spoke', Committee for the Scientific Investigation of Claims of the Paranormal, http://csicop.org/sb/9409/eyesthat.html

In America you drive what you are.
1 Affirmations, CafePress Internet Bumper Stickers, http://www. cafepress.com/ibs1/484752

In 2005 a US federal court established that the teaching of intelligent design in American public schools is unconstitutional.
1 The Pew Research Center, 'Reading the Polls on Evolution and Creationism', released 29 September 2005, http://people-press.org/ commentary/display.php3?AnalysisID=118
2 Michael J. Behe, *Darwin's Black Box* (New York: Simon & Schuster, Touchstone Books, 1996), pp. 51–97.
3 Edward J. Larson, *Summer for the Gods: The Scopes Trial and America's Continuing Debate Over Science and Religion* (Cambridge, MA: Harvard University Press, 1997), pp. 89, 107.

More than 37 million Americans, or one in eight of the population, live below the official poverty guidelines.
1 Paul Harris, '37 Million Poor Hidden in the Land of Plenty', *The Observer*, 19 February 2006, pp. 32–3.
2 Mark Trumbull, 'Life at America's Bottom Wage', *Christian Science Monitor*, 9 January 2007, http://www.csmonitor.com/2007/0109/p01 s02-usec.html
3 Federal Register, Vol. 72, No. 15, 24 January 2007, pp. 3147–8, http:// aspe.hhs.gov/poverty/07poverty.shtml. These figures are for the mainland states, including the District of Columbia. Rates for Hawaii and Alaska are higher.
4 Will Hutton, 'Britain Would Benefit From Clinton's Tough Love', *The Guardian*, 3 September 2006, p. 27.
5 Margy Waller, 'Heeding Clinton's Welfare Advice', *Philadelphia Daily News*, 6 February 2004, http://www.brookings.edu/views/op-ed/ waller/20040206.htm

As a protest against corruption in City Hall, Rabbit Hash, Kentucky, elected a black Labrador named Junior as its mayor.
1 Michael Les Benedict, personal communication.
2 Quoted in Lloyd Wendt and Herman Kogan, *Big Bill of Chicago* (Evanston, IL: Northwestern University Press, 2005), p. 545. See the Wikipedia article on 'William Hale Thompson', http://en.wikipedia.org/ wiki/William_Hale_Thompson
3 *Jurist: Legal News and Research*, http://jurist.law.pitt.edu/paperchase /2004/08/federal-appeals-court-upholds-former.htm

4 Chris Ayeres, 'In City Halls Across America the Cry Goes Up: Four Legs Good, Two Legs Bad', *The Times*, 13 December 2005, http://www. timesonline.co.uk/tol/comment/columnists/chris_ayres/article758389. ece

5 William Croyle, 'It's Donkey Against Pig for Rabbit Hash Mayor', *Cincinnati Enquirer*, 3 September 2004, http://www.enquirer.com/ editions/2004/09/03/loc_kyoldtimers03.html

65 per cent of American adults are overweight, 30 per cent are obese, and these proportions are growing.

1 John Hesketh to his brother, Pittsburgh, 1837, in Charlotte Erickson, *Invisible Immigrants: The Adaptation of English and Scottish Immigrants in Nineteenth Century America* (Leicester: Leicester University Press, 1972), p. 423.

2 American Obesity Association, 'Obesity in the US', http://www.obesity. org/subs/fastfacts/obesity_US.shtml. To find your BMI in countries using the metric system, you simply divide your body weight in kilograms by your height in metres squared. In the US you take your weight in pounds, divide it by your height in inches squared, then multiply by 704.5.

3 Kristina Nwazota, 'Obesity Edging Smoking as No. 1 Preventable Killer of Americans', *Online NewsHour*, http://www.pbs.org/newshour/extra/ features/jan-june04/obesity_3-15.html

4 See (author unknown), 'MSG – Slowly Poisoning America', http://www. rense.com/general52/msg.htm. This idea is a spin-off from a more serious study by Dr Russell L. Blaylock, *Excitotoxins – The Taste that Kills* (Santa Fe, NM: Health Press, 1994), in which obesity figures as a minor issue in an argument that these additives increase the prevalence of neurological disorders like Parkinson's disease, Huntington's chorea and Alzheimer's.

5 Eric Schlosser, 'Stuff the Kids', *The Guardian*, 24 April 2006, G2, p. 8.

6 Figures from Samana Siddiqi, 'Statistics on Poverty and Food Wastage in America', http://www.soundvision.com/Info/poor/statistics.asp

7 See, for example, W.H. Dietz, 'Does Hunger Cause Obesity?', *Pediatrics*, 95 (1995), pp. 766–7; Lee M. Scheier, 'What is the Hunger-Obesity Paradox?', *Journal of the American Dietetic Association*, June 2005, pp. 883–5.

8 Fujioka Kim, 'Obesity and Poverty: The Poorest of Us Also Weigh the Most', Associated Content: The People's Media Company, 2006, http:// www.associatedcontent.com/article/5576/obesity_and_poverty_the_ poorest_of.html

9 Quoted in Oliver Burkeman, 'Extreme Dining', *The Guardian*, 23 August 2006, G2, p. 8.

Thomas A. Edison, who invented recorded sound, thought jazz sounded better played backwards.

1 See Susan Currell, *The March of Spare Time: The Problem and Promise of Leisure in the Great Depression* (Philadelphia: University of Pennsylvania Press, 2005), p. 24.

2 'Culture Shock: The Devil's Music: 1920s Jazz', PBS, http://www.pbs.org/wgbh/cultureshock/beyond/jazz.html

3 Marybeth Hamilton, *In Search of the Blues: Black Voices, White Visions* (London: Jonathan Cape, 2006).

American conservatives hate political actors, though happy to back Ronald Reagan as President – not to mention Arnold Schwarzenegger as Governor of California.

1 The defence tactic of citing the Fifth Amendment, which prevents defendants from having to testify against themselves, was mainly deployed in the second wave of HUAC hearings involving Hollywood and other branches of the arts and entertainment industries, from 1951–4.

2 Ellen Hawkes, 'One Tough Cookie Who Refuses to Crumble', *Ms. Magazine*, Summer 2003, http://www.Talltalestogo.net/JGInterview.htm

3 Bill O'Reilly, 'People Who Need Perspective', *Jewish World Review*, 10 April 2001, http://www.jewishworldreview.com/cols/oreilly041001.asp

4 Arthur Miller, *Timebends: A Life* (London: Methuen, corrected paperback edition, 1988), p. 406.

5 Bill O'Reilly.com, FAQ, General Questions, http://www.billoreilly.com/pg/jsp/help/general/faq.jsp;jsessionid=2078723039023E086B625D1B E9821

The internet was an American invention for the military, designed to withstand a nuclear attack.

1 In 1972 renamed the Defense Advanced Research Projects Agency (DARPA), then changed back to ARPA in 1993, and back again to DARPA in 1996.

2 Barry M. Leiner, Vinton G. Cerf, David D. Clark, Robert E. Kahn, Leonard Kleinrock, Daniel C. Lynch, Jon Postel, Larry G. Roberts, Stephen Wolff, 'A Brief History of the Internet', Internet Society, http://www.isoc.org/internet/history/brief.shtml

Between 1995 and 2000, almost half the American population moved house; in 2005 alone, one in seven Americans changed their address.

1   Figures from 'Centrifugal Forces', *The Economist*, 14 July 2005.
2   Alexis de Tocqueville, *Democracy in America*, The Henry Reeve text, rev. Francis Bowen, ed. Phillips Bradley (New York: Random House Vintage Books, 1945), Vol. 1, p. 305.
3   US Census Bureau, 'Mobility of the Population of the United States: March 1966 to March 1967 (P20-171)', http://www.census.gov/ population/www/socdemo/migrate/p20-171.html
4   'Centrifugal Forces', op. cit.
5   US Census Bureau, 'State and County QuickFacts', http://quickfacts. census.gov/qfd/states/06/06065.html
6   'New York City Metropolitan Area: 2000–20005 Population & Migration', http://www.demographia.com/db-nycmigra.htm
7   'Centrifugal Forces', op. cit.
8   'Manufacturing Jobs Drop by a Third', *Buffalo Business First* , 20 March 2006; Infoplease, 'Top 50 Cities in the US by Population and Rank', http://www.infoplease.com/ipa/A0763098.html
9   'Centrifugal Forces', op. cit.
10 de Tocqueville, op. cit., Vol. 1, p. 304.

Americans spend upwards of $8 billion every year on self-help pro-grammes and products – four times the profits of the Ford Motor Company in 2005.

1   Figure from Steve Salerno, *Sham: How the Self-Help Movement Made America Helpless* (New York: Crown Publishers, 2005). Ford reported net profits of $2 billion for 2005. See Christine Tierney, 'Ford Profits Rise in the Fourth Quarter', *Detroit News*, 'Auto Insider', 23 January 2006, http://www.detnews.com/apps/pbcs.dll/article?AID=/20060123/ AUTO01/601230413/1148
2   George Carlin, 'People Who Ought to be Killed: Self-Help Books', *Complaints and Grievances* (Atlantic Audio CD), 11 December 2001.
3   Micki McGee, *Self-Help, Inc.: Makeover Culture in America* (New York: Oxford University Press, 2005), from the Introduction, *passim*.

In America, charity begins at home, and in states that vote Republican.

1   Andrew O'Hagan, 'A Journey in the South', *The London Review of Books*, 6 October 2005, pp. 3–12.

2   Ben Somberg, 'The World's Most Generous Misers: Tsunami Reporting Misrepresented US Giving', *Fairness and Accuracy in Reporting*, September/October 2005, http://www.fair.org/index.php?page=2676
3   Quoted in Somberg, op. cit.
4   Arthur C. Brooks, 'Are Americans Selfish? The Bond Between Faith, Philanthropy and Healthy Democracies', paper given at the Heritage Foundation, 16 February 2005, http://www.heritage.org/Press/Events/ev021605a.cfm; Independent Sector, 'Giving and Volunteering in the United States 2001', http://www.independentsector,ord/programs/research/GV01main.html
5   Beth Breeze, 'The Return of Philanthropy', *Prospect*, January 2005, reprinted by the Institute for Philanthropy, http://www.institutefor philanthropy.org.uk/IFP%20The%20Return%20of%20Philanthropy .pdf#search=%22%22tax%20relief%22%2B%22charitable%20givin g%22%2BInternational%20comparisons%22

Violent crime in the US has fallen by well over half since its peak in 1993, while it continues to rise in most of Europe.

1   James Alan Fox, 'Trends in Juvenile Violence: A Report to the United States Attorney General on Current and Future Rates of Juvenile Offending', prepared for the Bureau of Justice Statistics, United States Department of Justice, Washington, DC, March 1996.
2   US Department of Justice, Department of Justice Programs, 'Since 1994, Violent Crime Rates Have Declined, Reaching the Lowest Level Ever in 2005', http://www.ojp.usdoj.gov/bjs/glance/viort.htm. The Department of Justice figures are based on the National Crime Victimization Survey (NCVS), which interviews about 134,000 persons aged twelve and older in 77,200 households each year about their victimisations from crime. The NCVS is more accurate than the *reported* crime rate, since for various reasons many crimes do not get reported to the police.
3   John J. Donohue and Steven D. Levitt, 'The Impact of Legalized Abortion on Crime', *Quarterly Journal of Economics*, Vol. 116 (2001), pp. 379–420.
4   Steven D. Levitt and Stephen J. Dubner, *Freakonomics: A Rogue Economist Explores the Hidden Side of Everything* (London: Penguin Books, 2006), p. 138.
5   Ibid., pp. 137–8.
6   Robert J. Sampson, Stephen W. Raudenbusch and Felton Earls, 'Neighborhoods and Violent Crime: A Multilevel Study of Collective Efficacy', *Science*, Vol. 277 (1997), pp. 918–24.

7 Bureau of Justice Statistics, 'Cross National Studies in Crime and Justice' (Washington, DC: US Department of Justice, Office of Justice Programs), 2004, p. x.

Just over half of all Americans vote for President, and around one third vote between presidential elections.

1 Mike Bergman, 'US Voter Turnout Up in 2004, Census Bureau Reports', Press Release, US Census Bureau News, 26 May 2005, http://www. census.gov/Press-Release/www/releases/archives/voting/004986. html

2 United States Elections Project, 'Voter Turnout', http:/elections.gmu. edu/voter_turnout.htm; see also Samuel L. Popkin and Michael P. McDonald, 'Turnout's Not as Bad as You Think', *Washington Post*, 5 November 2000, p. B01.

3 Bergman, op. cit.

4 Calvin Woodward, 'Why Do So Few People Vote in the US?', Associated Press, 5 November 2006, Truthout Issues, http://www. truthout.org/cgi-bin/artman/exec/view.cgi/66/23633

5 Robert D. Putnam, 'Tuning In, Tuning Out: The Strange Disappearance of Social Capital in America', in Richard G. Niemi and Herbert F. Weisberg, eds, *Controversies in Voting Behavior* (Washington, DC: CQ Press, 2001), p. 61.

6 Mark Baldassare, 'California's Exclusive Electorate', *At Issue* (San Francisco: Public Policy Institute of California, 2006), http://www.ppic. org/content/pubs/atissue/AI_906MBAI.pdf;   http://www.ppic.org/ content/pubs/atissue/AI_906MBAI.pdf, pp. 6, 18.

In 2006 American venture capital investment outstripped European by nearly five to one.

1 Steve Hsu, 'No Startup Culture in Europe', *Information Processing*, 18 March 2006, http://infoproc.blogspot.com/2006/03/no-startup-culture-in-europe.html

2 The US total was actually 4.99 times Europe's, based on the average dollar–euro conversion for 2006 (as supplied by the Internal Revenue Service) of 1 dollar to 0.75800 euros. Figures from Dow Jones VentureOne, http://www.ventureone.com/ii/V1_EY_4Q06_EuropeFinan cingPR.pdf and http://www.ventureone.com/ii/V1-EY_4Q06_USFinPR. pdf

3 Kelvin Maney, 'Tech Start-ups Don't Grow on Trees Outside USA', *USA Today*, 27 June 2006, http://www.usatoday.com/tech/world/2006-06-27-silicon-culture_x.htm

4   David Vickrey, 'Germany's Innovation Dilemma', Atlantic Community Policy Workshop, 9 May 2007, http://www.atlantic-community.org/index/articles/view/Germany's_Innovation_Dilemma

5   PriceWaterhouse Coopers, National Venture Capital Association, 'Money Tree Report, Full-Year and Q4 2006 US Results', http://www.pwcmoneytree.com/MTPublic/ns/moneytree/filesource/exhibits/MoneyTree_4Q2006_Final.pdf

6   A list of the 'Most Active Venture Investors, Full-year, 2006' can be found on pp. 10–11 of the Money Tree Results cited above.

7   http://www.flagshipventures.com/companies/codonbiotech.html

8   https://www.intelportfolio.com/cps/co_profile.asp?co_id=1283

9   John W. Schoen, 'US Patent Office Swamped by Backlog', MSNBC On-Line, 27 April 2004, http://www.msnbc.msn.com/id/4788834/

America's approval rating has dropped to 58 per cent in Britain, 37 per cent in France and 15 per cent in Jordan.

1   The headline figures come from the Pew Global Attitudes Project, Trends in Global Opinion, 2006, 'America's Image in the World: Findings from the Pew Global Attitudes Project', http://pewglobal.org/commentary/display.php?AnalysisID=1019

2   Sidney Smith, review of Adam Seybert, *Statistical Annals of the United States* (1818), *The Edinburgh Review*, Vol. 33 (January 1820), p. 79.

3   James W. Caeser, 'A Genealogy of anti-Americanism', *The Public Interest*, 23 July 2003, http://www.travelbrochuregraphics.com/extra/a_genealogy_of_antiamericanism.htm

4   Smith, op. cit; Samuel Johnson, *Taxation no Tyranny* (London, 1775).

5   Paul Johnson, 'Anti-Americanism is Racist Envy', *Forbes Magazine*, 21 July 2003, http://members.forbes.com/global/2003/0721/017_print.html

6   Andrei S. Markovits, 'Introduction', *Uncouth Nation: Why Europe Dislikes America* (Princeton, NJ: Princeton University Press, 2006), http://press.princeton.edu/chapters/i8238.html

7   Josef Joffe, 'Question & Answer: Anti-Semitism and Anti-Americanism', Washington, DC, 5 May 2006, The Pew Forum on Religion and Public Life, http://pewforum.org/events/index.php?EventID=111

8   Barry Rubin, 'The Real Roots of Arab Anti-Americanism', *Foreign Affairs*, November/December 2002, http://www.foreignaffairs.org/20021101faessay9993/barry-rubin/the-real-roots-of-arab-anti-americanism.html

9   Markovits, 'Introduction', op. cit.

10 Joffe, op. cit.

Index

INDEX

INDEX